Choose Your Bearing

Contemporary Continental Ethics
Series editors: Bryan Lueck, Southern Illinois University Edwardsville and Lucian Stone, University of North Dakota

Normative Ethics from a Continental Perspective

The books in this series address pressing and difficult ethical questions from the perspective of Continental philosophy. They offer new ways of thinking about moral phenomena and raise challenging questions that have not been considered before. The series includes work in the field of normative ethics, both theoretical and applied. Space is also given to treatments of social, political and aesthetic questions that intersect with ethical considerations.

Editorial Advisory Board
Andrew Benjamin, Alphonso Lingis, Ladelle McWhorter, Eduardo Mendieta, Ann V. Murphy, Kelly Oliver, Danielle Petherbridge, Anthony Steinbock

Books available
Obligation and the Fact of Sense
Bryan Lueck
The Responsibility to Understand: Hermeneutical Contours of Ethical Life
Theodore George
The Fragility of Concern for Others: Adorno and the Ethics of Care
Estelle Ferrarese, translated by Steven Corcoran
Choose Your Bearing: Édouard Glissant, Human Rights and Decolonial Ethics
Benjamin P. Davis

Visit our website at: edinburghuniversitypress.com/series/epcce

Choose Your Bearing

Édouard Glissant, Human Rights and Decolonial Ethics

Benjamin P. Davis

EDINBURGH
University Press

Edinburgh University Press is one of the leading university presses in the UK. We publish academic books and journals in our selected subject areas across the humanities and social sciences, combining cutting-edge scholarship with high editorial and production values to produce academic works of lasting importance. For more information visit our website: edinburghuniversitypress.com

Edinburgh University Press Ltd
The Tun – Holyrood Road
12(2f) Jackson's Entry
Edinburgh EH8 8PJ

First published in hardback by Edinburgh University Press 2023

Typeset in 11/15 Meridien by
IDSUK (DataConnection) Ltd, and
printed and bound by CPI Group (UK) Ltd,
Croydon, CR0 4YY

A CIP record for this book is available from the British Library

ISBN 978 1 3995 2243 4 (hardback)
ISBN 978 1 3995 2244 1 (paperback)
ISBN 978 1 3995 2245 8 (webready PDF)
ISBN 978 1 3995 2246 5 (epub)

For my students

Contents

Acknowledgements

I have looked forward to the opportunity to thank those who have made this book possible. Alejandro Vallega introduced me to Glissant's work in February 2016. Thank you, Alejandro. Lucian Stone encouraged me to write about Glissant. Thank you, Lucian. Bryan Lueck believed in this book, and Carol Macdonald made it happen. Thank you both. I would also like to thank Christine Barton, whose copyedits made the book better. Finally, for legal reasons, I need to note both that the epigraph for this book comes from Edward W. Said, *Reflections on Exile* (London: Granta Books, 2000) and that the epigraph is an excerpt from REFLECTIONS ON EXILE by Edward Said. Copyright © 2000 by Edward W. Said, used by permission of The Wylie Agency LLC.

I wrote the manuscript from precarious posts in several places. I have people to thank from all of them.

From Atlanta: Dilek Huseyinzadegan, Rocío Zambrana, John Lysaker, John Stuhr, Michael Sullivan, Tom Flynn and Andrew Mitchell. Mike Chiddo, Catherine Fullarton, Grace Goh, Adam Blair, Jason Walsh, Abby Scribner, Mukasa Mubirumusoke, Osman Nemli, Katie Howard, Jordan Daniels, Dwight Lewis and Pellom McDaniels III. John Drabinski, for dialogue on Glissant. Ted Smith, for conversation about political commitment. Lauren Highsmith, for love and for your music. Eve and Meng Fei, for giving me a place to stay when I needed it. George Yancy, for checking in. Valérie Loichot, for sitting with me as we read Glissant in French. Cindy Willett, for egoless mentorship and for encouraging a project on Glissant and Levinas.

From St Paul: Garrett Johnson, Zeynep Ertekin, Corinne Freedman Ellis, Kristine Heykants and Raisa Elhadi. Samarjit Ghosh, for suggesting on the light rail that I take a look at *The Stuart Hall Project*. Jacob Neis and everyone at Next Chapter Booksellers. Eli, Zach and everyone at Spyhouse on Snelling. Helen Kinsella, for living a feminist life.

From St Louis: Harold Braswell, Steve Tamari, Rachel Brown, Sid Issar and Fannie Bialek. Gabby, for conversation over the years.

From Toronto: Allison Weir, Ralph Premdas, Jay Himat, Christopher Smith, Sam Tecle, Markus Dubber and Rohini Patel. David Scott, for conversation about Stuart Hall. Mark Kingwell, for hospitality and for generosity. Nikolas Kompridis, for a model of thinking, and for teaching me how to play tennis.

Thank you to those who responded to my emails with questions about human rights: Sam Moyn, Ayça Çubukçu, Jill Stauffer, Angela Naimou, Lyndsey Stonebridge, and everyone at *Humanity* for the work you are doing, and for allowing me to use a revised version of my article 'The Promises of Standing Rock' in this book. Joy James, for speaking truth. Jessica Whyte, for your illuminating work, and for espresso. Bernard Harcourt, for your generosity.

It is also worth noting that, in my critique of humanitarian organisations, I mean not at all to devalue those who have dedicated their life to the service of others but rather to observe the problematic structures in which they and I are implicated. I hope I have written this book in a tone that makes this note redundant. It is a better book for conversation with those actually working within these organisations. Thank you.

I would also like to thank those whose readings of Glissant I disagree with, because we are part of a larger debate: H. Adlai Murdoch and Neal Allar.

The CPA – a beautiful community of scholarship: LaRose Parris, Jane Gordon, Lewis Gordon, Nelson Maldonado-Torres. Kris Sealey, for support. AunRika Tucker-Shabazz, for your prayerful and wonderful engagements. Paget Henry, for staying on a call for three hours to answer my questions about Caribbean philosophy. Neil Roberts, for conversations in a Toronto park. Frieda Ekotto, for encouraging me to write more on Stuart Hall. Derefe Chevannes, for a walk down Beale Street.

My SLU colleagues, for conversation and for doing the work: Bukky Gbadegesin, Katrina Thompson, Shaneeka Favors-Welch, Emily Dumler-Winckler, Ms Dana Guyton. Clarice Thomas, for always seeing how I'm doing. Chris Tinson, for making clear the stakes of Black Studies at a Cardinals game.

A nod to Penny Weiss as well, for morning dialogues.

A few others have carried me along the way. Marcia Mikulak, for your example of thinking. Jacques Coursil, for conversation, for inspiration, for your example of a committed and imaginative life. Sarah Cahill, for your music, to which much of this book was written. Eric Aldieri, Aylin Malcolm and Jon Catlin, for ongoing conversations. Jeanne Fenlason, for lending me a book when I was young. Adam Lugsch-Tehle, for your generosity. Scott and Michaela, for hosting me in Philly and for encouraging me to go to Standing Rock. Teddy and Annabelle, for conversations by a bonfire. Ivy Kuhn, Erinn Miles, Josh Hill, Andrew Tyler Johnson, Bonnie Sheehey, Tamsin Kimoto, Leif Bergerud, Don Deere, Selin Islekel, Omar Rivera, Gregory Pappas, Rafael Vizcaíno, Mohammad Salama, Rebecca Rozelle-Stone, Chelsea Jack, Lindsay Poplinski, John Gray, Stephen Blair Venable, Douglas Ewart, Ben Schewel, Keri Schewel, Shahrzad Sabet, An Yountae, Beatrice Marovich,

Jeta Mulaj, Caleb Faul, Luvell Anderson and Seth Glasser. Andrea Pitts, for generosity as a colleague. Natalie Melas, for questions about how I read Glissant. Vincent Lloyd, for sustained mentorship and for encouraging me to write. Gerard Aching, for walks through Ithaca's gorges, for generosity, for cappuccinos, for affirmation. Lucy Benjamin, for enthusiasm, for inspiration. Miguel Gualdrón Ramírez, por un sentido de familia desde Fort-de-France. Shadi Anello, por un camino.

I would like to thank o povo Xukuru, the Lakota people, and the Anishinaabe people, for inviting me to your land. I have never felt more sane than when praying by water in the always multifaith, multiracial groups you bring together. Without your invitation, I am not sure that, in my life, I would have experienced that feeling of clarity, purpose, grounding and strength. Thank you for that gift.

To my students: Lizzy Wong, Megan Campbell, Callum Shepard, Veronika Nayir, Katie Delay, Dylan Alfi, Adhiraj Rana, Kabba Gizaw, Reshma Aser, Mariam Zaidi, Ulaa Kuziez.

Finally, I am grateful to my parents, for supporting my education, and to my brother, for all of our days working so hard and laughing so much.

Abbreviations

CD   *Caribbean Discourse: Selected Essays*. Translated by
J. Michael Dash. Charlottesville: University of Virginia
Press, 1989.

DA   *Le discours antillais*. Paris: Gallimard, 1997.

PhR   *Philosophie de la Relation*. Paris: Gallimard, 2009.

PO   *Poetics of Relation*. Translated by Betsy Wing. Ann
Arbor: University of Michigan Press, 1997.

PR   *Poétique de la Relation*. Paris: Gallimard, 1990.

TTM   *Traité du Tout-Monde*. Paris: Gallimard, 1997.

Preface

Looking back at the three or four years it took to write and revise this book, I can say that it has become something different from what I had originally envisioned. This project started as a relatively narrow intervention into how a line of Latin American philosophy that Enrique Dussel called 'the philosophy of liberation', what is increasingly called 'decolonial philosophy', took up the ethical vocabulary of Emmanuel Levinas. My argument remains that Édouard Glissant's relative ethics of opacity is more capable of speaking to today's ethical problems and possibilities than Levinas's absolute ethics of alterity. As I revised this book over the past year and read the work of, as well as engaged in conversation with, a few others – Gerard Aching, Kris Sealey, Nancy Mithlo, Neil Roberts, Allison Weir, LaRose Parris, Frieda Ekotto and Chris Tinson especially – I started to think of the book differently. In its placement in this series, and in the questions it raises, *Choose Your Bearing* can be read as asking Continental ethics and human rights discourse to take seriously Caribbean philosophy and Indigenous philosophy, and by extension Black Studies and Indigenous Studies, as sites of critical theory, epistemological correctives, and conceptual creation. What results from this engagement is a political theory that can no longer assume that the nation state protects rights, an ethical theory that can no longer withdraw into carefree abstractions, and a human rights discourse that can no longer maintain the goal of 'developing' humans, cultures and economies. Perhaps from such a renewed philosophy, one that looks back to Caribbean philosophy in the past century, we will gain ethical modes attuned to the rhythms of this century. At the very least, we will take one step toward a truer academic philosophy, one finally made to the measure of the world.

Benjamin P. Davis
September 2022
St Louis

To be 'for' human rights means, in effect, to be willing to venture interpretations of those rights in the same place and with the same language employed by the dominant power, to dispute its hierarchy and methods, to elucidate what it has hidden, to pronounce what it has silenced or rendered unpronounceable. These intellectual procedures require, above all, an acute sense not of how things are separated but of how they are connected, mixed, involved, embroiled, linked.

—Edward Said, 'Nationalism, Human Rights, and Interpretation'

Introduction: Starting from Responsibility and Human Rights

In a 2020 op-ed in *The Guardian*, Nemonte Nenquimo, a leader of the Waorani people, an Indigenous nation whose home is the Amazon rainforest, stated: 'This is my message to the western world – your civilization is killing life on earth.'[1] Could this be true? Could a way of life in one place not only harm people and damage environments in other places, but also destroy life itself across the planet? If this is true, then do those in the West have a duty to change their way of life? How could this change occur across societies? Are the concepts and ideas we currently use to speak about social justice, such as human rights, sufficient to bring about this needed social change, change that would honour and preserve life on earth?

This book's argument rests on the following premises: as a result of European colonisation, the way of life in any Western country today relies on resource extraction and commodity production in other countries it thereby renders poor.[2] This international division of labour involves practices that deny the human rights – the political, economic and cultural rights – of the workers who mine the minerals, sew the clothes, and otherwise provide the basic substances for life in the West. Fair trade programmes and wage increases do not change the fact that some spend their days hunched over sewing machines while others continually update their wardrobes.

Even a cursory reading of international news, or literature from a variety of places, makes clear that the West's way of life depends on resource extraction that violates human rights in different parts of the planet.[3] Poor people the world over often make ethical appeals asking people in the West to change their basic habits of living in order to allow for others to live, to live with dignity, and to live amidst sustaining land and water. By leveraging rights claims in pronouncing what dominant powers have tried to silence, philosophers such as W. E. B. Du Bois and Édouard Glissant have also called for the West to change its political and economic foundations.

In this book, I argue that Western societies need to re-examine how we understand responsibility. I contend that human rights claims provide a sufficient tool for conducting this re-examination. Through listening to the rights claims of dispossessed people across the world, we can begin to understand our duties not only to one another, but also to life itself.

* * *

Several thoughtful critics have consistently raised concerns about using the concepts of responsibility and human rights in order to achieve the scale of social change needed for the survival of our species. Internationally, the discourse of responsibility often takes the form of capitalist development, leading the post-colonial theorist Gayatri Spivak to observe that today '[d]evelopment is the dominant global denomination of responsibility'.[4] Further, the 'protection' that Western powers claim to offer through 'the responsibility to protect', exemplified in US military operations in the Middle East, has in practice increased the gap between ethical ideals and political realities on earth. Indeed, the responsibility to protect has been little more than a 'cosmetic' effort that fails to address the true causes of war.[5] Overall, through the rhetoric of global responsibility, the US projects 'low-minded imperial ambitions in high-minded humanitarian tones', as the historian Samuel Moyn puts it.[6] In part with the above concerns and histories in mind, in her study of how invoking responsibility functions in human rights advocacy, the political scientist Kathryn Sikkink points out that 'the norms appear to require that one *not* talk about the responsibility of a wider range of actors because such talk might take the pressure off the state'.[7] Invoking responsibility might, she continues, even 'risk blaming the victim, underplay the structural causes of injustice, or crowd out other more collective forms of political action'.[8] A prominent example that proves all of these critics right is BP's hiring of the public relations firm Ogilvy & Mather to promote the idea of the 'carbon footprint', a concept that shifts our focus away from oil companies and an energy landscape based on fossil fuels and toward how much we as individuals drive, travel, and otherwise use oil. In other words, the corporations that increasingly govern the values of our world promote an understanding of responsibility not in structural but in individual terms.[9]

Why, then, start from responsibility? I begin from responsibility because it cannot be avoided. As Spivak reminds us, to be human is to be 'already inserted into a structure of responsibility'.[10] Even if responsibility is currently carried out largely in personal ways, and even if responsibility is often understood as tying us only to our nuclear family or country, it can also be understood as a route or a path. In this way, responsibility forms an occasion for relating differently. The question becomes how to re-describe and re-think responsibility such that the actions that responsible ethical actors pursue collectively are different from 'development' and 'protection' internationally and victim-blaming and individualisation interpersonally.[11]

From taking responsibility as a starting point, a second question emerges: Precisely who is responsible for changing their habits and institutions for the sake of life on our planet? Is it simply everyone who lives in what Nenquimo called the Western world? *Choose Your Bearing* specifically addresses the task of creatively becoming more responsible to elites, those whom the memory studies scholar Michael Rothberg calls 'implicated subjects', meaning people who 'occupy positions aligned with power and privilege without being themselves direct agents of harm; they contribute to, inhabit, inherit, or benefit from regimes of domination but do not originate or control such regimes'.[12] Implicated subjects initially tend to deny that they are part of an elite. 'For the members of the elite who wish to help make changes in existing relationships', Glissant observes, 'the obligation is absolute to deny that there is such an elite class in order to deny the system' (DA 698/ CD 206). But responding to differences in social class, Glissant teaches, should look less like 'aiding' the oppressed and more like directly challenging the economic and political foundations of the elite class in the first place. 'If they declare their commitment to liberation without also negating themselves (calling themselves into question) as a group', he continues, 'they cannot fight against the system that created their class and will only fall into step with the system' (DA 698/CD 206, translation modified).

In their class positions and through their daily actions, implicated subjects benefit from and reinforce domination. On my reading of implicated subjects, they include men who through their gender identification gain authority in patriarchal contexts, citizens who through their civic status gain access to social services in nation states, students who through their education at prestigious universities have access to political power, and many others – I invite my reader to consider their own positioning. For responsibility to be effective under these conditions, it must be active. Passivity tends toward complicity. Surveying twentieth-century histories of how fascism takes over countries, the historian Nitzan Lebovic notes that a fascist mob 'needs the cooperation of the elite more than it needs to be in the majority'.[13] Glissant adds about implicated subjects who assimilate themselves to practices of domination, 'Everything must grind to a halt so that exploitation can take place', and 'the elite is given the responsibility of "maintaining" this condition of stasis' (DA 693/CD 202).

In a recent study of responsibility, the political theorist Antonio Vázquez-Arroyo argues that a politically effective sense of responsibility needs to include not only reflection on 'how one is responsible for the historical structures of power bearing one's name and from which one differentially benefits' but also an active break from those unjust structures.[14] Reflection and breaking, he continues, require 'calibrating one's response, in the midst of emotional and often visceral reactions when one is asked to take responsibility for the actions performed in one's name and for the structures of power that constitute the stage in which one enjoys certain rights, privileges, and status'.[15] Responsibility today requires a recalibration – not an overwhelming guilt but an active break with elite class affiliations, a break that is understood as part of a larger transformation of governing institutions. Several practical questions emerge. How can implicated subjects take responsibility for the 'historical structures of power' from which they continue to benefit? How should elite actors recalibrate their responses to injustice? What exactly is the 'stage' on which responsibility is to be enacted? Because it raises these questions, this book speaks especially to students, those whose goals and orientations are soon to become more expansive through showing up for protests, making art in community and living in new places. It is a study especially relevant to classrooms, faith groups, café discussions and other settings of conversation about how justice-oriented actors understand themselves to be responsible amidst the overlapping political and environmental crises of the present. These conversations, which would do well to start from and remain in dialogue with the dispossessed, are steps on a larger path of action.

* * *

I now need to answer a second question: Why start from human rights? This question requires a more extended answer, because while structures of responsibility form a part of life for all humans, human rights discourse is a recent political fabrication. For that reason, while human life will always be conditioned by needing to respond to others, we could always choose another strategy if leveraging human rights claims failed to realise ethical ideals and achieve political gains.

In his sixth and eighth theses on Feuerbach, Karl Marx teaches that the truth of something does not lie only in its abstraction. Rather, the truth of something is its social truth.[16] The social truth of human rights contains several problematic articulations. Indeed, the reason to take human rights movements seriously with a view toward decolonial pursuits is not because there is a natural or historical alignment between these movements. Following World War II, the human rights movement began as distinct from efforts toward decolonisation. Relatedly, there are conceptual reasons why decolonial theory remains suspicious of human rights discourse. In his 2009 article 'Who Speaks for the "Human" in Human Rights?', the decolonial thinker Walter Mignolo gives an answer to the question his article's title asks:

From the sixteenth century to the Universal Declaration of Human Rights, He who speaks for the human is an actor embodying the Western ideal of being Christian, being man and being human. In other words, 'human' in human rights is an invention of Western imperial knowledge rather than the name of an existing entity to which everyone will have access.[17]

Mignolo's argument is that the European origin and scope of human rights belie their claim to universal application. For Mignolo, human rights exemplify 'the provincialism of the universal'.[18] For his part, the philosopher Nelson Maldonado-Torres diagnoses 'the coloniality of human rights'.[19] He argues that the decolonisation of human rights requires firstly a decolonisation of the human. On this account, scepticism toward human rights is part of the decolonial turn's scepticism toward the coloniser's historical denial of full humanity to the colonised. Discussing Mignolo as well as Spivak, Maldonado-Torres notes that 'their common concern is that there is a pattern in which the definition of human rights leads to the creation of experts who are designated to speak to the colonized and other marginalized peoples about the rights that they possess'.[20] Other philosophers have examined how human rights claims operate in particular places, and they have found that Maldonado-Torres's analysis is correct. Thinking with Spivak and attending to Palestine, Jasbir Puar has observed that '[t]he white woman's burden from the nineteenth century is regenerated for contemporary deployment through liberal feminist frames within human rights discourses'.[21] Writing about the violence nation states bring onto Indigenous peoples in Latin America, Julia Suárez-Krabbe concludes that while '[r]ights can contribute to protect the lives and wellbeing of some', '[b]ecause they are framed within a specific dominant ontology, and sustain a particular political horizon, human rights and development limit radical social change'.[22]

Beyond decolonial theory, in the field of international relations, Neve Gordon and Nicola Perugini ask us to keep in mind the second Bush administration's justification of wars in the name of human rights as well as Amnesty International's use of the discourse to advocate for the Western occupation of Afghanistan. Gordon and Perugini have thus shown how the concept of human rights has become an epistemic and moral framework subtending 'a culture of *ethical violence* . . . in which human rights, humanitarianism, and domination are intricately tied'.[23] Their critique updates, in regard to contemporary humanitarians, what Du Bois wrote about missionaries in *Color and Democracy*, a text to which I will return in concluding this book. Du Bois put it this way: 'Even if among these people of kindly intent there should be some who really succeed in doing an appreciable amount of good, the good they do often is not sufficient to compensate for the bad for which the system back of them is responsible.'[24] With such insights in mind, the critical theorist Randall Williams starts his book *Divided World: Human Rights and Its Violence* from Du Bois's writings in the 1940s, drawing on additional Marxists to highlight 'the oppositional relation between two major postwar political forms, human rights and decolonization'.[25]

We can see, then, that insightful critical theorists have demonstrated how human rights can presuppose an oppressive, hierarchical and ironically provincial anthropology, operating through paternalistic declarations, designations and calls for development. In other words, we can see that in practice, when citizens of the West invoke human rights, they are often speaking for others instead of standing with them, or they are citing human rights only to justify colonial occupations and violence. Here the decolonial critiques of responsibility and human rights overlap: the critical point is that both can substitute minimal moral reform for maximal political transformation.[26]

But the social truth of human rights is also found in the Amnesty International tote bag on an otherwise conservative campus in Atlanta, in the community events board in a progressive church in Minneapolis, and in the Human Rights Campaign bumper sticker on a car outside a bar in Houston. That is to say, the discourse of human rights articulates the terrain of justice-oriented actors today. It is the language from which many of us begin, especially as students and in faith groups, not quite knowing where to go from there. For this reason, human rights are broadly legible starting points for conversations about politics.[27] 'Human rights norms and organizations remain the chief source of idealistic passion in the world', Moyn writes – 'at least among its well-meaning cosmopolitan elites.'[28] A key strategic question in turn, Moyn continues, is 'what to do with the progressive moral energy to which human rights have been tethered in their short career. Is the order of the day to reinvest it or to redirect it?'[29]

I contend that reinvesting in human rights claims is worthwhile in order to strengthen the oppositional (decolonial) elements within them. This is a method with broad historical precedent, including how the diplomats of recently independent states variously mobilised rights claims at the United Nations following World War II. While associating human rights and empire is now what the historian Roland Burke calls 'an academic commonplace', this was not the case even and especially among the self-understanding of newly postcolonial states in the 1950s.[30] At the South-South dialogue that was the Bandung conference of 1955, for instance, many delegates agreed on the universality of human rights. Neither the critique that human rights violated cultural particularity nor the sense that human rights were a colonial instrument was present at Bandung. It was quite the opposite. '[A]t this point in history', Burke explains, 'in the eyes of European, colonial powers, human rights were a threat to their colonial holdings and legacies more than a neocolonial tool.'[31] As Burke further argues regarding the relationship between human rights and decolonisation, 'Human rights became a perennial aspect of anti-imperial and postcolonial phraseology not for its conceptual clarity, but for its versatility as a language with all-purpose emancipatory potential.'[32] More specific precedents include, for instance, Jamaican Premier Norman Manley's early 1961 human rights policy, which his government understood as in line with the larger regional project of the West Indies Federation, and the Xukuru nation's 2018 victory in the Inter-American Court of Human Rights against the state of Brazil, which the Xukuru understood as a wider victory for Indigenous peoples. Indeed, the Xukuru have continued to use the language of human rights not only to make claims on the state, but also as a way to name ongoing wrongs and to motivate additional struggles.[33] With this robust, but often overlooked, decolonial history of human rights in mind, the legal theorist José-Manuel Barreto has stressed, in regard to state violence and exploitative capitalism, that contemporary social movements 'have in human rights a powerful discourse to resist them' as well as 'to fathom a new world order pervaded by global justice'.[34]

* * *

In addition to learning from the historical examples Burke, Barreto and others highlight, *Choose Your Bearing* looks to the cultural theorist Stuart Hall to gain its methodological foundation for beginning from human rights. Hall allows us to see how human rights can serve as a starting point to develop an ethics for a new Left – to motivate a politics – in the present. His sixth, seventh and eighth lectures on cultural studies in 1983 inform how I read human rights in the present. In Lecture 6, 'Ideology and Ideological Struggle', Hall treats the function of ideology through the philosopher Louis Althusser's concept of 'articulation'. 'The theory of articulation', Hall explains, 'asks how an ideology discovers its subject rather than how the subject thinks the necessary and inevitable thoughts which belong to it.'[35] That is, ideologies work in at least two ways: they not only limit our understanding of the world, but they also empower us to find a place in it. In Hall's words, ideologies enable us 'to begin to make some sense or intelligibility of [our] historical situation, without reducing those forms of intelligibility to [our] socioeconomic or class location or social position'.[36] The example he gives here is religion, arguing that religion has 'no necessary political connotation'.[37] While religion conditions individuals ('subjects'), those articulations are historically contingent. They can always be transformed through re-articulation. 'To use a geographical metaphor', he goes on, 'to struggle around religion in that country' – a country where religious influences predominate – 'you need to know the ideological terrain, the lay of the land . . . If you want to move religion, to rearticulate it in another way, you are going to come across all the grooves that have articulated it already.'[38]

Hall continues with a key point that I will extend to how human rights have been articulated in the US: '[R]eligion has become the *valorised* ideological terrain, the domain into which all the different cultural strands are obliged to enter.'[39] As a consequence, 'no political movement in that society can become popular without negotiating the religious terrain. Social movements have to transform it, butt into it, inflect it, develop it, clarify it – but they must engage with it.'[40] Reading human rights as Hall reads religion, I argue that human rights discourse – even as a limiting ideology for the reasons Spivak, Mignolo, Puar, Williams and others have documented – allows actors to make sense of our historical situation, providing a topographical map to guide our responses to an unjust present. Human rights claims thus can also serve as an empowering ideology, if they can be re-articulated to motivate further ethical, political and spiritual commitment.

Hall's discussion of the Marxist philosopher Antonio Gramsci's concept of hegemony in Lecture 7, 'Domination and Hegemony', develops Hall's previous claims regarding religion. '[B]ecause hegemony is the establishment of the leading position on a variety of sites of social and political struggle', he says, 'it includes domains that are usually ignored by Marxists, like the discourses of morality.'[41] 'Anybody who wants to command the space of common sense, or popular consciousness, and practical reasoning', he goes on, 'has to pay attention to the domain of the moral, since it is the language within which vast numbers of people actually set about their political calculations.'[42] 'The Left has rarely talked about that space in which the difference between the "good" and the "bad" is defined', meaning 'it has rarely attempted to establish the language of a socialist morality'.[43] In stronger terms, Hall argues that the Left 'has abstained from engaging on a front where it ought to be present'.[44] Here are his summary lines, said in central Illinois a few years into Ronald Reagan's first term:

A hegemonic politics operates in the cultural apparatuses, the discourse of moral languages, in the economic struggle, in the political space (including electoral struggles as well as other forms). It tries to occupy each and every front and understands that victory is not the great battle which ends with the final collapse of the enemy. Victory is the seizing of the balance of power on each of those fronts of struggle. It is commanding the balance of power on each of those ideological forces at each point in the social formation. That is a lesson which few on the Left have understood, but one which the bourgeoisie (especially in its contemporary forms) absolutely understands. They do not leave the cultural, intellectual, and moral spaces alone. They do not ignore the academies because there are relatively few people involved. They do not refuse to do battle on the terrain of sexual, social, and religious problems because that is not the domain of politics and power. They know that if they are going to make a difference in history, they are going to have to make a difference on all those fronts.[45]

Hall's response to neoliberal hegemony, to social values created by market logics, does not simply look to apply previous models of social change. '[W]e have lived through a succession of periods in the Western world when nonproblematic forms of the class struggle and the class belongingness of ideologies have simply refused to appear', he states in his final lecture, returning to name the problem that a methodological attention to cultural forms tries to solve.[46] 'There are only two responses to this situation: Either continue to use theory to guarantee that somewhere down the road such correspondences will appear, or undertake the exceedingly difficult task of bringing theory into line with the complexities of the empirical problems you have to explain.'[47] His lectures continually emphasise the latter approach: theory has to look to strange places and use various imaginative approaches to be able to understand empirical problems in the present. But that does not mean that theory should avoid the compromises that come with intervening into the predominant terrain.[48] Critical theory can try either to posit an alternative to existing vocabularies or to modify those vocabularies on their own terms. Hall consistently advocates for the latter, calling for a politics that 'strengthen[s] and deepen[s] the oppositional elements of already existing cultural forms'.[49] This is different from 'inviting people to abandon the forms in which they are involved and to suddenly move over to a different place, into a different formation'.[50] Hall would warn against any utopian suggestion of an absolute break, event or interruption. He teaches that such suggestions tend to fail not only because they are not persuasive to actors who do not want to depart from their habitual lives, but also because ethical theorists are not as good as we think we are at diagnosing which cultural forms are problematic. For him, all cultural forms are contradictory.[51]

* * *

One of the examples Hall gives of a cultural form that is worth strengthening and deepening is the discourse of rights. '[T]he

language of rights', he says, 'cannot belong *only* to the bourgeoisie.'[52] Civil rights are an example. While the liberal and
institutional ground on which civil rights are contested might
lead to containment, he acknowledges, they are nevertheless 'real and effective moments of protest, resistance, and
struggle'.[53] He also names human rights, noting that bourgeois rights meant more than merely gaining rights for some
classes, because they also 'open[ed] the possibility for classes
which had been excluded by the ways in which that ideology
functioned, to claim the universality of such rights'.[54] 'Those
excluded others', he says, 'could struggle to place themselves
within a language which claimed to speak of *human* rights.'[55]
Human rights thus provide an example of his claim that sometimes people who are being excluded from gaining rights do
'not need another term; they needed *that* term, the term
which the bourgeoisie already understood, in order to conduct the struggle'.[56]

Both Hall's call for a method that deepens the oppositional
elements of existing cultural forms instead of appealing to a
transcendental ethics of interruption and his example of rights
language to illustrate this point raise problems for many theorists. Some worry that using rights language individualises
struggle and cannot sufficiently challenge the state, a concern
I address further in Chapter 2.[57] Hall has a similar concern,
going on to acknowledge that 'the franchise is eventually won
in a form which, while allowing [those previously excluded]
access to political power, also individualises and fragments
their political representation (one person, one vote)'.[58] Rights
can also limit (or delimit) mobilisations, thereby containing
radical definitions of democracy 'by articulating them, stitch-
ing them into place within, ideologies of liberalism'.[59]

Acknowledging these concerns, Hall nevertheless points us
to struggle on the ever-contested social terrain. '[T]he meaning
of all these terms', he says about rights as well as democracy in

that final lecture, and the struggles about the definitions and implications of those terms, 'changed from the seventeenth to the nineteenth century. The same terms refer to different realities. They can even represent different interests, different demands, different sites of struggle, as the historical conditions in which they are mobilized, the social forces to which they are attached, change.'[60]

I suggest that human rights can speak to the domain of the moral, the terrain of ethics through which most people live out their (often unacknowledged) political commitments. Because human rights have been articulated in a widely accessible document – the Universal Declaration of Human Rights – actors can debate this text. Because human rights also belong to a longer, generally under-studied radical tradition – David Walker, José Carlos Mariátegui, Claudia Jones, Malcolm X, Patricia Monture and Paul Gilroy come to mind – actors can apprentice themselves to this tradition and thus join these conversations.[61] These debates and conversations can lead to community-guided political actions. This book itself is a reflection inspired by, and an elaboration on, the radical rights claims made by those noted a few lines above; below, I will briefly elaborate on how reflecting on the Universal Declaration can inspire debates about the habits and structures through which we live.

* * *

When we take the Universal Declaration as a starting point, we can note how extractions of goods that allow for 'normal' daily life to proceed in some places involves the exploitation of resources (and ultimately lives) according to colonial patterns.[62] Many resources, from the beans for our morning lattes to the lithium for our hybrid cars, are still being extracted by the most precarious people for shipment to the

West. Although political power shifted during formal decolonisation, to a considerable extent economic power remains in the hands of elites in colonising countries. For instance, after independence, leaders of Ghana and Nigeria have had to face the problem that the control of cocoa and oil markets remains in London, New York and Houston. It is in considering such a problematic that Ghana's first prime minister, Kwame Nkrumah, said, 'Neo-colonialism is . . . the worst form of imperialism. For those who practise it, it means power without responsibility and for those who suffer it, it means exploitation without redress.'[63] Studying the production of commodities such as cocoa and oil, as well as cobalt from the Congo that goes into our electronic devices, allows us to see endurances of the practices of forced labour that the Universal Declaration of Human Rights prohibits in Article 4 and aims to provide a bulwark against in Article 22.[64]

Moreover, when we read Article 13, Part 1 – 'Everyone has the right to freedom of movement and residence within the borders of each state' – we can ask: What are the necessary conditions for having this right? For the coffee or avocado farmer who picks beans or fruits during his or her day, what does this right mean? If we consider this meaning, and our responsibilities for carrying out this right, we quickly see that what is needed is much more than a 'fair trade' programme, which still looks like people in the West drinking the best coffee (saved for export) and travelling to the coffee-producing countries (say as tourists or studying abroad) while the people in the rest of the world stay in one place for much of their lives given their economic exigencies.

Article 3 of the Universal Declaration of Human Rights states: 'Everyone has the right to life, liberty and security of person.' This line could be taken up to intervene in the US context because 'liberty' is couched between life and security of person. While Republicans in the US have elevated liberty over and above life and security of person, the Covid-19 pandemic has brought into relief, once again, the need for life and security if one is to have liberty in a meaningful way. Article 3 is a secular statement, agreed upon widely enough to make it into the Universal Declaration. It could be cited and used to push local mobilisations for socialised medicine in the US, deployed in places like churches where 'life' is already articulated strongly (if often in conservative senses) and where human rights are often already taken seriously. It is noteworthy that Pope Francis, following a Catholic tradition that suddenly embraced human rights in the middle of the twentieth century, employs the language of human rights.[65] Meanwhile, the Human Rights Campaign is the largest LGBTQ advocacy group in the US. It is rare that the Pope and the queer advocates agree on the language of struggle. Of course, they have different understandings of what human rights imply. But if we take seriously Hall's argument for deepening oppositional elements in already existing cultural forms, then some critiques, here that the Catholic Church is too conservative or that the HRC is too corporate, appear as unhelpful. The point, Hall teaches us, is to shift the meaning of (often problematic) inherited language in order to make political gains. We do not get to choose this language, and we desperately need to have cultural conversations, on the widest possible level, in order to make these political gains. Hall reminds us that '[p]eople have to have a language to speak about where they are and what other possible futures are available to them'.[66] While 'emergent cultural forms do not contain their own guarantees', they nevertheless 'contain real possibilities'.[67]

Many of us, after having conversations with others to examine our daily lives and to consider how they relate to the rights listed in the Universal Declaration, will find that we participate in patterns that violate human rights. In response, many of us remain invested in the ever-difficult task of 'unlearning imperialism'.[68] We are left with some questions: Can we participate differently? Is there a way to live in our daily lives – as externally determined as they feel from trying to provide for our families and to pay our bills and debts – such that we do not violate but in fact protect the rights of others and of the earth itself?[69]

Thesis and Chapter Outline

The thesis of this book is that rights claims made by the dispossessed entail duties for citizens of wealthy countries to live differently. The particular claim I take as my focus is Glissant's call for a 'right to opacity', which I explain in Chapter 1. In Chapter 2, I use the philosopher James Griffin's distinction between primary and secondary duties in order to argue that the primary duties corresponding to the right to opacity include participation in coalitional protest against the state and corporate forces that violate rights. I then treat the prayer camps at Standing Rock in 2016 as places where actors articulated rights claims resonant with the right to opacity. These examples show how the right to opacity functions in practice. In Chapters 3 and 4, I further argue that the secondary duties corresponding to the right to opacity include, beyond coalitional participation, a broader sense of solidarity extending to basic areas of life: what food we eat, what jobs we take, what clothes we wear, when and how we travel or decide not to travel, and how we form kinship relationships. Having treated the ethical strengths of rights claims in the first four chapters, in Chapter 5 I consider one important limitation of human rights claims, namely, that they can foreclose other political visions. To make this point, rather than prescribing a universal relation between human rights and politics, or conversely rejecting the usefulness of rights in all cases, I examine a particular context: W. E. B. Du Bois's brief use of human rights and then abandonment of the discourse for its complicity with capitalism and colonialism in the 1940s. Examining Du Bois's relationship to human rights can inform how we recalibrate our relationship to rights and responsibilities in the situations in which we find ourselves today.

While this book overall keeps considerable faith in human rights as a starting point for a Left/decolonial ethics and politics, it concludes with the acknowledgement that if human rights are tools for making political gains in addition to rethinking ethical duties and responsibilities, then a strategic leveraging of human rights claims also needs to know when not to deploy the discourse and instead seek other paths. As a whole, *Choose Your Bearing* can be read as an extended inquiry into what Tiffany King calls the 'new and old forms of speech' that decolonial social movements engage, create, abandon and require.[70] In other words, this book can be read as dwelling with what ethical theory could become when it is inflected by protest and prayer.[71] *Choose Your Bearing* is ultimately a call for the West – which Glissant understands as a project more than a place (DA 14/CD 2) – to transform its understanding of value itself.

* * *

To begin this book, I have suggested that human rights contain no guarantee, but that they speak to where many people are and suggest futures available to them. They are a starting point to strengthen and deepen already present oppositional commitments. Because the language of human rights is already operative across many campuses, churches and other political spaces, it can be leveraged to contest oppressive sexual, social, religious and educational norms. Naming human rights violations is a way to speak to the 'bad'. Defending human rights goals is a way to affirm the 'good'. Most importantly, more than just starting conversations, at their best human rights claims can inspire political commitment. Making connections from everyday life to the Universal Declaration invites actors to show up to protest a pipeline or to decline the offer of an internship in oil and gas. If we think about what we can do collectively to challenge human rights violations, we will begin to consider local, direct actions.[72] We can boycott companies that violate human rights and we can challenge these forces more directly. We can divest our money from pipeline-funding banks and investments, and we can occupy those financial institutions in order to bring attention to how they support a fossil fuel economy that violates Indigenous rights to drinking water and religious practices per Universal Declaration Articles 3, 18 and 25.[73] We can remind each other of the agency we still have.

Justice-oriented actors have in human rights claims a call to participate in activism around land here and now. Ongoing rights work connected to decolonial movements in the Americas demands honouring treaty rights and repatriating land. It also involves shifting currently predominant conceptualisations of obligation, particularly around debt and migration. A decolonial sense of responsibility would contribute to a larger reckoning with historical and ongoing (colonial) hierarchies of humanity. A clear example of the need to reframe obligation lies in the fact that Western financial bodies are willing to forgive some of Ukraine's debt but not that of Barbados.[74] A further example lies in the fact that the United States and many European countries continue to deny the rights of entry, healthcare, education and citizenship to migrants who have been forced to move for reasons of war, famine or conflict that Western agricultural or military practices caused.[75] Thought in terms of connecting movements and reframing obligations, the practice of human rights becomes about not just designating and delegating power, but about building power in the face of ongoing state violence.

'Resistance presupposes power', the political philosopher Joy James clarifies.[76] She goes on:

Those who differentiate between power and domination in order to link power to communal goals for social and cultural freedoms, economic sufficiency, and radical democracy posit a vision of political community as the context for human development. Recognizing the diverse experiences and powers of oppressed peoples is essential in order to challenge subordination and exploitation. Viable political communities reflect the diversity and plurality of humanity. With foundations in justice and equity, a law of human rights posits one humanity: the right to participate in self-governance, to experience freedom, to live without violence and economic degradation.[77]

This is the promise of human rights work today, James teaches: to build power in 'risk-taking commitments' that affirm decolonial options.[78]

* * *

In the following chapter, I read Glissant's 'right to opacity' as a summary concept inviting practices that militate against the status quo of violent, rights-violating resource extraction and commodity production. Spivak writes about the globalised present, 'Today Marx's ghost needs stronger offerings than Human Rights with economics worked in . . . or even responsibility (choice or being-called) in the Western tradition.'[79] Following Glissant, *Choose Your Bearing* presents a 'stronger offering' in Spivak's sense: not human rights to justify development economics, but human rights as a gateway to political commitment, where responsibility is understood as a relational practice – between autonomous choice and heteronomous being-called – of participation, solidarity and feasibility.[80] Connecting human rights discourse to decolonial philosophy by explaining duties corresponding to the right to opacity, this book highlights the ethical paths that remain open to us if we not only choose to listen to the claims of others, but also allow them to bear on us.

Notes

1. See Nemonte Nenquimo, 'This is my message to the western world – your civilization is killing life on earth', *The Guardian*, 12 October 2020, <https://www.theguardian.com/commentisfree/2020/oct/12/western-worldyour-civilisation-killing-life-on-earth-indigenous-amazon-planet>.

2. See Walter Rodney, *How Europe Underdeveloped Africa* (New York: Verso, 2018). See also Samir Amin, *Accumulation on a World Scale: A Critique of the Theory of Underdevelopment* (New York: Monthly Review Press, 1974).

3. My method here follows Enrique Dussel in his *Ethics of Liberation*. There Dussel writes that 'the Other . . . the oppressed or excluded face, the nonintentional victim . . . reveals himself or herself as the cry for which one must have ears to be able to hear . . . The Other is the possible victim and caused by my functional action in the system. I am re-sponsible' (Enrique Dussel, *Ethics of Liberation: In the Age of Globalization and Exclusion* (Durham, NC: Duke University Press, 2013), p. 384). It is noteworthy that I will follow Dussel's point here in spirit if not in Levinas's vocabulary of 'the Other'.

4. Gayatri Spivak, 'Responsibility', *boundary 2* 21, no. 3 (1994): p. 21.

5. Mojtaba Mahdavi, 'A Postcolonial Critique of Responsibility to Protect in the Middle East', *Perceptions* XX, no. 1 (2015): p. 7; Siddharth Mallavarapu, 'Colonialism and the Responsibility to Protect', in *Theorising the Responsibility to Protect*, ed. Ramesh Thakur and William Maley (Cambridge: Cambridge University Press, 2015), p. 306.

6. Samuel Moyn, *Human Rights and the Uses of History* (New York: Verso, 2017), p. 2.

7. Kathryn Sikkink, *The Hidden Face of Rights: Toward a Politics of Responsibilities* (New Haven: Yale University Press, 2020), p. 5.

8. Ibid.

9. See Rebecca Solnit, 'Big oil coined "carbon footprints" to blame us for their greed. Keep them on the hook', *The Guardian*, 23 August 2021, <https://www.theguardian.com/commentisfree/2021/aug/23/big-oil-coined-carbon-footprints-to-blame-us-for-their-greed-keep-them-on-the-hook>.

10. Gayatri Spivak, 'Supplementing Marxism' in *Whither Marxism: Global Crises in International Perspective*, ed. Bernd Magnus and Stephen Cullenberg (New York: Routledge, 1994), p. 117.

11. As the social scientist Yascha Mounk notes in his recent study about narratives of the welfare state and the conservative emphasis on personal responsibility in the US, 'Over the last decades, the concept of responsibility has shrunk to a punitive core' (Yascha Mounk, *The Age of Responsibility: Luck, Choice, and the Welfare State* (Cambridge, MA: Harvard University Press, 2017), p. 21). In my view, the Left still needs to envision a concept of responsibility that functions as a legible and popular alternative to this punitive concept.

12. Michael Rothberg, *The Implicated Subject: Beyond Victims and Perpetrators* (Stanford: Stanford University Press, 2019), p. 1. I thank Patricia Hill Collins for asking me, at a conference in 2016, to consider further to whom my work is addressed.

13. Nitzan Lebovic, 'Introduction: Complicity and Dissent, or Why We Need Solidarity between Struggles', *CLCWeb: Comparative Literature and Culture* 21, no. 3 (2019): p. 2.

14. Antonio Y. Vázquez-Arroyo, *Political Responsibility: Responding to Predicaments of Power* (New York: Columbia University Press, 2016), p. xvi.

15. Ibid. p. xvii.

16. In regard to Marx's method, Stuart Hall says that there is 'the necessary moment of abstraction', but 'you cannot stop there – which a great deal of theory does'; in turn '[y]ou need to return to the problem you really wanted to solve, but now understanding that it is the product of "many determinations," not of one . . . you return to a world of many determinations, where the attempts to explain and understand are open and never eliding – because the historical reality to be explained has no known or determined

end' (Stuart Hall, 'Through the Prism of an Intellectual Life', in *Essential Essays Volume 2: Identity and Diaspora*, ed. David Morley (Durham, NC: Duke University Press, 2019), p. 311).

17. Walter D. Mignolo, 'Who Speaks for the "Human" in Human Rights?', *Hispanic Issues On Line* (2009): p. 10.

18. Ibid. p. 11.

19. See Nelson Maldonado-Torres, 'On the Coloniality of Human Rights', *Revista Crítica de Ciências Sociais* 114 (2017): pp. 117–36.

20. Ibid. p. 130.

21. Jasbir Puar, *The Right to Maim: Debility, Capacity, Disability* (Durham, NC: Duke University Press, 2017), p. 99.

22. Julia Suárez-Krabbe, *Race, Rights and Rebels: Alternatives to Human Rights and Development from the Global South* (London: Rowman & Littlefield International, 2016), p. 10.

23. Nicola Perugini and Neve Gordon, *The Human Right to Dominate* (Oxford: Oxford University Press, 2015), p. 77.

24. W. E. B. Du Bois, *Color and Democracy* (New York: Oxford, 2007), p. 326.

25. Randall Williams, *The Divided World: Human Rights and Its Violence* (Minneapolis: University of Minnesota Press, 2010), p. xxi. While some might say that Williams's and my arguments work against each other, in fact we share many premises and differ only slightly in our conclusions. As I will demonstrate in Chapter 2, I follow Williams's call 'to shift our analytical perspective from one that assumes imperialism is a problem *for* international law, to one that grasps their mutually constitutive relationship', such that 'anti-imperialist theorizations direct us to look *outside the law* for sources of revolutionary, international transformations' (ibid. pp. xx, xxx). 'In this decolonizing register', Williams goes on, 'the displacement of the juridical makes possible a critical reckoning oriented toward the building of local, national, regional, and international movements in a counter-counterrevolutionary mode' (ibid. p. xxx). Looking beyond the Universal Declaration of Human Rights, Williams highlights 'alternative forms of universality', conceptions that, in addition to 'practices of freedom', were 'much more directly

rooted in the actualities of struggle' (ibid. p. xviii). By examining how rights claims carry with them a moral weight that bears on the desires and practices of those in the West, I am also looking outside the law. Further, the Indigenous rights claims that inspired this book certainly emerged from the actualities of struggle. It is for these reasons that I see my argument and that of Williams to have much more productive resonance than one might initially assume. Indeed, the following chapters' inquiry into solidarities beyond one-time participation in events offers a way to consider the political implications of rights claims beyond what Williams accurately calls a 'short-term urgent rescue model' that 'consistently reproduces an international division of humanity and works against the formation of a truly international practice of solidarity' (ibid. p. 38).

26. Cf. Samuel Moyn, *The Last Utopia: Human Rights in History* (Cambridge, MA: The Belknap Press of Harvard University, 2010), p. 171.

27. To continue the example of the Amnesty International bags on campus, when one student sees another with a bag claiming 'I Am a Human Rights Defender' or 'Build Bridges Not Walls', it can lead to further questions: What does that mean to you? How do you defend human rights around here?

28. Moyn, *Human Rights*, p. 101.

29. Ibid.

30. Roland Burke, *Decolonization and the Evolution of International Human Rights* (Philadelphia: University of Pennsylvania Press, 2013), p. 113.

31. Ibid. p. 114.

32. Roland Burke, Marco Duranti and A. Dirk Moses, 'Introduction: Human Rights, Empire, and After', in *Decolonization, Self-Determination, and the Rise of Global Human Rights Politics*, ed. A. Dirk Moses, Marco Duranti and Roland Burke (Cambridge: Cambridge University Press, 2020), p. 6.

33. For a discussion of Manley's relationship to human rights and decolonisation, see Steven L. B. Jensen, 'Manley, Human Rights, and the End of Colonial Rule in Jamaica', in Moses et al.,

Decolonization, p. 250. My knowledge of the Xukuru case comes from personal communication with Marcos and Diego Xukuru. I would like to thank o povo Xukuru for their guidance.

34. José-Manuel Barreto, 'Decolonial Thinking and the Quest for Decolonising Human Rights', *Asian Journal of Social Science* 46, nos. 4–5 (2018): p. 499.

35. Stuart Hall, *Cultural Studies 1983* (Durham, NC: Duke University Press, 2016), p. 142.

36. Ibid. p. 143.

37. Ibid.

38. Ibid.

39. Ibid. p. 144.

40. Ibid.

41. Ibid. p. 173.

42. Ibid.

43. Ibid.

44. Ibid. p. 174.

45. Ibid. pp. 177–8. These lines recall his 1979 essay 'The great moving right show', his diagnosis of the radical right: 'What makes these representations popular', he writes about the radical right's rhetorical moves around law and order, enemies of the state, the threat of anarchy and the idea of the 'enemy within', 'is that they have a purchase on practice, they shape it, they are written into its materiality. What constitutes them as a danger is that they change the nature of the terrain itself on which struggles of different kinds are taking place; and they have pertinent effects on these struggles. Currently, they are gaining ground in defining the "conjunctural". That is exactly the terrain on which the forces of opposition must organize, if we are to transform it' (Stuart Hall, 'The Great Moving Right Show', in *Selected Political Writings*, ed. Sally Davison et al. (Durham, NC: Duke University Press, 2017), pp. 176, 186). I read Hall's final 1983 cultural studies lecture, 'Culture, Resistance, and Struggle' as an elaboration on the kind of oppositional struggle he called for at the end of the 1979 'The Great Moving Right Show'.

46. Hall, *Cultural Studies 1983*, p. 185.

47. Ibid.

48. Here I also follow Edward Said's claim that human rights are a way to see, and to argue for, connections across the planet: 'To be "for" human rights means, in effect, to be willing to venture interpretations of those rights in the same place and with the same language employed by the dominant power, to dispute its hierarchy and methods, to elucidate what it has hidden, to pronounce what it has silenced or rendered unpronounceable. These intellectual procedures require, above all, an acute sense not of how things are separated but of how they are connected, mixed, involved, embroiled, linked' (Edward Said, 'Nationalism, Human Rights, and Interpretation', in *Reflections on Exile and Other Essays* (Cambridge, MA: Harvard University Press, 2002), p. 430).

49. Hall, *Cultural Studies 1983*, p. 189.

50. Ibid. Examples of twentieth-century Continental ethics that call for a radical abandonment of present forms of life include Alain Badiou's call for fidelity to the 'event' that interrupts everyday life and Emmanuel Levinas's prescription of passive, prayerful reverence toward the Other.

51. Hall, *Cultural Studies 1983*, p. 188.

52. Ibid. p. 181.

53. Ibid.

54. Ibid. p. 182.

55. Ibid.

56. Ibid. pp. 183–4.

57. Recent work I have found instructive on these points includes Jessica Whyte, *The Morals of the Market: Human Rights and the Rise of Neoliberalism* (New York: Verso, 2019) and Jayan Nayar, 'The Non-Perplexity of Human Rights', *Theory & Event* 22, no. 1 (2019): pp. 267–305. See also Joseph R. Slaughter, *Human Rights Inc.: The World Novel, Narrative Form, and International Law* (New York: Fordham University Press, 2007), p. 91.

58. Hall, *Cultural Studies 1983*, p. 183.

59. Ibid.

60. Ibid.

61. For rights claims in the work of these figures, see for example David Walker, 'Appeal' (1829); José Carlos Mariátegui, 'The Problem of Land' (1928); Claudia Jones, 'We Seek Full Equality for Women' (1949); Malcolm X, 'The Ballot or the Bullet' (1964); Patricia Monture, 'The Roles and Responsibilities of Aboriginal Women' (1992); Paul Gilroy, *Against Race* (2000) and *Postcolonial Melancholia* (2005).

62. I have previously written about the connection between human rights and decolonisation in Benjamin P. Davis, 'What Could Human Rights Do? A Decolonial Inquiry', *Transmodernity: Journal of Peripheral Cultural Production of the Luso-Hispanic World* 9, no. 5 (2020): pp. 1–22.

63. Kwame Nkrumah, *Neo-Colonialism: The Last Stage of Imperialism* (London: Heinemann, 1965), p. xi. Nkrumah's is another way of stating the problem of coloniality. 'Coloniality', Nelson Maldonado-Torres explains, drawing on Aníbal Quijano, 'refers to long-standing patterns of power that emerged as a result of colonialism, but that define culture, labor, intersubjective relations, and knowledge production well beyond the strict limits of colonial administrations' (Nelson Maldonado-Torres, 'On the Coloniality of Being', *Cultural Studies* 21, nos. 2–3 (2007): p. 243).

64. Summarising Ngugi wa Thiong'o's important attention to Western cultural impositions in addition to economic control, Robert J. C. Young writes, 'Ngugi has drawn on Fanon to add to Nkrumah's analysis the additional component of the neocolonial elite, the often western-educated ruling class who identify more closely with the west than with the people of the country that they rule; in return for an affluent life-style, they facilitate the exploitative operations of western national and multinational companies' (Robert J. C. Young, *Postcolonialism: An Historical Introduction* (Oxford: Wiley, 2016), p. 48).

65. The *Vatican News* got right to the point in their perfect title: see Francesca Merlo, 'Pope: Human rights first, even if it means going against the tide', *Vatican News*, 10 December 2018, <https://www.vaticannews.va/en/pope/news/2018-12/pope-francis-message-human-rights-day-international-conference.html>.

66. Hall, *Cultural Studies 1983*, p. 206.

67. Ibid.

68. I borrow this phrase from Ariella Aïsha Azoulay, *Potential History: Unlearning Imperialism* (New York: Verso, 2019). In *Potential History*, Azoulay makes several insightful critiques of both human rights discourse and the United Nations. For example, she distinguishes between official invocations of human rights and a different set of performative rights: 'Rights are reconsidered in this book as protocols for a shared world, an alternative configuration to the dominant discourse of human rights that is conceived and considered from the perspective of differential sovereign powers and emblematized by the Universal Declaration of Human Rights . . . This sovereign universal human rights discourse based on abstract equality renders obsolete and irrelevant the real, concrete inequalities perpetrated by imperialism and inherent in the position of citizens in a differential body politic' (ibid. p. 54). I hope that by the end of this book it is clear how much I have learned from this criticism as well as this vision of rights as 'protocols for a shared world'.

69. For my extended discussion of reading human rights with a view toward ethical changes in daily life, see Benjamin P. Davis, 'Human Rights and Caribbean Philosophy: Implications for Teaching', *Journal of Human Rights Practice* 12, no. 4 (2021): pp. 136–44.

70. Tiffany Lethabo King, *The Black Shoals: Offshore Formations of Black and Native Studies* (Durham, NC: Duke University Press, 2019), p. 44.

71. Standing Rock will be my principal example of protest and prayer. I also have in mind prayers in the work of Aimé Césaire and Frantz Fanon. Both of arguably their most well-known prayers reflect a remarkable receptivity to the world and to a world in the making, a world that could be, a world not yet: Césaire in his 'robust prayer' [*ma prière virile*] says 'make of me a man of closure / make of me a man of beginning / make of me a man of reaping / but also make of me a man of sowing'; and Fanon, in his 'final prayer', says, 'O my body, make of me always a man who questions!' See Aimé Césaire, *Journal of a Homecoming/Cahier d'un retour au pays natal* (Durham, NC: Duke

University Press, 2017), pp. 128/129; Frantz Fanon, *Black Skin, White Masks*, trans. Charles Lam Markmann (London: Pluto Press, 2008), p. 181. In reading protest and prayer together into ethics, I follow a long line of Caribbean philosophy that combines politics and aesthetics, what Paget Henry describes in terms of historicism and poeticism (Paget Henry, *Caliban's Reason: Introducing Afro-Caribbean Philosophy* (New York: Routledge, 2000), pp. 93, 112). Glissant himself acknowledges this lineage, reading Césaire as combining 'political activity' and 'poetic creation' (PhR 132).

72. My method is also informed by the work of Lewis Gordon. See for example Lewis Gordon, 'Shifting the Geography of Reason in an Age of Disciplinary Decadence', *Transmodernity: Journal of Peripheral Cultural Production of the Luso-Hispanic World* 1, no. 2 (2011). See also his emphasis on collective responsibility: Lewis Gordon, *Fear of Black Consciousness* (New York: Farrar, Straus and Giroux, 2022), p. 158. Cf. the kind of pedagogy LaRose Parris calls for in *Being Apart: Theoretical and Existential Resistance in Africana Literature* (Charlottesville: University of Virginia Press, 2015), p. 165.

73. See Emma Howard, 'A beginner's guide to fossil fuel divestment', *The Guardian*, 23 June 2015, <https://www.theguardian.com/environment/2015/jun/23/a-beginners-guide-to-fossil-fuel-divestment>; see also Green Portfolio, 'Is your hard-earned cash funding fossil fuel development?', 12 April 2022, <https://greenportfolio.com/blog/banking_and_climate_change/>.

74. '[B]y failing to fully account for how the exceptional costs of climate change affect national wealth, the I.M.F. and the World Bank have wound up driving countries in need toward profit-reaping hedge funds and banks, to borrow billions of dollars, often at credit-card-like interest rates. Throughout, the debts have been collected. They were collected as the shadow of the 2008 financial crisis lingered and as a pandemic decimated tenuous health care systems and tourist-reliant economies. They continue to be collected despite a climate crisis that is caused almost entirely by the copious fossil fuels that those same

creditor nations burned to industrialize and achieve their own wealth, the very wealth that undergirds the I.M.F. Caribbean nations are being asked, in a sense, to pay not only their own debts but the rest of the world's debts, too, for all the progress it made while leaving the Caribbean behind . . . Debt is written off in Ukraine, as it was for Germany after World War II. Other countries, though, the ones subjugated throughout history, have seen their humanitarian crises ignored . . . Perhaps the suggestion that lenders forgive debt isn't about kindness but about obligation – about seeing it as a kind of back tax that they owe to society and to frontline societies, in particular' (Abrahm Lustgarten, 'Oceans of Debt', *The New York Times Magazine* (31 July 2022): pp. 31, 49, 47).

75. See for example Lea Coffineau, 'Migration as a Claim for Reparations: Connections between political agency and migration', *Public Seminar*, 7 December 2020, <https://publicseminar.org/essays/migration-as-a-claim-for-reparations/>.

76. Joy James, *Resisting State Violence: Radicalism, Gender, & Race in U.S. Culture* (Minneapolis: University of Minnesota Press, 1996), p. 243.

77. Ibid.

78. Ibid.

79. Gayatri Spivak, 'What's Left of Theory?', in *An Aesthetic Education in the Era of Globalization* (Cambridge, MA: Harvard University Press, 2012), p. 197.

80. For a critique of the legal 'liability model' of responsibility, see Iris Marion Young, *Responsibility for Justice* (Oxford: Oxford University Press, 2011), pp. 95–122. For an elaboration of the (heteronomous) Levinasian being-called model of responsibility, including a helpful comparison of that model to the (autonomous) Sartrean model of responsibility, see François Raffoul, *The Origins of Responsibility* (Bloomington: Indiana University Press, 2010), pp. 121–219.

1 The Right to Opacity in Theory

Toward an Alternative Ethical Vocabulary

Contemporary ethical theory needs to speak to globalisation and coloniality. Globalisation has generated social relations in which lifestyles and values are somewhat shared.[1] Across the world, from the beginning of European colonial rule to the present, a combination of legal, economic, educational, as well as military and police forces have imposed, promoted and maintained some forms of life, such as the heterosexual, patriarchal family, at the expense of alternative ways of life.[2] A key question for decolonial ethics is how to relate to others in a way that affirms cultural rights in response to these standardising impositions. In this chapter, I argue that Édouard Glissant's framing of an ethical relation as emerging from 'contacts' with others, defending the 'opacity' of others and ultimately standing in solidarity with others, is more fruitful for decolonial pursuits than Emmanuel Levinas's framing of an 'encounter' with a single Other, whose difference is understood in terms of 'alterity', and who is ultimately served through reverence. I start from Levinas because the philosophy of liberation, decolonial ethics and decolonial political theology continue to use his vocabulary: difference is framed in terms of alterity, and the ethical relation is exemplified in bearing witness. Calling into question Levinas's ethical vocabulary also shows the limitations of contemporary ethical theory that relies on his terms.

Levinas's concept for difference is 'alterity', 'the radical heterogeneity of the other' such that this other is 'absolutely other'.[3] He reserves the term 'religion' for the face-to-face 'ethical relation', 'a relation without relation' in which 'the encounter with the Other opens the infinite'.[4] He asserts: 'The Other remains infinitely transcendent, infinitely foreign; his face in which his epiphany is produced and which appeals to me breaks with the world that can be common to us.'[5] The Other is a rupture, breaking the possibility for a shared world of relation and communication. The language Levinas uses to describe the ethical relation is not compassion or care, but extreme and hyperbolic terms such as obsession, persecution, trauma and substitution. He insists further that the Other is not different with only 'a relative alterity' and in doing so avoids considerations of cultural difference.[6] Building on these descriptions of alterity, his conceptualisation of responsibility ultimately relies on what John Drabinski describes as a 'blanched' encounter – without the colours and textures of race, gender or nation.[7] In sum, Levinas's indeterminate language of alterity and encounter leads to a religious non-relation with one Other as opposed to shared strivings in a world held in common with particular, differently embodied others. His vocabulary gives us individual substitution, but not collective solidarity.[8] Following Levinas's own clarification in an interview – 'My task does not consist in constructing an ethics' – we can say that Levinas is a thinker of the ethical but not of ethics. As Drabinski puts it, Levinas 'is not concerned with producing a plan of responsible ethics'.[9] Could we say the same about those writing in his wake?

Reading Levinas and developing the philosophy of liberation, Enrique Dussel presents the ideal ethical actor, 'the supreme man of Alterity', as 'he who is capable of opening

himself to the Other'.[10] Dussel cites biblical figures as historical examples who perform this ethics of alterity: the Samaritan, the prophet and the martyr who witnesses or testifies
to the Other.[11] Following the trajectory of Levinas's ethical
vocabulary from alterity to substitution, and adding Walter
Benjamin's concept of the 'victim', in his later *Ethics of Liberation* Dussel presents ethical action as being 'persecuted by the
power that produces such victims'.[12] Dussel's contribution is
to bring Levinas's 'Other' down to earth. Dussel's 'Other' is
not metaphysical but historical: the poor, exploited and dehu-
manised victims of unjust systems. What demonstrates that
the system is not ethical is the cry of the victim itself.[13] The
task of an ethics of liberation in turn is to respond to the 'call'
of the community of victims, the 'call for solidarity and for
the responsibility of "organic intellectuals" who are invited to
collaborate responsibly in the scientific *critique* of the system
that oppresses them'.[14] Following Levinas, Dussel goes further
than critique: the ethical actor is one who becomes 'caught as
prey, as a "substitute" victim who "bears witness" (*martys* in
Greek) *within* the system, and who thereby stands in for the
absent presence of the victims'.[15]

More recently, in presenting a decolonial ethics, Nelson
Maldonado-Torres describes coloniality in terms of 'the violation of the meaning of human alterity', and An Yountae,
in presenting a political theology that takes seriously both
Continental and decolonial concerns, argues that mysticism
and politics come together because 'the act of self-loss or self-
emptying, is not escapism or an evasion of one's ethical responsibility' but rather is an action that 'gives birth to a new subject
who is conditioned by alterity'.[16] Both Maldonado-Torres and
Yountae develop their uses of alterity in conversation with
Dussel's reading of Levinas. But adopting the language of alterity can start decolonial responses to others off on the wrong
foot. Maintaining a framework of alterity means inheriting

the epistemological puzzles that come with Levinas's concept. For example, how can actors communicate with an Other who remains infinitely strange? These puzzles quickly become political problems: without a world held in common, actors can worship an Other, but not work with others.

The concern driving this chapter is that the language of alterity sets up responsibility as individual passivity regarding a single Other, not collective action 'in confrontation with elites, authorities, and opponents', as the political scientist Sidney Tarrow describes the direction of successful modern social movements.[17] If an individual conditioned by alterity does not link with others in collective confrontation, then one's religious response to alterity – self-sacrifice and bearing witness – functions to purify one's soul more than to resist capitalist exploitation or state repression. Dussel's above take on Levinas's substitution reads as if the criterion for ethical action is being caught in a dominant system, not challenging it successfully. Is it not more likely that this altruistic actor becomes merely another victim and not a substitute one? The idea that 'good social justice champions die with the validation that they tried and that perhaps the next generation can benefit from their labors', Nancy Mithlo reflects on a lifetime of resistance, is a 'delusionary justification' with 'the ultimate effect of martyrdom and sacrifice'.[18] She calls into question this approach: 'But isn't this assumption of suffering and death in reality a means of perpetuating bias and discrimination? Doesn't this encouragement to keep charging up the same hill in the end exhaust and destroy activists?'[19]

In sum, because an ethics of alterity suggests individual (in)action and practical impossibility, and because it is played out in reception and sacrifice, not resistance and solidarity, it fails to affirm collective possibilities in the present and for the future. If, as Simon Critchley summarises, '[e]thics, for Levinas, is critique', and if this critique is severed from the contaminations of politics, then we can say that Levinas – and those who adopt his terms without modifying them significantly – provides an ethics, a critique, that is not making a bid for political power.[20] Keeping ethics and politics clearly separated is precisely Levinas's intention. But if this separation is not a problem in Levinas's conceptual landscape, it becomes a problem for decolonial ethics. In failing to inform a confrontation with political power, the language of alterity limits the ways to achieve the very goal of liberation and decolonial philosophy: the negation of the system that produces victims.

Alterity and Encounter Read in Context

To understand the precise limits that come with the term, we can start by raising questions of any ethics of alterity. In what context does another remain absolutely other? To what extent is this extreme positing of difference helpful for theorising contemporary ethics (and not simply 'the ethical')? And, is it correct that alterity prevents, or even militates against, totalisation?[21] Context matters. Colonial projects – erasures and productions – have resulted in a number of shared, standardised practices across the globe. '[U]nder globalization', Stuart Hall writes, 'everywhere is becoming more diasporic. It is not because people like to travel.'[22] That is, globalisation *forcibly* mediates differences. Consequently, formulations of absolute difference, such as alterity, are increasingly less relevant as starting points for a vocabulary informing how to relate to one another. Claims of absolute difference carry assumptions already belied by the reality of today's actors, who share models of life.[23] Examples clarify this point.

In her ethnography of rural north-eastern Brazil, and calling into question some of Levinas's claims, the anthropologist Nancy Scheper-Hughes observes regarding religious practices that '[n]ot everything can be dissolved into the vapor of absolute cultural difference and radical otherness'.[24] She underscores the ways in which 'we are not so indefinably "other" to one another', including how she, like the subjects of her ethnography, 'instinctively make[s] the sign of the cross when [she] sense[s] danger or misfortune coming'.[25] In turn, where 'matters of faith (in the broadest sense), morals, and values' are 'at least partially shared', she remains 'not afraid to speak and engage [her] Brazilian *companheiras*'.[26] Scheper-Hughes, a New Yorker by birth, shares the sign of the cross with her companions because of the impositions of Catholicism as well as the ways it has been taken up and lived out – by her family and by her ethnographic subjects. In making contact with others, even those from a remote location and a different culture, her experiences of persons and faces belie a claim to a singular Other's transcendental alterity.

Based not on his ethnography but on his phenomenology of globalisation in an urban setting, Eduardo Mendieta makes a point similar to that of Scheper-Hughes. He describes the appearing of people less as completely foreign, as Other, and more as concretely different, as others. For instance, the numbing repetitions of faces in advertisements, screens and billboards in New York City limit some of their demands on the phenomenologist. In this context of globalised images, he concludes, 'alterity is deflated, and detranscendentalized'.[27] The clearest summary remains that of the anthropologist Michel-Rolph Trouillot: 'There is no Other, but multitudes of others who are all others for different reasons.'[28]

* * *

In a world of increasing 'contacts among cultures', to use Glissant's phrase, it has become difficult to maintain claims to (absolute) alterity (PR 39/PO 26). When people feel that their practices, values and deepest commitments are 'partially shared', and when their experiences are technologically medi-ated, ordinary speech and non-reverential engagements tend to follow, including a range of affective gestures and expo-sures, from holding the door for another to police brutality. These are the shared conditions that a contemporary vocabu-lary of ethics must take into account.

Contacts with others in a globalised world feature marks of politics – weighing, calculating and deciding – that have already leaked in. For example, a journalist pays attention to one individual and not another on the city's light rail as they make their way to work, then to a different person from the transit station to their preferred café, then to the barista and not the woman experiencing homelessness as they order their morning latte. By the time they are at their desk and opening their emails, they have proceeded through a series of selective attendings. In none of these cases do they hold their morning plans in abeyance after facing another. Their attention to oth-ers was limited in the first place, because they spent much of the train-ride reading a newsletter on journalism ethics and trying to 'get ahead' on a few emails before their workday began. The daily contacts and frictions between them and those with whom they came into contact on the train, at the station, in the café and at their office are far removed from the kind of prayerful orientation to the Other that an ethics of alterity prescribes. But in a context of mendacious 'news' spread on social media, actors invested in challenging colonial patterns today rely on the work of investigative journalism. A journalist who becomes a contemporary Samaritan upon having a religious encounter on the train might be less able to do their work effectively, and thus less helpful for informing patterns of social life.

This is the question I am getting at: If the language of alter-ity and encounter does not reflect the reality of urban life in a globalised world today – for reasons of selective attention, pace and calculation – and if Mendieta is right that alterity is de-transcendentalised in these settings, then can any engagement therein really be called ethical? Not on Levinas's terms, but perhaps so if we move away from Levinas's vocabulary.

In light of the historical mediations and relative (not absolute) differences that Scheper-Hughes and Mendieta describe, we can acknowledge that Levinas's transcendental framing of encounter and alterity is not an accurate starting point for thinking about contemporary contacts, much less communities and coalitions. What Levinas's ethics gains in conceptual severity it loses in applicability. Under consideration here is a kind of already 'applied' ethics, then. One question becomes how to define ethical relations among differences without importing transcendental baggage. In the remainder of this chapter, I articulate initial concepts for a more grounded and politicised vocabulary of ethics. Giving up an appeal to alterity does not necessarily cede to totalisation, reification or appropriation. Another way to theorise relations is with Glissant's concept of opacity.[29]

Situated between understanding others as transparent and comprehensible, on the one hand, and as inscrutably Other, on the other hand, opacity offers a way to frame difference that could inform a collective politics. An example that illustrates the politics of *not* comprehending others is found in world travel. Respecting the opacity of various knowledge practices across cultures might look like not travelling in the first place, because such travel increases demands to cater to US tastes and (lacking) language abilities, thus bulldozing regional knowledges (often literally, say to build more chain hotels). The pains caused by elite travel are present especially when locals understand knowledge as related to the land, such as when the land being developed into hotels includes sacred burial grounds. As Mariana Ortega notes, taking up travel in a slightly more figurative sense through her reading of María Lugones, '[I]n some cases whites or members of dominant groups have to decline world-travelling, as doing so may be more harmful than beneficial.'[30]

What Glissant ultimately invites is not a turn back to the self or a self-contained subject, but rather an expansion of ethical responsibilities outward in pluralities, toward concretely different others in a process of making, maintaining and defending ways of life alternative to the colonial models that globalisation standardises. In addition to providing a means to think about challenging capitalist denials of cultural rights (as in building hotels for tourists on Indigenous land), the politics of opacity does not first and foremost seek recognition from the repressive state. Rather, Glissant's call to reclaim a 'right to opacity' invites us into collective challenges to the state's mechanisms of recognition and comprehension.

Contacts, Relays and Opacities

'Contacts among cultures – one of the givens of modernity', Glissant writes, 'no longer come across the huge spans of time that have historically allowed meetings and interchanges to be active but almost imperceptibly so' (PR 39/PO 26). These contacts occur on our daily commutes and bear on the lives of others across the globe. 'Whatever happens elsewhere has immediate repercussions here', and vice versa (PR 39/PO 26). The journalist's use of public transportation instead of driving their own car has the immediate repercussion, however small, of decreasing the demand for oil production in several resource-rich 'elsewheres'. Repeated contacts render difference more quotidian. When others are not held in reverence or discounted in abjection, the possibility of collaboration (as well as condemnation) emerges.

Most of ethical life is lived away from extremes – in the contact zones between abjection and reverence. Contacts can involve what Mendieta calls 'an uncoupling of identities', a process that both deflates one's loyalty to one's family or nation and introduces what is strange or felt as contradictory.[31] This is the ethical/political direction in which Glissant's 'contacts' points us – to relations and entanglements already underway, ones that can undermine a filial loyalty to our most familiar and normal forms of life. But here is the paradox, upon which I will elaborate in later chapters: to expand responsibilities beyond born-into attachments, one should not do what the anthropologist Courtney Bender rightly criticises as borderless 'zooming around', in which physically (in 'progressive' vacations, such as the trip to Vietnam through the travel programme of *The Nation* magazine), spiritually (in visualised prayer) or otherwise imperialism is reproduced as 'those in the United States could travel quickly and effortlessly to other parts of the world'.[32] That would be an ethical effort that, like the flight of neoliberal capital to tax havens, as Scheper-Hughes puts it, 'implies a parallel flight from local engagements, local commitments, and local accountability'.[33] Realising one's international responsibilities will involve local and particular engagements.

Glissant's emphasis on particularity helps actors see how ethical engagements should play out. He calls for rejecting any sense of a single, hierarchical Humanity (*l'Humanité*) and instead recognising many humanities (*humanités*) – a recognition of what decolonial thinkers are calling a 'pluriverse', where many different conceptions of 'worlds' exist on a single planet.[34] 'Every expression of humanities', Glissant writes, 'opens onto the fluctuating complexity of the world. Here poetic thought safeguards the particular, because only the totality of truly secure particulars guarantees the energy of Diversity' (PR 44/PO 32, translation modified). He continues with a specification: 'But in every instance this particular sets about Relation in a completely intransitive manner, relating, that is, with the finally realized totality of all possible particulars' (PR 44/PO 32).

These lines raise two important practical points. First, a decolonial responsibility works to defend particular cultures, where language is a kind of proxy. Importantly, these cultures must be defended on their own terms and should be defended for the sake of all, because the loss of one language impoverishes all (see PR 110/PO 95). The goal is to protect a totality, not to defend one's specific language or culture. Such a parochial defence would be its own kind of monolingualism or ethnocentrism. Second, it is worth staying with Glissant's line about an 'intransitive manner'. I read this phrase not as suggesting that there is a lack of motion or transition, but rather that the manner is intransitive in a grammatical sense – no object is taken. This linguistic point becomes political insofar as it describes a way of action. To live in a completely intransitive manner precludes projection or imposition onto something as well as comprehension of something. In its emphasis on intransitivity, Glissant's concept of 'contacts' differs from tourist travel, which takes cultures and traditions as objects of consumption. What, in turn, are ethical actors to make of Glissant's exhortation to carry out 'relating . . . all possible particulars'? We can understand this line through a key metaphor in *Poetics of Relation*, the weave (*trame*).

The promise of the weave is that it operates differently from the projection and comprehension that has defined the modern/colonial West.[35] Glissant writes that 'this poetics of Relation interweaves [*se trame*] and no longer projects' (PR 45/PO 32). 'Each of its parts patterns activity implicated in the activity of every other. The stories of peoples [*Les histoires des peuples*] have led to this dynamic' (PR 45/PO 33, translation modified). But this dynamic in which the weave is made is chaotic and generally unjust. The implication of (hi)stories is far from a simple good. The material histories of cultures are now in contact because of deeply violent and traumatic pasts (and presents), what Glissant calls a tragedy on a global scale, a tragedy to which ethics must respond (DA 686/CD 197).

From understanding 'entanglement' as both descriptive and prescriptive, ethical actors can deepen their planetary political consciousness and gain a path for action. The descriptive sense of entanglement designates the 'worldwide commercial market' (PR 166/PO 152). While not theorising Glissant, Michelle Murphy summarises the violent histories that produced our present connections: 'No single being on this planet escapes entanglements with capitalism, colonialism and racism, even as their violent effects are profoundly concentrated in hotspots of hostility.'[36] The forces of globalisation are sometimes hidden, masked by what Glissant calls 'flash agents', such as advertisements and slogans that conceal how consumer products are made (PR 155/PO 141). Flash agents are 'caught up in dailiness [*prise dans le quotidien*]' (PR 215/PO 199). For instance, behind every iPhone – and what the Apple billboards dotted around US cities never reveal – are factories in Shenzhen and mines in Kinshasa. Every here requires a there. In practice, 'there' signals production and exploitation in a global division of labour, meaning that 'places of dispossession, countries in the throes of absolute poverty, are excluded from this participation [*ce partage*]' (PR 151/PO 137, translation modified). *Partage* is important. One could say that the factories of Shenzhen are implicated in globalisation. Given the alienation of the workers and forced aspects of their labour, however, this is not participation in any fair sense. It is exploitation and exclusion.

To understand 'the entanglements of worldwide relation' as emerging from 'commonplaces' is to cultivate a mode of 'planetary consciousness' (PR 44, 219/PO 31, 202, translation modified). This is a mode of consciousness formed in the face of both 'suicidal political regimes' and anthropogenic climate change seen in 'floods and hurricanes', two forces of politically induced global precarity that can 'call forth international solidarity' (PR 212/PO 196). On ethical and political grounds, we can acknowledge that the models of life that have forcibly become predominant in the West cannot solve our own problems, because the West, on Glissant's definition, is first and foremost a projection, a trajectory of dispossession (DA 14/CD 2). That is, the West – particularly in its economic form of capitalism and related military form of occupation – is first and foremost transitive: it takes as its objects the labour of peoples while rejecting their unofficial histories, refusing to listen to them on their own terms and in their own languages. The practical question becomes how to think about ethical relations that support not transitive projections but intransitive weaves.

Crucially, in addition to his description of entanglements, Glissant prescribes entanglement. '[T]he West', he declares, 'has produced the variables to contradict its impressive trajectory every time', so 'the West is not monolithic, and this is why it is surely necessary that it move toward entanglement' (PR 205/PO 191). His prescription comes with a crucial proviso. 'The real question', he goes on, 'is whether it will do so in a participatory manner [*le mode des participations*] or if its entanglement will be based on old impositions' (PR 205/PO 191), what he later calls the 'old definitions' (TTM 231). How is this participatory entanglement achieved? I suggest that Glissant's concept of 'relays', leading to his 'right to opacity', forms this participatory mode of action both amidst (descriptive) and toward (prescriptive) entanglements. After elaborating on relays, I will return below to the question of how Glissant's right to opacity avoids the old impositions and definitions.

Understanding relays requires distinguishing between flash agents and active agents. For Glissant, flash agents always carry a negative political connotation. They hide the aforementioned places of dispossession (PR 213/PO 197). Examples include the images projected through television, advertising and cell phones, all of which have greatly individualised modern/ colonial experience. Such images call to a life of 'noncontact [*non-relation*]' instead of international solidarity (DA 434/CD 143). They do so through standardising ways of life and relationships taken as ideal, a fantasy of transitivity or objectification. Flash agents 'dictate fashion and commonplace – these two modern embodiments of interrelation' (PR 180/PO 166). They 'transform into a neutral relay . . . the very thing that formerly functioned as an active relay' (PR 192/PO 178). By hiding violence, flash agents neutralise, preventing their viewers from understanding political histories. Apple products, as they tell you, are 'designed in California' but made in China and sourced in the Democratic Republic of the Congo, as they do not tell you. In turn, they are promoted through advertising that targets individuals through broad strokes, say through a photograph that is assumed to have wide appeal when placed on a Minneapolis billboard. This is why when Glissant talks about flash agents he uses the language not of a *trame* but of a *faisceau*, not a weave and less a 'network' than a beam of light – those incessant, distracting beams that can be challenged in achieved weaves of opacities (PR 180, 189/PO 166, 175).

Unlike the universalising light of *faisceaux*, the links of a *trame* are located and grounded. Active relays interweave, moving from particular places and protecting their particularity instead of imposing generally. Glissant teaches that 'intervention "in Relation" can only really happen "in a place" . . . There is no generalisable strategy of action in Relation that can be developed' (PR 192/PO 178). Providing an instance of an active relay, the political scientist Sanford Schram discusses how individuals who are precarious in the face of the injustices of state-backed capitalism use mixed-media relays to communicate their shared struggles. Relays between narratives, figures and images 'highlight the processes by which collective action can potentially address individual claims without doing an injustice to them'.[37] 'Coalitional politics', he goes on, 'arguably has not just its own ethics but a distinctive aesthetic.'[38] Coalitional politics moves through a certain aesthetic, meaning a certain way of sharing sensibilities. Stories are relayed, heard and relayed again, and in that process the ethical actor's sensibilities become more critical, as when one hears again and again of police violence against water protectors or Black Lives Matter activists.

A way of relaying without imposing, without demanding assimilation or imposing hierarchical ways of life, is a *partage* in the sense Glissant endorses. How active relays share knowledge is different from the way that colonisation makes certain knowledge shared, seen for instance in the way Portuguese is the official language in Brazil. Colonial sharing of knowledge is forced, moving through flash agents as well as other imperial agents, such as teachers in residential schools. By contrast, sharing in a weave involves giving freely and choosing to be heard and incorporated, such as when one shares one's experience of struggle with another in order to form a coalition. The Precarias of Spain provide an example. Their method includes a kind of activism/research in which practitioners ask each other, 'What is your precarity?' and 'What is your strike?', thus relaying from an individual's response to a shared sense of precarity – and in turn manifesting that precarity publicly.[39] Glissant says in a famously obscure line, 'Relation relinks (relays), relates' (PR 187/PO 173). A relay, we must not forget, is a simple term. In track and field, runners form a relay team in that they share a baton. In this way, relation is constituted by participatory relays of knowledge (*de connaissance partagée*) (PR 20/PO 8). Its active relays are intransitive. Such relays are not analysed from above but shared on the ground in *partage* to the extent that they are both communicated and heard. Both the teller and the listener participate in this relay. On this foundation of a particular place and among particular actors, we can begin to build participation as a presupposition of a new sense of responsibility.

Glissant's 'active relays' are elements of demanding a right to opacity. The relay and the right to opacity are connected in that the former establishes the latter. Here, the aesthetics informs the politics, as Glissant suggests in describing 'the open circle of our relayed aesthetics, our unflagging politics [*nos politiques inlassables*]' (PR 220/PO 203). The translation is helpful because it asks us to consider how practices of relaying lived experience could be anti-nationalistic – 'unflagging' not as avoiding fatigue but instead read more literally, as taking down flags, the symbol of nationalism *par excellence*. After all, an inversion of the US flag has long been a staple of Indigenous protests in the US. And we have seen it recently in Black Lives Matter marches in the wake of police murders of Breonna Taylor, George Floyd and too many others. I will return to the example of the flag in the following chapter.

Considering consequences or fruits is another way to differentiate between a relay neutralised by a flash agent and an active relay in relation. Whereas neutralised relays lead to standardisation, active relays protect particularity, working toward establishing what Glissant would describe in *Poetics*, echoing *Caribbean Discourse*, as 'the right to opacity' (PR 203, 204, 209/ PO 189, 190, 194). It is worthwhile to stay with how we hear this phrase. Glissant's famous line in *Caribbean Discourse* is translated as 'We demand the right to obscurity [*Nous réclamons le droit à l'opacité*]' (DA 14/CD 2). With respect to reading *Poetics* as an echo of *Caribbean Discourse* – as he says it is (PR 28/PO 16) – it is important to read his reiteration of this claim at the end of the earlier text. 'Relation', he writes, 'is built on the voices of all people, which I have called their opacity, which is nothing, after all, but an expression of their freedom' (DA 803/CD 255–6, translation modified). How, then, does opacity relate to freedom? And how is it connected to responsibility? In his recent *Glissant and the Middle Passage*, Drabinski asks further, 'What does it mean to have a *right* to opacity? The critical sense of this phrase – *the right to opacity*', he continues, 'lies in its anticolonial force, and therefore its resistance to certain senses of knowing and understanding that would seek to absorb, reactivate, and possess'.[40] An initial political question is how this 'resistance' comes about – whether it is inherent or achieved. I contend that the right to opacity is an invitation, and ultimately an achievement, more than it is a given. Glissant's own words demand careful attention.

'[T]hat which protects the Diverse', Glissant begins, 'we call opacity' (PR 75/PO 62). Some of Glissant's readers have nearly equated this 'protective' opacity with resistance, as if a community's opacity were ontologically given. These readers have claimed that the opacity of a culture is a self-defence against both the standardisation of globalisation and the transparency-seeking epistemologies of the West and its functionaries – anthropologists, philosophers, diplomats, aid workers and so on. For one, Neal Allar has claimed that opacity 'protects the subject from the invasive grasp of (neo)colonial thought', providing 'a protective shield'.[41] For another, H. Adlai Murdoch has argued that opacity 'is an epistemologically-grounded world vision that allows each subject the right to his or her own unknowability'.[42] Reading opacity this way risks making it into a new infinity or alterity. Allar's and Murdoch's arguments come very close to Levinas's claim that 'Infinity does not permit itself to be integrated' and that 'the Infinity of the Other' in fact 'prevents totalization'.[43] A sense of transcendence remains.[44]

I want to place emphasis on an aspect of opacity different from the epistemological focus of Allar and Murdoch. Materialists and historians would raise questions of their claims. For the materialist, concepts do not themselves act in the world. Opacity, when it means cultural practices and visions marked by differences, cannot itself 'protect' precarious populations, nor can it 'allow' a right that prevents epistemological violation (e.g. the mining of Amazonian Indigenous knowledge for pharmaceuticals). A historian would note that this 'opacity' has not historically prevented domination. To read opacity as a built-in protection, then, is not itself politically helpful in the face of state-caused dispossessions today. After all, colonial projects have not needed to understand others in order to decimate them. Suggesting an impossibility of epistemological comprehension is not the same as preventing political comprehension – seen, for instance, in attempted cultural absorption and genocidal elimination. How, then, could opacity have a political edge?

Repeating the line from *Caribbean Discourse* in the 'For Opacity' chapter of *Poetics*, Glissant writes, 'We demand the right to opacity [*Nous réclamons le droit à l'opacité*]' (PR 203/PO 189). He concludes this chapter with another kind of echo, translated as 'We clamour for the right to opacity for everyone [*Nous réclamons pour tous le droit à l'opacité*]' (PR 209/PO 194). In both cases, I would translate the verb as 'reclaim'. This translation, and the reading it implies, differs from those who have argued that opacity is itself a check against power. Emphasising the fact that opacity exists as re-claimed, as demanded again, suggests it has to be achieved repeatedly. Through this sense of re-claiming opacity, we can hear immediate resonance with Indigenous efforts to re-claim land, such as the historically successful and ongoing *retomadas* in Brazil. We can link the re-claiming of the right to opacity to Glissant's call in *Poetics* to the 'protection of the land, by mobilizing everyone' (PR 160/PO 146). And we can understand this link further when we achieve this mobilisation alongside the other two practices he calls in this section 'rallying points' – a relating to natural surroundings and a defence of 'the people's language, Creole' (PR 160/PO 145–6).

It is crucial to note that Glissant's is not a mobilisation based on ethnicity or filiation. The point, rather, is to practise a mode that links not 'to the intolerance of a root but, rather, to an ecological vision of Relation' (PR 160/PO 146). Reclaiming the right to opacity invites a politics at once oppositional and relational, a re-claiming of land against state and market forces. While it is oppositional in this way, it also works across filial boundaries through multiracial coalitions. Re-claiming the right to opacity challenges comprehension – the classic colonial 'gesture of enclosure' – not by itself but through the 'participation and confluence' it invites (PR 206/ PO 192, 191).[45]

I suggest that how Glissant situates participation with others amidst land (itself active and historical) avoids falling back on the old impositions and definitions of what politics and land are. In *Traité* he writes, 'Let's run this risk. Our responsibility in this matter is collective, and our action should be so too. We must make our place immeasurable, that is, link it up with the Immeasurability of the world. Let's also look at its beauty. My hope lies in this voice of the landscapes [*J'espère en cette parole des paysages*]' (TTM 232). By situating human life within landscape, Glissant again refuses to fall back on the 'old definitions'. Glissant's 'poetics of landscape', as Katherine McKittrick explains, 'creates a way to enter into, and challenge, traditional geographic formulations without the familiar tools of maps, charts, official records, and figures'; it is through 'a poetic-politics', McKittrick continues, that Glissant 'conceptualizes his surroundings as "uncharted", and inextricably connected to his selfhood and a local community history'.[46]

* * *

In a paradox, while the term 'opacity' itself implies incomprehensibility, Glissant's concept of opacity needs to be legible to actors. Quite simply, Glissant distinguishes opacity from obscurity, writing clearly, 'The opaque is not the obscure' (PR 205/ PO 191). More precisely, the opaque 'is that which cannot be reduced [*Il est le non-réductible*]' (PR 205/PO 191). As I read it, the epistemological point regarding opacity is not that it is obscure (as the ontological readings can suggest) but rather that it involves irreducibility – the fact, for instance, that Indigenous cultural traditions and knowledge practices are not reducible to global standards or models. But we should be careful not to conflate epistemology and politics. And we should not raise ontology to the level of political action. To avoid comprehension – to militate against the transitivity of the West – is not primarily an epistemological or an ontological question. It is first a political question. Perhaps this is why Glissant calls the chapter *Pour l'opacité* and not simply *L'opacité*. Opacity must be cultivated, fostered and ultimately achieved in active, quotidian relays that lead to becoming-with and standing-with others. I will elaborate on this claim in Chapter 2.

To read opacity in terms of practice – in terms of actively relaying, making a demand and re-claiming – is also to distinguish it from alterity, which presents ethics as passive and receptive, as being subjected to and through the infinite demand of an Other. Making a demand or re-claiming a right marks an activity, suggesting that something is to be taken or taken back. If the right to opacity is demanded, then we can see how it is a helpful term for understanding a range of decolonial rights claims. For instance, Indigenous nations' demands for epistemological respect – not to be studied as ethnographic subjects, for example – fit under a claim for the right to opacity. To bring the right to opacity into further relief, it is helpful to compare Glissant's claim with human rights discourse more broadly.

The Right to Opacity and Human Rights

The project of globalisation aims at what Mendieta calls the 'actualization of one global design'.[47] He argues that this actualisation occurs not only through corporate advertising and military invasion, but also, and perhaps most egregiously because most insidiously, in the 'continuation of the [modern] civilizing project by the United States, under the flag of the war against all wars that is benignly called the crusade for human rights and its condition of possibility, globalization'.[48] Running so counter to humanitarian currents of human rights, this claim deserves examination. Is Mendieta correct? Are human rights another iteration of what the political theologian Catherine Keller calls the West's 'crusader complex', such that we can speak, as Maldonado-Torres does, of 'the coloniality of human rights'?[49]

Globalisation is the condition for the possibility of human rights because human rights emerged as a post-World War II international project, as a way to shift from politics to morals and from structural transformations to reforms – from maximal demands, including decolonisation, to minimal demands, such as calling out a corrupt leader of a newly independent nation state.[50] Indeed, human rights gained traction much later, and in a much more minimal way, than what scholars linking the term to the Greeks or Romans argue. As the historian Samuel Moyn notes, 'The roots of contemporary human rights are not to be found . . . in Greek philosophy or monotheistic religion, neither in European natural law nor early modern revolutions', and 'neither in horror against American slavery nor Hitler's Judeocide'.[51] Rather, on Moyn's account, human rights emerged in the 1970s as 'a *moral* alternative' to political struggle, and thus as compatible with liberal individualism as opposed to collective decolonial politics. He summarises: 'Human rights were minimal, individual and fundamentally moral; not maximal, collective and potentially bloody.'[52]

The difference between the practice of Glissant's right to opacity and the traditional (elite) channels of human rights practice hinges on different conceptions of responsibility. A decolonial responsibility must start from and refer back to the claims of marginalised peoples and dominated classes – those on the underside of ordinary catastrophes (DA 802/CD 255). The right to opacity is connected to what Glissant calls 'a collective sense of responsibility' (DA 802/CD 255). This sense of responsibility is part of a 'struggle for independence' and 'the possibility of achieving modern forms of participatory democracy, however much one distrusts this form of government when one considers the disastrous incarnations it has produced in the past' (DA 802/CD 255). The right to opacity stresses the need for ethical actors to stand, suffer and strive with others.

The right to opacity is a rights claim that works toward organising communities. In regard to the history of human rights, it fits within third-generation rights. First-generation, civil-political rights include the right to speech or assembly. Second-generation, social-economic rights include the right to healthcare, education and fair wages. The first two generations represent Cold War tensions. Third-generation rights came out of decolonisation. They are collective or solidarity rights that communities use not only to make claims on the state but also to suggest ways of life. Third-generation rights usually lack the state recognition sometimes afforded to the first two generations, but, as I will argue in the next chapter, they remain relevant for political organisation today. Further, different from how a state is often the primary duty-bearer of first- and second-generation rights, justice-oriented actors have broad duties related to third-generation rights.[53]

In addition to how a right to opacity might function as a third-generation right to inform communal organising, there is a second reason why it is worthwhile to stay with the right to opacity. What it loses in its esoteric rights claim – *Demanding exactly what?* an international lawyer might fairly ask – it gains in the breadth of the duties pursuant to it. 'The content of a right defines the content of its correlative duties', the philosopher James Griffin explains.[54] '[W]hat one person has a right to demand, some other agent has a duty to supply.'[55] This is the paradigmatic framing of rights and duties, what he calls 'primary duties correlative to rights'.[56] The primary duties following from the right to opacity include not studying Indigenous people or settling on their land, in both cases objectifying them in a transitive project. Other related primary duties are standing with people making claims to cultural rights when they invite justice-oriented implicated subjects into their struggles. Beyond primary duties there are also 'secondary duties', Griffin goes on to say, meaning 'duties to promote human rights, duties to monitor their observance, and duties to ensure compliance with them, when that is indeed feasible'.[57]

Considering secondary duties around the right to opacity should be more than a matter of legalistically naming required actions. With Glissant, it is a task for the imagination, a task for thinking in relays and communities about the broad reaches and resonances of a claim. Through such an imaginative consideration, it becomes apparent that the secondary duties around the right to opacity include a variety of actions – how we travel or engage locally, consume or boycott, dress in fashion or wear out our clothes. When we gather these implications together, the secondary duties around a right to opacity encompass enough actions to demand a re-examination of our way of life, in its entirety, in what is now called the Global North, what Glissant means by the projecting, transitive 'West'. The right to opacity is a rights claim emerging from the Global South. Actors in the Global North should understand themselves as duty-bearers of this claim.

The right to opacity could weigh on its (elite) obligation-bearers in the following way. If forces of standardisation – such as a US-driven model of politics and justice, US restaurants, US and European fashions, US- and Europe-driven commodity extraction, and US and European tourism – combine to suppress and negate local cultures and the flourishing of their peoples in favour of a world of McDonald's, English and 'democracy' while keeping most people poor via a global division of labour, then human rights around culture, education, work, freedom of thought, movement and security are being violated by everyday practices in the Global North. If one is serious about challenging the forces of standardisation and transparency, such that various peoples maintain their cultural rights, then one would work less to address specific bad actors or specific instances of human rights failures and more to address the forces that cause broad human rights violations in the first place.

For example, the student who is occupying Chase Bank in a direct action does more for international human rights than the student who spends their spring break 'aiding' a Mayan community in Guatemala. Operating from New York City, the hip non-profit Charity: Water goes as far as to note about Guatemala that '[t]his multi-cultural country has a rich Mayan heritage and diversity'.[58] But its humanitarians follow the footsteps of soldiers – we recall, painfully, the 1954 CIA-led coup in Guatemala, which led to what journalists frankly called 'brutal military dictatorships and a genocidal civil war against its Indian population' as well as the killing of nearly 200,000 people.[59] Like occupying soldiers, humanitarians continue to displace Mayan and other languages in favour of English and Spanish. A decolonial sense of responsibility to the thirsty in Guatemala would motivate challenges not only to so-called humanitarian responses but also to the states and companies that caused the need for such humanitarianism in the first place. This is why the right to opacity calls for political participation.

We can further use the right to opacity as a device to analyse and group together past struggles.[60] One instance of the secondary-duties approach to the right to opacity is Elizabeth Heyrick's pamphlet in the early 1820s, 'Immediate, not gradual abolition', which called for an end to the consumption of sugar; consumption of sugar fuelled the slave trade. Another is the Dutch Angola committee's call in the 1970s to boycott coffee produced in rights-violating conditions in Angola. The committee's pamphlet cited a United Nations working group's conclusion that 'the most inhuman form of forced labor prevails in the Portuguese colonies in Africa'.[61] Even more recently, in the early 2000s, the Coalition of Immokalee Workers asked consumers to boycott Taco Bell in order to support their efforts, as producers of ingredients for the fast-food chain, at getting paid a living wage despite their status as immigrants. These boycotts are part of the secondary duties around a right to opacity because the differences of others are controlled and denied when those others are forced to work for the consumption of wealthy metropolitans instead of being able to cultivate their own cultural practices. From a stress on both the primary and secondary duties related to the right to opacity, we move toward not interpersonal substitution but international solidarity.

For all of the discussion of Glissant as a post-structuralist thinker of uncertainty, and for all of his crucial work in interrogating the Western drive to comprehend others, he is certain about the forces, logic and bulldozing effect of globalisation/ coloniality – that 'the worldwide commercial market' finds you '[n]o matter where you are' (PR 166/PO 152). 'These are not vague forces that you might accommodate out of politeness', he asserts (PR 166/PO 152). '[T]hese are hidden forces of inexorable logic that must be answered with the total logic of your behaviour [*il faut répondre par une logique totale de ton*

comportement]' (PR 166/PO 152). 'You must choose your bearing [*Il faut choisir l'allure*]' (PR 166/PO 152). Glissant's call is
not simply to acknowledge one's postcolonial complicity and
to stop there. It is a question of one's total logic, of the positions
one takes vis-à-vis the state and its forces (one's primary duties)
as much as of one's style, meaning how one comports oneself
in daily life (one's secondary duties). This is not a return to a
settled bearing. It is an imaginative ethics that invites a 'gamble
on the unknown' (PR 21/PO 8). In beginning from duties, we
understand the right to opacity as first and foremost a demand
to choose our bearings, to take sides, among the damned or the
dominant amidst the dazzle of globalisation/coloniality. This is
a question of a lived position in daily life. This is a question of
ethics and not of the ethical.

Before elaborating on how the right to opacity plays out in
practice, it is worth considering one of its limitations. A shift
in vocabulary from encounter and alterity to contacts and
opacity, as Glissant himself acknowledges, 'does not provide
us with the concrete arms to fight an economic war, a total
war, in which all peoples are implicated today' (DA 16/CD 3,
translation modified). In other words, a shift in ethics does
not necessarily lead to a shift in political economy. 'But each
critical approach to the mode of contact existing among peoples and cultures', Glissant maintains, 'makes us suspect that
one day men will perhaps arrest themselves' (DA 16–17/CD 3,
translation modified). Whereas Levinas argues that '[t]he face
arrests totalization' and that '[w]hen man truly approaches
the other he is uprooted from history', Glissant suggests that
actively relaying entangled and violent histories could raise
consciousness and lead to challenging oppressive forces.[62]

Contacts among cultures can allow for a moment of hesitation such that colonial forces can be perceived not as natural (or
neutral) but as ideological. This negative moment still leaves us
susceptible to the limitations of any ethics of interruption – that

it presents a provocation but not a politics. In turn, if hesitation is to become resistance, it might begin by taking up opacity not as an ontological given but as an achievement that must be demanded politically. Contacts among cultures can allow a moment of pause from which ethical actors begin to participate in a positive process of standing-with others. Re-claiming the right to opacity in this way challenges the colonial models of globalisation. The right to opacity is about building and taking risks with others – 'Let it be a celebration', Glissant writes so beautifully (TTM 29).[63] In the next chapter, I elaborate on my theorisation here by discussing the 2016 protests at Standing Rock as an example of the right to opacity in practice. At Standing Rock, the prayers, dances, marches and direct actions created a celebration.

Notes

1. For a description of the present in terms of globalisation/coloniality, see Benjamin P. Davis, 'Globalization/Coloniality: A Decolonial Definition and Diagnosis', *Transmodernity: Journal of Cultural Production of the Luso-Hispanic World* 8, no. 4 (2018): pp. 1–20.

2. For a discussion of heterosexuality in relation to coloniality, see María Lugones, 'Heterosexualism and the Colonial/Modern Gender System', *Hypatia* 22, no. 1 (2007): pp. 186–209. Cf. Ann Laura Stoler, 'Intimidations of Empire: Predicaments of the Tactile and Unseen' and 'Tense and Tender Ties: The Politics of Comparison in North American History and (Post) Colonial Studies', in *Haunted by Empire: Geographies of Intimacy in North American History*, ed. Ann Laura Stoler (Durham, NC: Duke University Press, 2006), pp. 1–22, 23–68.

3. See Emmanuel Levinas, *Totalité et infini: Essai sur l'extériorité* (Leiden: Martinus Nijhoff, 1971), pp. 25, 30. Henceforth TI. For the translation, see Emmanuel Levinas, *Totality and Infinity: An Essay on Exteriority*, trans. Alphonso Lingis (Pittsburgh: Duquesne University Press, 1969), pp. 36, 40. Henceforth EE.

4. TI 78–79, 141/EE 80, 134.

5. TI 211/EE 194.

6. TI 211/EE 194.

7. John Drabinski, *Levinas and the Postcolonial: Race, Nation, Other* (Edinburgh: Edinburgh University Press, 2011), p. 68. Cf. Joy James's claim: 'To romanticize or falsify the disciplined body', she writes, 'one need only present it as unstructured by race, sex, and class' (James, *Resisting State Violence*, p. 42). For a discussion of how alterity prevents considerations of gender, see Sonia Sikka, 'The Delightful Other: Portraits of the Feminine in Kierkegaard, Nietzsche, and Levinas', in *Feminist Interpretations of Emmanuel Levinas*, ed. Tina Chanter (University Park: The Pennsylvania State University Press, 2001). See also Cynthia Willett, *Maternal Ethics and Other Slave Moralities* (New York: Routledge, 1995), pp. 62, 81; Falguni Sheth, *Toward a Political Philosophy of Race* (Albany: State University of New York Press, 2009), p. 174.

8. See Emmanuel Levinas, *Otherwise than Being or Beyond Essence*, trans. Alphonso Lingis (Pittsburg: Duquesne University Press, 1998), pp. 15, 43, 53, 112, 118, 124, and 196, n. 21.

9. See Emmanuel Levinas, *Ethics and Infinity*, trans. Richard A. Cohen (Pittsburgh: Duquesne University Press, 1985), p. 90; Drabinski, *Levinas and the Postcolonial*, p. 101.

10. Enrique Dussel, *Liberación Latinoamericana y Emmanuel Levinas* (Editorial Bonum: Buenos Aires, 1975), p. 28. Translation mine.

11. Ibid. pp. 28–9.

12. Enrique Dussel, *Ethics of Liberation: In the Age of Globalization and Exclusion*, trans. Bustillo et al. (Durham, NC: Duke University Press, 2013), p. 288.

13. Ibid. pp. 383–5.

14. Dussel, *Ethics*, p. 326. Dussel has noted the limitations of Levinas. See Enrique Dussel, '"The Politics" by Levinas: Toward a "Critical" Political Philosophy', in *Difficult Justice: Commentaries on Levinas and Politics*, ed. Asher Horowitz and Gad Horowitz, trans. Jorge Rodriguez (Toronto: University of Toronto Press, 2006), p. 81.

15. Dussel, *Ethics*, p. 326. To contextualise my intervention in conversation with other fields, I note that my concern with decolonial philosophy's inheritance of Levinas's vocabulary of 'the Other' resonates with Jasbir Puar's concern that 'liberal interventions are invariably infused with certitude that disability should be reclaimed as a valuable difference – the difference of the Other – through rights, visibility, and empowerment discourses – rather than addressing how much debilitation is caused by global injustice and the war machines of colonialism, occupation, and U.S. imperialism' (Puar, *The Right to Maim*, p. xvii). That said, Puar and I depart to a considerable extent in our analyses of the possibilities and limitations of rights discourse.

16. Maldonado-Torres, 'On the Coloniality of Being', p. 257; An Yountae, *The Decolonial Abyss: Mysticism and Cosmopolitics from the Ruins* (New York: Fordham University Press, 2016), p. 44.

17. Sidney Tarrow, *Power in Movement: Social Movement and Contentious Politics* (Cambridge: University of Cambridge Press, 2011), p. 6.

18. Nancy Mithlo, *Knowing Native Arts* (Lincoln: University of Nebraska Press, 2020), p. 231.

19. Ibid.

20. Simon Critchley, *The Ethics of Deconstruction: Derrida and Levinas* (Edinburgh: Edinburgh University Press, 1999), p. 5. I follow Wendy Brown's imperative for critical theory here: 'Critical theory aims to render crisis into knowledge, and to orient us in the darkness. Critique that does not affirm life, affirm value, and above all affirm possibilities in the present and the future, while certainly possible, is not making a bid for political power and hence cannot be understood as political' (Wendy Brown, 'Untimeliness and Punctuality: Critical Theory in Dark Times', in *Edgework: Critical Essays on Knowledge and Politics* (Princeton: Princeton University Press, 2005), p. 15).

21. See TI 30/EE 40. My claims in this chapter are not intended to suggest that 'alterity' could not, in any context or time, be the most helpful term. Following Stuart Hall, I do not think of conceptual vocabularies as time-out-of-mind entities; they are tools, and as with any tool, context and purpose always matter.

My claim is that in regard to contemporary social movements in the Americas, where many of us are increasingly living multiple (diasporic) identities, 'opacity' is more fruitful for thinking, analysing and organising than 'alterity'. We can also consider, for instance, the flexibility of 'opacity' to describe emotional life, as in Tina Campt's stunning essay 'The Opacity of Grief' (see Tina M. Campt, 'The Opacity of Grief', *Bomb Magazine*, 26 January 2022). Nevertheless, for a compelling use of 'alterity', see for example Mohammad Salama's forthcoming book on the Qur'an, *God's Other Book*.

22. Hall, 'Through the Prism of an Intellectual Life', p. 319.
23. For the language of 'models', see Aníbal Quijano, 'Coloniality of Power, Eurocentrism, and Latin America', *Nepantla: Views from the South* 1, no. 3 (2000): pp. 533–80.
24. Nancy Scheper-Hughes, *Death Without Weeping: The Violence of Everyday Life in Brazil* (Berkeley: University of California Press, 1992), p. 29.
25. Ibid.
26. Ibid.
27. Eduardo Mendieta, *Global Fragments: Globalizations, Latinamericanisms, and Critical Theory* (Albany: State University of New York Press, 2007), p. 21.
28. Michel-Rolph Trouillot, 'Anthropology and the Savage Slot: The Poetics and Politics of Otherness', in *Recapturing Anthropology: Working in the Present*, ed. Richard Fox (Santa Fe, NM: School of American Research Press, 1991), p. 39.
29. Mary Gallagher puts it this way: 'Glissant considers as the condition of an enduring diversity what Levinas stigmatizes for his part as the apotheosis of reduction: namely the acceptance and understanding of difference in a relational context envisaged as a totality' (Mary Gallagher, 'Ethics in the Absence of Reference: Levinas and the (Aesthetic) Value of Diversity', *Levinas Studies* 7 (2010): p. 122). Cf. Bernadette Cailler, 'Totalité et Infini, Altérité et Relation: d'Emmanuel Levinas à Édouard Glissant', in *Poétiques d'Edouard Glissant*, ed. Jacques Chervrier (Paris: Presses de l'Université de Paris-Sorbonne, 1999).

30. Mariana Ortega, *In-Between: Latina Feminist Phenomenology, Multiplicity, and the Self* (Albany: State University of New York Press, 2016), p. 138.

31. Mendieta, *Global Fragments*, p. 29.

32. Courtney Bender, *The New Metaphysicals: Spirituality and the American Religious Imagination* (Chicago: University of Chicago Press, 2010), p. 180.

33. Nancy Scheper-Hughes, 'The Primacy of the Ethical: Propositions for a Militant Anthropology', *Current Anthropology* 36, no. 3 (1995): p. 417.

34. See for example Arturo Escobar, *Designs for the Pluriverse: Radical Interdependence, Autonomy, and the Making of Worlds* (Durham, NC: Duke University Press, 2018).

35. Decolonial theorists have argued that coloniality is constitutive of modernity, such that 'modernity' by itself is an inadequate term. See for example Aníbal Quijano, 'Coloniality and Modernity/Rationality', *Cultural Studies* 21, no. 2 (2007): pp. 168–78.

36. Michelle Murphy, 'Against Population, Towards Afterlife', in A. E. Clarke and Donna Haraway (eds), *Making Kin Not Population: Reconceiving Generations* (Chicago: Prickly Paradigm Press, 2018), p. 121. Henceforth MKNP.

37. Sanford F. Schram, *The Return of Ordinary Capitalism: Neoliberalism, Precarity, Occupy* (Oxford: Oxford University Press, 2015), p. 69.

38. Ibid.

39. Isabell Lorey, *State of Insecurity: Government of the Precarious* (New York: Verso, 2015), pp. 97–8.

40. John Drabinski, *Glissant and the Middle Passage: Philosophy, Beginning, Abyss* (Minneapolis: University of Minnesota Press, 2019), p. 13.

41. Neal Allar, 'The Case for Incomprehension: Édouard Glissant's Poetics of Relation and the Right to Opacity', *Journal of French and Francophone Philosophy* XXIII, no. 1 (2015): pp. 43, 44, 43.

42. H. Adlai Murdoch, 'Édouard Glissant's Creolized World Vision: From Resistance and Relation to *Opacité*', *Callaloo* 36, no. 4 (2013): p. 885.

43. TI 78/EE 80.

44. In a recent essay, Li Chi-she reads opacity in terms of alterity, arguing that in *Poetics* Glissant 'considers seriously what alterity could mean in terms of the specificity of the island experience in Martinique' (Li Chi-she, 'Opacity', *Philosophy Today* 63, no. 4 (2019): p. 861). Glissant does invoke 'alterity' in *Poetics*, but he associates its acceptance with 'The thought of the Other', which he criticises or takes some distance from (PR 169/PO 154). I would disagree, then, with Chi-she's claim that in *Poetics* Glissant 'proposes a philosophical vision of radical alterity' (Chi-she, 'Opacity', p. 865). That is not his preferred term, even if he does, at times, capitalise 'the Other' – for instance when he describes the work of Michel Leiris as an 'ethnology of Relation' and 'an ethnography of the relation to the Other [*à l'Autre*]' (TTM 131; see also TTM 248). In my view, Glissant to some extent, perhaps to an insufficient extent, grounds ethics in a politics, illustrated in his reading of Jacques Berque, 'He always thought of the approach to the Other *in* a vision of world solidarity' (TTM 183).

45. See Gerard Aching, 'The "Right to Opacity" and World Literature', *1616: Anuario de Literatura Comparada* 2 (2012): pp. 40, 45.

46. Katherine McKittrick, *Demonic Grounds: Black Women and the Cartographies of Struggle* (Minneapolis: University of Minnesota Press, 2006), p. xxii.

47. Mendieta, *Global Fragments*, p. 91.

48. Ibid. p. 94.

49. See Catherine Keller, *Cloud of the Impossible: Negative Theology and Planetary Entanglement* (New York: Columbia University Press, 2014), p. 268; Maldonado-Torres, 'On the Coloniality of Human Rights'.

50. See Jessica Whyte, *The Morals of the Market: Human Rights and the Rise of Neoliberalism* (London: Verso, 2019). See esp. Chapters 3, 4 and 5.

51. Moyn, *Human Rights*, p. 98.

52. Ibid. p. 99, emphasis mine; p. 98. Moyn addresses the questions of maximal claims in his book, *Not Enough: Human Rights in an Unequal World* (Cambridge, MA: The Belknap Press of Harvard University Press, 2018).

53. Joseph Slaughter notes that the problem of the narrative of three generations of rights is that it presents 'a smooth evolution of human rights legislation from the eighteenth to the twentieth centuries; it has also regularly been invoked to celebrate the UN's legislative activity as a process of consensus-building, and to naturalise, as part of a telos of human progress, the West's prioritisation of civil and political rights over social, economic, cultural, environmental and solidarity rights. Although the generational schema comprehends certain international legislative trends, it is misleading when used to plot a neat, Eurocentric genealogy of contemporary human rights, or to intimate that civil and political rights are (and always have been) divisible from and more fundamental than social, cultural and economic rights' (Joseph R. Slaughter, *Human Rights, Inc.: The World Novel, Narrative Form, and International Law* (New York: Fordham University Press, 2007), pp. 15–16).

54. James Griffin, *On Human Rights* (Oxford: Oxford University Press, 2008), p. 167.

55. Ibid.

56. Ibid.

57. Ibid.

58. 'Guatemala',   <https://www.charitywater.org/our-projects/guatemala>.

59. Stephen Schlesinger, 'Ghosts of Guatemala's Past', *New York Times*, 3 June 2011, <https://www.nytimes.com/2011/06/04/opinion/04schlesinger.html>. See also Stephen Schlesinger and Stephen Kinzer, *Bitter Fruit: The Story of the American Coup in Guatemala* (Cambridge, MA: Harvard University Press, 2005).

60. I thank Adrienne Davis for this suggestion of using the right to opacity as an analytic tool to understand past struggles.

61. See 'Coffee for Holland means blood for Angola', <http://psimg.jstor.org/fsi/img/pdf/t0/10.5555/al.sff.document.nizap1026_final.pdf>. For a summary argument that 'human rights were pivotal in the arguments against Portuguese colonialism', see Miguel Banderia Jerónimo and José Pedro Monteiro, 'The Inventors of Human Rights in Africa: Portugal, Late Colonialism, and the UN

Human Rights Regime' in *Decolonization, Self-Determination, and the Rise of Global Human Rights Politics*, ed. Moses et al., p. 311.

62. TI 314, 45/EE 281, 52.

63. See also Allison Weir, 'Collective Love as Public Freedom: Dancing Resistance. Ehrenreich, Arendt, Kristeva, and *Idle No More*', *Hypatia* 32, no. 1 (2017): pp. 19–34.

2 The Right to Opacity in Practice

The Critical-Reformist Tension

This chapter begins from and stays with two tensions regarding theorising the state. The first is perhaps the constitutive tension in scholarship on human rights: the understanding of the modern state as both predatory and protective. In his 2013 *Universal Human Rights in Theory and Practice*, Jack Donnelly observes that 'the modern state has emerged as both the principal threat to the enjoyment of human rights and the essential institution for their effective implementation and enforcement'.[1] He goes on to place his faith in human rights to prohibit 'a wide range of state interferences' and thereby to carve out 'zones of state exclusion'.[2] In this way, 'human rights place the people above and in positive control of their government', a position achieved through 'extensive rights of political participation'.[3] Donnelly's trajectory moves toward 'the moral standing of the state', concluding with 'paths of incremental change'.[4] His position epitomises what I will call 'the critical-reformist tension', which notes and criticises state-caused rights violations before returning to a call for state reform. This first tension is important because many justice-oriented actors feel it today. It leads to conflicting demands for practice. It is carried out in practice when students consider the risk of working as radical artists, activists or community organisers only to go to law school before garnering stable jobs in government or accepting positions at prestigious NGOs.

James Griffin's 2008 *On Human Rights* typifies a thin version of the critical-reformist tension. Griffin's analysis of human rights violations centres not state violence but relations between rights, such as how a state's enforcement of welfare rights can violate liberty rights.[5] Ultimately, he argues that 'states are the main agents of security of person' and that 'in some states one can vote and enjoy the protection of the police and army without being a citizen, but only citizenship makes their possession secure'.[6] In stressing police protection, Griffin lacks a robust accounting for Indigenous displacement and police violence. His focus on security, which comes at the expense of attending to state predation on made-precarious peoples, recalls A. Dirk Moses' recent observation that 'the security imperative can justify permanent occupation, that is, colonial rule'.[7] This point brings me to the second tension.

A series of ongoing governmental permissions for and limits on capitalistic resource extraction on the land of the Standing Rock Sioux can leave human rights actors' heads spinning. The Standing Rock Sioux and other local, national and international actors have made numerous rights claims challenging the Dakota Access Pipeline. The United States has recognised some of these claims and dismissed others. The emotions of activists can be as mercurial as the state's vicissitudes. We celebrate court orders to conduct an environmental review of the pipeline's impact only to grit our teeth when an appeals court allows the pipeline to continue carrying oil. But changing the behaviour of the state is only one way of understanding the purpose of rights claims. Other approaches to human rights open new analytical and practical possibilities.

The second tension is the strain actors place on rights discourse when they stretch it beyond its immediate application of appealing to the state. Considering Standing Rock as a recent example of rights theory and praxis can shed light on an old problem in rights discourse, namely, how to theorise the 'failure' of rights to change the institutions on which they are making claims.[8]

In this chapter, I present a typology of three approaches to human rights: paradigmatic, critical and organisational.[9] Each approach offers a different way of taking up Glissant's right to opacity. Reflecting on different orientations to rights that were present at Standing Rock, I have read my typology back into recent literature, which I track carefully below. Because the actions at Standing Rock only make sense as categorised once the categories have been introduced, I start from recent texts before returning to Standing Rock. My purpose is to lay out the theoretical presuppositions of three ways actors implicitly or explicitly think about human rights so as to offer three distinct, but sometimes overlapping, paths of action. This typology aims to help practitioners avoid what Theodor Adorno called *begriffslose Praxis*, meaning political practices lacking clear conceptual orientation.[10] Making clear and distinct these paths, as well as the theorisations on which they rely, could inform the choices of those who are standing at forks in their own roads.[11] At stake is the orientation of human rights work today.

Today, Jayan Nayar makes clear, claims to human rights operate in light of 'the post-Arendtian realization' that the concept of human rights, 'rather than applying to all Humans by virtue of some universal quality of being Human', is in practice 'inescapably linked to state-territorial contexts of political belonging and its rationalities of inclusions and exclusions, rights and rightlessness'.[12] '[Hannah] Arendt's preference for civil rights as opposed to human rights', Ayça Çubukçu adds in a recent essay on solidarity, 'is based on the unstable assumption, nay assertion, that the primary function of the state is the *protection* of its citizens and their rights.'[13] Çubukçu then pauses in a critical way: 'But how and why could Arendt, writing as a denationalized German Jew who only barely escaped Nazi Germany, assert this?'[14] I extend Çubukçu's question to scholars of our time: How can many leading human rights theorists – witnessing consistent state violence – slide rather easily back into calling for a gradually reformed state?[15] Why do they maintain that, subjected to the right pressures, an entity that has always been predatory will tend toward being universally protective? In the context Nayar outlines, and with Çubukçu's push in mind, another relevant question becomes, in Nayar's words, 'how to (re)think Human Rights out of the bordered geopolitics of inclusion and exclusion in a world of a globalized, territorially-bounded and segregated "sovereign" state system?'[16]

My response to Nayar's question requires three parts. I begin by outlining additional examples of the critical-reformist tension, paying attention to how theorists conceptualise the role of activism vis-à-vis the state. I then distinguish between three theoretical approaches to human rights: (1) a state-oriented approach that uses the language of rights, exemplified in Benjamin Gregg's 2016 *Human Rights State* – what I call *the paradigmatic approach*; (2) an approach with multiple orientations and an ambivalent relationship to rights, exemplified in Left critical theory and decolonial theory – what I call *the critical approach*; and (3) a community-oriented approach that uses the language of rights, exemplified in Valeria M. Pelet del Toro's 2019 scholarship on legal work in Puerto Rico – what I call *the organisational approach*. Finally, I show how these approaches were deployed in 2016 at Standing Rock. Because they challenged state-led dispossession, capitalist resource extraction and rights denials caused by both the state and corporations, rights claims at Standing Rock provide examples of how Glissant's right to opacity operates in practice.

This chapter's main contribution is to draw out the organisational approach, which can be situated between liberal theories advocating rights talk while assuming the state as ideally protective (Griffin, Donnelly, et al.) and critical theories interrogating the use of rights and its assumed normative conditioning and paternalism (Left critical theory, recent decolonial theory, etc.). An examination of the organisational approach considers how, taken up organisationally, human rights become a shared language for affirming and legitimising political communities that are alternatives to the modern state form. Practised this way, human rights claims become starting points – active relays, in Glissant's terms – for broader political action. What the organisational approach stands to give activists today is both a way to disentangle human rights talk from a territory-bound state addressee and a way to think about the work of human rights without tying the successes and failures of that work to state reform.

Commenting above that Griffin provides a 'thin' example of the critical-reformist tension, I imply that there are 'thicker' examples – examples that problematise the threat of the state more extensively. From its introduction onward, Kathryn Sikkink's 2017 *Evidence for Hope* speaks to instances where states violated human rights as well as to histories of 'state repression'.[17] At the beginning of the book, she describes activism as a way to challenge successfully the governments that perpetrate human rights violations, such that states repress activism: 'Efforts to weaken human rights activism suggest that governments perceive organizations that promote human rights to be effective.'[18] But her framing of activists and states is, in the final instance, collaborative; together, 'activists and states' can add 'new feature[s] to the human rights institutional landscapes'.[19] That is, although Sikkink begins her hopeful book with examples of activists on the fringes of their societies, one of her criteria for social progress is the establishment of human rights norms in official structures. By her lights, this centripetal motion, from activist margins to state centres, is what constitutes successful social change: 'Human rights struggles led to concrete laws and institutions that have altered the fabric of the world we live in today.'[20] Her aim, then, is to appeal to and reform repressive governments – she finds promising the call for 'state accountability'.[21] *Evidence for Hope*'s last chapter, accordingly and like Donnelly's, fleshes out the 'policy implications' of her argument.[22]

We can consider as a second example Lindsey Kingston's 2019 *Fully Human: Personhood, Citizenship, and Rights*. Kingston observes that states are 'the venue for human rights practice'.[23] However, the key concept in *Fully Human*, 'functioning citizenship', seems to challenge the state-oriented paradigm. Kingston perceptively argues that 'reliance on state duty-bearers leaves little political space for effectively responding to statelessness, instead offering another tool of marginalization and oppression to hold over minorities and political dissenters'.[24] She approaches the conclusion of her book by suggesting that functioning citizenship 'problematizes our reliance on states and legal nationality for protecting rights, constituting political communities, and ultimately determining one's worthiness as a fellow human being'.[25] That said, she ultimately returns to the state, maintaining that the promise of functioning citizenship is to move beyond 'mere legal status to facilitate mutually beneficial, rights-protective relationships between the state and the individual'.[26] Advocates, then, 'must work within' the international system.[27] Hence her concluding prescription: 'State duty-bearers and the international community as a whole must be subjected to continued pressure to respect the norms expressed by international human rights law and frameworks', and this pressure takes the form of a 'lobby for human rights'.[28]

The critical-reformist tension leaves justice-oriented actors in a space of conflicting demands, one that often presents more questions than answers. If the state is a protector of rights – the *only* entity that can secure rights, as Griffin has it – but also a violator, then for whom does it secure rights and by what criteria? If these criteria show repeated failures to protect the rights of some, and indeed repeated intentional denials of the rights of others, then why should activists continue to pursue this reformist approach? More specifically, we can ask: In regard to Sikkink's call for accountability, to whom is this accountability directed? And for what reason does the state consistently refuse to give an account of its rights denials to certain groups? Is the 'pressure' to which Kingston suggests we subject the state duty-bearers *itself the kind of reliance* she seems to want to call into question? And if so, does not such pressure reproduce the tools of marginalisation and oppression that Kingston emphasises we need to problematise?

How we answer these questions relies on what conception we have of the state in the background of our theories. The critical-reformist tension emerges for Donnelly, Sikkink, Kingston and others who adopt a modern theory of the state. Following Kant and Hegel, modern European political theory presents the state as a means to freedom. The language of rights sustains political action that aims at state reform, thus bringing the state more in line with its own concept of providing universal rights. According to this ideal theory, the activity of civil society should be guaranteed through state-sanctioned rights to political participation (e.g. to assembly), which functions as a conscience of the state. If the task of activism is to call the state to its better self, then states' weakening of activism is both a moral and political failure to live up to their responsibilities.

While scholars exemplifying the critical-reformist tension admit that the state has historically denied and continues to deny rights to certain individuals – including those it claims it has a duty to protect, such as its own citizens – many scholars still prescribe institutional reforms as part of a larger call for modern states to live up to their ideal concept. For these liberal theorists, the framing of the state as both violator and protector of rights is not a contradiction that gives pause so much as evidence that more work needs to be done. The critical-reformist tension, qua *tension*, then, is less a contradiction in their own work and more an imposition from a critical perspective that calls into question the modern model. This critical perspective claims that an empirical field saturated with violence belies the state as a worthwhile regulative ideal.

In doubling down on the critical impulse and abandoning calls to reform, critical theorists draw upon a historical record where 'reform' has meant only more insidious reinstallations of hierarchies of race, gender, labour and so on. A first example is seen in the ostensible abolition of slavery in the US, which in turn allowed for incarceration as an afterlife of slavery, given the 13th Amendment's infamous 'except as a punishment for crime'.[29] As Joy James puts it, 'Given the Thirteenth Amendment, the convict lease system, and the modern prison industrial complex, the United States has never known democracy severed from captivity.'[30] A second example of the deceptive history of 'reform' occurred as colonial states responded to invocations of human rights in the 1940s. Fabian Klose summarises this history as follows in regard to Great Britain:

Reform and development became important pillars of British colonial policy and served several functions. The main objective of the announced reforms was to improve the economic and social situation in the colonies, in order to be able to better exploit existing resources for the reconstruction of Great Britain.[31]

And in regard to France:

> Like the federal structures, the reforms were reduced to a cosmetic minimum and made apparent the irresolvable contradiction between the equality principle and France's hegemonic position. The constitution of the Fourth Republic was the attempt to proclaim the end of colonialism without really losing the overseas territories and to implement reforms without forfeiting any power.[32]

Further, when confrontations arose in colonised areas, colonial powers refused to call them wars:

> Great Britain and France refused to give their colonial confrontations in Kenya and Algeria the official status of 'armed conflict'. In order to block the applicability of humanitarian law and the intervention of international actors, they believed it was necessary to avoid any designation that could be interpreted as meaning armed confrontation, or even war, no matter the circumstances . . . The war without rules became a war without a name [through] the neutral terms 'emergency' and 'civil disturbance'.[33]

In sum, official, colonial language functioned to cover up and criminalise resistance.[34] With the above examples in mind, many critical theorists remain suspicious of both calling for reform and adopting official vocabularies.

Recent scholarship resonant with this critical line has underscored the need for historical and geographical specification of any theory of the state, assumed or explicit. This scholarship includes Saidiya Hartman's critique of 'predatory state forms', John Crabtree and Francisco Durand's notion of 'state capture', and Robert Nichols's genealogy of state-led dispossession.[35] Other theorists have linked ongoing anti-Black police violence and occupations of Indigenous land in the US to the aforementioned colonial patterns of both cosmetic reform and refusal to describe confrontations as 'war'. Drawing on traditions of Black and Indigenous theory and resistance, respectively, Joy James and Nick Estes have argued that the modern understanding of the state assumes that activism is a feature of correctable *conflicts* as opposed to ongoing *wars*.[36]

* * *

For the remainder of this chapter, I narrow my focus to the consideration of the state in the Americas, and to the United States in particular. In the Americas, state formation and continuation cannot be separated from colonisation and enslavement.[37] My narrowed focus is a methodological consideration indicating that, given the difficulties of attending to 'the state' in the abstract, it is more fruitful to attend to what a state has been and is – the historical and actual relationship between form and content. It is worthwhile to consider the words of not just those who theorise the state but also those who have suffered it.

In regard to the state in the Americas, Glen Coulthard, reading Frantz Fanon, has called on theorists 'to transcend the fantasy that the settler-state apparatus – as a structure of domination *predicated* on our ongoing dispossession – is somehow capable of producing liberatory effects'.[38] According to James's, Estes's, and Coulthard's arguments, enduring patterns of slavery, genocide, misogyny and colonisation provide evidence for the case that denial of rights to some is not an incidental, and therefore correctable, feature attendant to the American state, including the United States and Canada. On the contrary, these patterns indicate that the state's denial and violation of rights is an essential element constitutive of the state. If this argument is right, then it forecloses the paradigmatic response to human rights violations, namely, that rights violations result only from an imperfect state, which can be improved by reforms hoping to realise the ideal state.

The critical-reformist tension is not just about theorising the state; it is also about theorising the relationship between the state and what challenges it. In addition to asking theorists exemplifying (and practitioners adopting) the critical-reformist tension to take sides, there is a clear practical implication of the critical argument: if reliance on the state is problematic and in fact often exacerbates human rights violations, then the orientation of political actors should shift, appealing to other sources of recognition. In this spirit, we can consider the promises of human rights theory and practice beyond policies and institutions that presuppose the state as the duty-bearer corresponding to rights claims.

What possibilities emerge from bracketing law and policy as the presupposed *telos* of human rights theory and practice? This bracketing is not mutually exclusive with looking at law as a cause, instantiation, or result of that theory and practice. It is a method that can still learn from, for instance, the academic lawyer Steven Ratner's claim that international law should be a source of information for political philosophers because the rules of law are 'both a formalized instantiation, and in some cases even a causal factor, of the moral problems of global justice'.[39] But the fruits of this interdisciplinary understanding, in my view, are different from Ratner's (and Donnelly's, Sikkink's, Kingston's – the modern, liberal position's) hoped-for 'more institutionally sensitive . . . policy-guiding set of principles of international public morality'.[40] For Ratner, the lawyer's task is 'oriented toward analyzing and solving concrete problems through the institutions we have (even if reformed somewhat)'.[41] Starting from Glissant in the previous chapter, I make a case for giving the political philosopher (as well as the lawyer and the activist) a more imaginative task, namely, to analyse and respond to concrete problems without firstly or necessarily tying that analysis and response to predominant institutions. For this reason, the organisational approach not only has means and ends different from the liberal, paradigmatic approach, but also endorses a broader role for rights claims than the critical approach's strategic reduction of international law to a 'mere tool', that is, 'to the tactical, instrumental deployment of legal argument', to cite Robert Knox's formulation.[42]

Three Approaches to Human Rights

The Paradigmatic Approach

Benjamin Gregg's 2016 *The Human Rights State* exemplifies what I call 'the paradigmatic approach' to human rights, which presupposes the state as the duty-bearer corresponding to human rights claims and ties the success of those claims to the reform of the state. Gregg maintains the importance of the state despite the radical potential with which he begins the book. He imagines 'politics' early in the text 'as robust openness to possibilities never before realized, possibilities bordering on utopian'.[43] After this opening gesture, which suggests social forms that humans have yet to achieve, he returns to the state, the modern political form, in his presentation of the human rights ideal 'as an integral element of the state'.[44] Gregg also exhibits the critical-reformist tension: while he acknowledges that 'in many cases, the state of government or some other authority is itself the violator', he then appeals – in a move surprising given his utopian opening – 'to a classical Greek topos': the state is 'the spear that alone can heal the wound it caused'.[45] Gregg explains his appeal: 'A realistic utopia, a practical cosmopolitanism, requires reconceptualizing human rights in ways that facilitate their advance by heightening their practicability.'[46] The organisational approach to human rights attempts to reconceptualise human rights in a way that heightens their practicability, but it appeals to sources of recognition different from Gregg's 'healing' state.

Differences between paradigmatic, critical and organisational approaches are brought into relief through Gregg's
discussion of Médecins Sans Frontières (MSF) as an example
of institutions in civil society that 'establish pockets within a
nation state in which the NGO recognizes, for its own purposes, at least some individuals as bearing human rights'.[47]
For Gregg, '[t]hese humanitarian zones have the capacity to
form a kind of human rights state'.[48] For others, such as Jessica
Whyte, MSF is one of the NGOs that draws 'on an account of
rights developed by the neoliberals since the 1940s', namely,
the bifurcation of civil society (as free and checking the state)
and politics (as violent and coercive).[49] Gregg's assurance that,
in his vision, the human rights state is to keep its traditional
function of protecting capitalist markets and commercial
organisations suggests that his project is also drastically different from Whyte's vision of human rights as well as from the
vision I am articulating in conversation with Glissant.[50]

Overall, Gregg places his book as working against a kind of
'charity model' of human rights, which removes agency from
individuals by thinking that the state endows each individual
with certain rights. Instead, he takes individuals as authors
of their rights: human rights are 'something that members of
a political community might themselves author and grant to
themselves', and they do so 'within or alongside a particular
nation state, targeting it for transformation into a state that
embraces human rights as part of its internal constitution'.[51]
Hence his title: the human rights state, as a 'device or mechanism of advocacy', is 'a metaphorical community directed at
a corresponding nation state'.[52] Gregg has a twofold aim.[53]
His view of the promise of human rights is directly different
from both a critical and an organisational approach, as we will
see: 'The human rights project aims to change state behavior
and the behavior of groups within the political community;

it counters efforts and trends that leave the state out of that project.'[54] Accordingly, the human rights state and the actual, modern state exist at the same time. If the individual is part of both states, we are left wondering: How does the individual, as a member of both states, make rights claims for themselves (self-authorisation) and toward the state (recognition)?

Gregg's metaphor for individual action, as part of 'social movements', is a backpack.[55] The backpack is his way of explaining how 'human rights [could be] bound to the person of a human being and no longer to national territories'.[56] Just as a student carries a backpack wherever they go, so too, according to this argument, the individual should perform human rights by taking a 'human rights backpack' wherever they go.[57] 'A person claims toward others – performs for others – a right to have rights first of all as a right to oppose one's exclusion in practice from the law on paper.'[58] '[A] human rights backpack establishes the bearer's political agency in a cosmopolitan sense, at least aspirationally', Gregg continues.[59] 'Backpackers do not wait for recognition by the corresponding nation state to practice recognition among themselves.'[60]

Yet for a performance that Gregg calls 'an agonistic politics' and that involves self-authorship, in *The Human Rights State* there is a remarkable reliance on reformist advocacy appealing to the authority of the state: 'The human rights project . . . here takes the form of persuading nation states to recognize the human rights that members of a human rights state have assigned themselves . . . The project does not undermine a nation state.'[61] Some scholars would observe that this call for persuasion assumes that activism occurs in a context of conflict and not of war (e.g. James and Estes). Other critics of rights discourse would worry that the goal of persuasion of the powerful state is a chimera because rights claims function to implicate actors in the state much more than to challenge the trajectory of state-based practices (e.g. Coulthard).

The Critical Approach

Contra the paradigmatic approach that Gregg exemplifies, some have argued for a suspension of any assumed faith in rights. '[O]ne of our worries about legalism', Wendy Brown and Janet Halley explain in their 2002 *Left Legalism/Left Critique*, 'pertains to its impulse to call the question too peremptorily.'[62] 'The question' refers to theories of social change. Brown and Halley's worry is that rights claims and other legalist approaches foreclose other forms of political change that are part and parcel of any Left agenda, a worry this book's final chapter will address in more historical detail. '[T]he left's current absorption with legal strategies', they assert, 'means that liberal legalism persistently threatens to defang the left we want to inhabit . . . limiting its normative aspirations.'[63] What for the paradigmatic approach is a binary between civil society and the state is theorised together in the critical approach, which worries that every appeal to rights that looks to reformed policies 'commits itself to normativizing deployments of state power'.[64] For instance, radical queer kinships are swept aside by a legalising discourse to expand marriage as the officially sanctioned form of adult intimacy. Brown adds to these points in her 2004 article '"The Most We Can Hope For . . .": Human Rights and the Politics of Fatalism', arguing that claims to human rights displace 'dissonant political projects' that 'may offer a more appropriate and far-reaching remedy for injustice defined as suffering and as systematic disenfranchisement from collaborative self-governance'.[65] Bernard Harcourt, in his 2020 *Critique & Praxis*, makes a similar point, arguing that 'today, the single greatest challenge to critical theory is liberal legalism: the idea that we should conform to the rule of law as a way to avoid political strife'.[66]

Brown and Harcourt represent a strand of the critical approach that follows a European tradition of critical theory. Both argue that the best response to legal liberalism is critique. 'Critique', for Brown, 'emerges in the German philosophical tradition starting with Kant and continuing through Hegel, Marx, and the Frankfurt School'.[67] '[T]he birth certificate of critical philosophy', Harcourt says, lies with Marx's famous 1845 note that the point of philosophy is not just to interpret the world but to change it; critical theory then continues through the Frankfurt School.[68] Like the paradigmatic approach to human rights, this mode of the critical approach adopts a tradition that conceptualises the state as an entity that can be improved through pressures such as rights claims. Donnelly would say that activists work in civil society to create zones of state exclusion; Sikkink, Kingston and Gregg would argue that civil society works to align the state and the people in rights-*protective* relationships (e.g. 'the human rights state'). The critical move is to ask: participation and protection for whom? That is, who constitutes 'the people'? Crucially, this move can occur on different lines. Brown, Harcourt and other critical theorists who build on Kant, Hegel, Marx and the Frankfurt School emphasise 'the ambivalent politics of human rights'.[69] Other critical theorists who start from American theorists and histories condemn human rights more strongly.

As noted in this book's introduction, Nelson Maldonado-Torres has stressed that, to this day, 'there is a pattern in which the definition of human rights leads to the creation of experts who are designated to speak to the colonized and other marginalized peoples about the rights that they possess'.[70] In response to this paternalism and parochialism, the decolonial move would be not 'the extension of existing universalisms' by promoting European norms around rights but rather 'a series of struggles aimed at bringing about the humanity of the colonized and in that process letting them discover or define what they take the universality of humanity to be'.[71] Any appeal, any request for recognition, gives away where those appealing think power resides. Maldonado-Torres's consciousness-oriented approach places power with communities struggling under coloniality, leaving them to define their own sense of who they are. The language of rights, according to this decolonial approach, places power in the hands of the state, leaving the community to be little more than a potential recipient of charity.[72] '[I]n our efforts to *interpolate* the legal and political discourses of the state to secure recognition of our rights to land and self-determination', Coulthard writes in regard to Indigenous struggles for recognition by Canada, 'we have too often found ourselves *interpellated* as subjects of settler-colonial rule'.[73]

If the decolonial rebuttal is correct, then rights claims often do the opposite of what scholars like Gregg think they are doing in challenging a charity model. Gregg's point is that claims to rights perform an inclusion of excluded communities into rights protections, and that they do so while being directed at the state. Brown and Harcourt think that the politics of rights is ambivalent because it cannot separate itself from a liberal imaginary that maintains oppressive norms. Extending this critique, Maldonado-Torres condemns human rights discourse for speaking for the dispossessed more than standing with them. But if human rights claims serve primarily to re-install violent state structures, then why do some peoples resisting ongoing colonisation, such as the Xukuru nation, continue to mobilise rights claims in their struggles? And why would they do so beyond specific strategic measures such as their 2018 victory against the state of Brazil at the Inter-American Court of Human Rights? The Xukuru's invocations of rights at their annual assemblies provide examples of theorising rights claims that are empowering but not first oriented to the state – rights claims that do not presuppose the state as the addressee. With this theory and practice in mind, I will next draw out what I call *the organisational approach* to human rights. In doing so, I will keep in mind Glissant's insight that while the role of discourse is to organise, the role of poetics is to unfold (TTM 134). Perhaps a more imaginative human rights discourse today would combine these roles, organising and unfolding (moving, relaying, changing, exchanging) in different situations for different purposes.

The Organisational Approach

In her 2019 'Beyond the Critique of Rights: The Puerto Rico Legal Project and Civil Rights Litigation in America's Colony', Valeria M. Pelet del Toro presents legal advocacy in Puerto Rico as a case of rights claims that are empowering and that do not tie their success to state reform. Viewed from the criterion of state reform, rights discourse in Puerto Rico has failed. But viewed from a different perspective, 'rights talk has historically provided a framework for effective organizing and community action'.[74] Del Toro aligns with the critical approach when she notes that through a variety of legal initiatives, lawyers in Puerto Rico worked with the efforts of local leaders 'to reexamine their relationship to the law of the colonial oppression and aimed to give Puerto Ricans the tools they needed to have their movements speak for themselves'.[75] In this way, rights claims raise consciousness and voices. In addition to litigation, the activities of Puerto Rico's first public-interest law firm included 'community and public education, media work, and community organizing'.[76]

Importantly, del Toro theorises rights discourse in a way different from both Gregg and recent critical theory. She contends that 'it is important to recognize the role of rights talk here: as a gateway to political engagement'.[77] In employing rights in this way, 'Puerto Ricans were fighting for their voices to be heard, challenging those who told them to step aside, and devising new political visions for their society . . . they were engaging in nation building, key to ensuring any type of decolonization.'[78] For del Toro, rights talk is not a barrier but a bridge to further political action as power is built among a community. This theorisation of rights is also an important point of departure from the paradigmatic approach: for Gregg, human rights advocacy is political in its performance. For del Toro, rights claims are a *gateway* to politics. For both Gregg and del Toro, rights claims are made in a situation where an oppressed group struggles against an external power for recognition of something its members already recognise in one another. Crucially, however, del Toro drops the expectation of a state response. For her, the success of rights claims is not tied to recognition by the state.

Del Toro's case study proves that rights discourse can be fruitful less as an appeal to the state and more as a form of organisation – as an entrance point, or gateway, to political action. '[A]s an advocate', she writes summarising the suggestion of a lawyer in Puerto Rico, 'you might opt for litigation not because it will give you the outcome you want, but because it will give you the exposure you need to educate the public on a given issue'.[79] Looking backward, rights claims are a way to remember violent histories. They challenge official histories by preventing 'political repression and state violence' from being forgotten, thus 'defending and validating the kind of dissent that was lethal in Puerto Rico'.[80] Looking forward, rights claims can be imaginative in addition to being part of strategic litigation: '[R]ights talk helped give Puerto Ricans the impetus to articulate new demands, visions, and realities for themselves. This process facilitated a public space for Puerto Ricans to debate and contend with issues like government repression, censorship, politically-based murders, and sexual harassment, among others.'[81] Rights claims, in being broadly legible, are in this way starting points for public conversations. They are language to organise further efforts.

To summarise the above three different theoretical approaches to human rights: the paradigmatic approach suggests making right claims so as to reform the state as a correctible duty-bearer. The critical approach maintains an ambivalent relationship with rights. It often demands jettisoning the language of rights in favour of community-oriented movements. The organisational approach calls for employing the language of rights in making broadly legible claims that organise people who work together to voice new demands and to make new political realities. Both the critical and the organisational approaches prescribe methods that call into question the critical-reformist tension in contemporary human rights scholarship today, dwelling on the state as a violator instead of returning rather quickly to appeal for its 'protection'. The organisational approach carries promise because it suggests a path forward more clearly than the critical approach does. The organisational approach offers a vision for using rights claims that are not necessarily oriented to predatory state forms, but that instead function as rallying cries, mobilising locally and garnering international attention for ongoing struggles.

The Three Approaches at Work and the Promises of Standing Rock

As an example of how the paradigmatic, critical and organisational approaches to human rights defend cultural rights, what Glissant calls the right to opacity, we can consider the 2016 protests at Standing Rock. To consider Standing Rock is to dwell not with elite theoretical speculations but with grounded, ongoing practical efforts, particularly those of marginalised communities of resistance.[82] This extended consideration follows Mariana Ortega's methodological suggestion that decolonial theory would do well to look not to a transcendental 'beyond' but to immanent practices already underway.[83] (She has Dussel in mind in making her critique.) Examples of ongoing efforts include horizontal labour practices, co-operative modes of production, queer kinship units and horizontal political organisation. From this underside of globalisation, legible modes could offer bearings with social traction to the elite, or, when that fails, coalitional challenges to the powerful in our age of exclusion.

The US responded to activism at Standing Rock by using the aforementioned methods of colonial Britain and France: invocation of emergency measures, criminalisation of resistance, and a refusal to define Standing Rock as an iteration of an ongoing war between the US and the Standing Rock Sioux. The latter claim takes on heightened significance given the 1851 and 1868 Fort Laramie Treaties between the US and the Standing Rock Sioux, because treaties are agreements between sovereign nations. Given the international attention that focused, albeit briefly, on Standing Rock, the state violence at Standing Rock exemplifies what the historian Patrick William Kelly has called a 'sovereign emergency'.[84] Understood this way, we can place the state violence at Standing Rock not only in the wake of European colonial violence in the 1940s, but also in connection with that of Brazil, Chile and Argentina in the 1970s, reflecting in our time what Kelly documents as the 'growing sense of the limits of national borders and the urgent need to respond to acts of obscene state repression'.[85] State repression at Standing Rock, such as the police water cannons deployed against water protectors on freezing nights, combined with occasional state action to halt the pipeline, makes clear that Coulthard is right in *Red Skin, White Masks* when he emphasises that Indigenous activism has made American colonial powers in the twentieth century shift from 'the genocidal exclusion/assimilation double' to 'a seemingly more conciliatory set of discourses and institutional practices that emphasize our *recognition* and *accommodation*'.[86] Justice-oriented theorists and actors today, especially those who have not suffered state displacement and occupation, would do well to hear his 'seemingly' and keep top of mind that the state's violence is alive and well.

Activism at Standing Rock was a response to the Dakota Access Pipeline (DAPL), which was originally planned to run ten miles north of Bismarck, North Dakota. Due to public pressure in Bismarck, an overwhelmingly white city, DAPL was re-routed to the north border of the Standing Rock Sioux reservation. This also meant that the DAPL would now run under the Missouri River. In its modified arrangement, DAPL transports crude oil from North Dakota's Bakken oil fields, running under the Missouri River as well as Lake Oahe, near the Standing Rock Sioux Reservation, and crossing four states on its way to Illinois, where in 2020 there are still billboards on the highway supporting DAPL. From near Patoka, Illinois, the oil travels in the Energy Transfer Crude Oil (ETCO) pipeline to refineries in Nederland, Texas, along the Gulf of Mexico, where it is prepared for export. The Missouri River is the Standing Rock Sioux tribe's primary source of water. For this reason, among others, DAPL was generally considered to threaten the human rights of the Standing Rock Sioux. In a September 2016 piece in *The Guardian*, Rebecca Solnit described the movement at Standing Rock as situated 'at the confluence of environmental and human rights'.[87] And Amnesty International summarised, adding a critique of state forces: 'The pipeline project is a violation of Indigenous people's human rights – and so is the excessive police response to protests against the project.'[88]

In 2016 Indigenous activists organised communities of resistance in response to DAPL, which could be read as a signifier for uprooting global capital backed by state power. As Nick Estes has pointed out, given that the word *Lakota* translates to *friend* or *ally*, 'one ceases to be Lakota if relatives or travelers from afar are not nurtured and welcomed . . . It was this Indigenous generosity – so often exploited as weakness – that held the camp together.'[89] How we understand 'community' at Standing Rock is important. Those who ended up working together at Standing Rock did not share a lineage, nor did they come from the same place. It was not, then, a filial or geographic community. Rather, it was a normative community – a community of shared practices and ecological responsiveness, where more-than-oppositional orientations of resistance (taking a stand against DAPL) created the community. Thus, prayer camps at Standing Rock offered a sense not of racial or national belonging, but of political belonging. Working together, for instance by cutting and distributing firewood to stay warm after direct actions, also created bonds. In this way, activist participation does not presuppose a ready-made community. It is more accurate to say, just as one shows up to a community-organising meeting or a march and thus creates the organisational unit, participation generates the community.

Another important normative feature of Standing Rock was the multiple rows of tents organised for 'two-spirit' individuals. The two-spirit rows challenged a simple gender bifurcation. For months kinship units across genders, generations and races allowed for some to participate in direct-action protests while others prepared camp, worked with journalists and legal support, and rested. Noticeably, several camps featured no billboards or televised advertisements – what Glissant would call neutralising flash agents of capitalism. This is not to say that camps at Standing Rock were outside of globalisation and its standardising models. But it underscores that Standing Rock featured sites of resistance that offer practical alternatives worth choosing as 'bearings', in Glissant's terms, for an ethics in the present.

For an example of how these bearings are lived out, we can consider how activists at Standing Rock inverted the US flag.

Common to Indigenous and Black Lives Matter protests in the US, this tactic is worth thinking about more extensively. In a standard US socialisation, the flag is given ultimate concern. Through direct political socialisation, students in US public schools pledge allegiance to the flag on a daily basis, hands on their hearts. Pledging is not only an affective practice, but is also an act of embodied piety – days are oriented through a beginning that heartfully worships this icon (indeed, this idol). It is in this context of patriotic religiosity, and on land where claims to sovereignty are contested, that the inversion of the flag takes on its heightened significance.

For some this example already wades too deeply into symbolic, not material, politics. But symbolism remains important because of the learning process it reflects. The inversion of the flag exemplifies what Ortega has called 'becoming-with', namely, 'the possibility that my relations with others with whom I fight oppression is an experience that stands to change both who I am and my understanding of the worlds I inhabit'.[90] Becoming-with is not becoming-other or being-for-the-other. Its stress is not on subsuming or serving difference, but on building with it. One is able, Glissant writes, 'to conceive of the opacity of the other for me, without reproach for my opacity for him. To feel in solidarity with him or to build with him or to like what he does', he continues, 'it is not necessary for me to grasp him. It is not necessary to try to become the other (to become other) nor to "make" him in my image' (PR 207/PO 193).

The critique of the nation state implicit in practices of becoming-with at Standing Rock makes a bid for political power in its affirmations of life. The 'NO' of the slogan 'NO DAPL' exemplifies an appreciation and affirmation of life, including the water that makes life possible – a key rallying point at Standing Rock was the claim 'Water is Life'. The communal formulation of 'NO DAPL' emerged from the solidarity of standing-with as many chose to 'stand with Standing Rock', as the saying went. The negation at play here – the 'NO' of 'NO DAPL' – is crucial to seeing how this claim enacts a right to opacity understood as a political activity and achievement. This 'NO' emphasises what Allar summarises as 'the right *not* to be understood'.[91] The right to opacity is the right not to be understood or recognised. It is not a right tied to an individual subject, nor is it a natural right that, in John Locke's sense, pre-exists any government. Instead, it is a right that is articulated in both opposition (NO DAPL) and affirmation (becoming-with and standing-with). It is a right achieved through shared political pursuits. To prevent the pipeline is to prevent one instantiation of a standardising, colonising force. To resist this 'standardized dilution' (TTM 192), in Glissant's terms, is to affirm cultural practices different from those globalisation imposes. Through participation and solidarity, opacity is demanded. The work of ethics at Standing Rock suggests a 'participatory manner' against 'old impositions' (PR 205/ PO 191). In great contrast to the norms suggested by credit card commercials and airport lounges, at Standing Rock the rules were simple: no alcohol, no drugs, no swearing, and dress simply – this is a prayer camp, so act accordingly. Start from prayer, respect, honesty and humility, and situate yourself in the ancestral and grounded wisdom of the people and the place. To understand further the practices that the right to opacity groups together as a retrospective analytic device, we can examine the rights claims that circulated at Standing Rock.

The urgent question for those invested in activism is not whether the events at Standing Rock constituted human rights violations, but how to respond to those violations. Responses at Standing Rock were not monolithic. Different members of the Standing Rock Sioux advocated for different models. All three approaches to human rights were present at Standing

Rock: legal strategies were used in efforts to reform the state (paradigmatic); anarchists and others engaged in direct actions against the state with no rights claims in sight (critical); and activists invoked rights claims as they reached out to other international struggles while linking those claims to distributions of free food and medical care that not only pointed to, but also embodied, alternative political forms (organisational). Further, sometimes not only separate organisations, but also individual groups and actors, adopted all three approaches. The work of the Lakota People's Law Project (LPLP) attorney Chase Iron Eyes, for instance, muddles any easy application of the theoretical approaches to practice. Iron Eyes was arrested for *trespassing* (on the ancestral land of his people!) and instigating a 'riot'. He continued to host tribal leadership, pray with water protectors, and provide legal services. Today his efforts with the LPLP serve to protect 'the First Amendment Rights of Native peoples and their allies'.[92]

Exemplifying the paradigmatic approach, on 27 July 2016 – the day after the US Army Corps of Engineers approved DAPL's path through the Missouri River – the Standing Rock Sioux filed a complaint in federal court. On 19 August 2016, to protect the pipeline, North Dakota Governor Jack Dalrymple declared a state of emergency and invoked the Emergency Management Assistance Compact (EMAC), normally summoned during natural disasters, allowing federal, state and local law enforcement agencies to share equipment and personnel. (This echoed Maryland Governor Larry Hogan's 2015 invocation of EMAC to repress Black-led activism against the police killing of Freddie Gray.) Also in August of 2016, the Standing Rock Sioux issued an official appeal to the United Nations (UN) that focused on the violations of the UN Declaration on the Rights of Indigenous Peoples (UNDRIP), noting that DAPL violates Article 32 of the UNDRIP, which requires states to obtain the consent of an Indigenous people before developing projects affecting their land.[93]

On 9 September, the US Army Corps of Engineers decided, under pressure from the Justice and Interior Departments, to postpone issuing permits to dig on federal land by the Missouri River north of the Standing Rock reservation. In a 22 September press release, presumably responding to both the appeal of the Standing Rock Sioux and the heightened international visibility of the human rights violations at Standing Rock, Victoria Tauli-Corpuz, the United Nations Special Rapporteur on the rights of Indigenous peoples, called on the US to halt the construction of DAPL. She also cited the UNDRIP, saying that the US should 'consult with the affected communities in good faith and ensure their free, and informed consent prior to the approval of any project affecting their lands'.[94] In line with the paradigmatic approach, where rights and the political participation they sanction are leveraged to bring the state in line with its own concept, Tauli-Corpuz stated: 'The US authorities should fully protect and facilitate the right to freedom of peaceful assembly of Indigenous peoples, which plays a key role in empowering their ability to claim other rights.'[95] Standing Rock Sioux chairman David Archambault II made a similar appeal in his 24 October letter to Attorney General Loretta Lynch, asking for the respect of treaty rights, appealing to the Justice Department to investigate violations of civil rights, noting the militarisation of law enforcement, and listing myriad state violations of guaranteed rights, including rights to speech, privacy and assembly.[96] All along as these rights claims were being invoked, water protectors mobilised in different ways.

On 4 December, the Obama administration effectively halted construction of the pipeline by rejecting a permit to drill underneath the Missouri River. (Exemplifying how the charity model sneaks its way into the paradigmatic approach, Solnit called this rejection a 'gift from the US Army Corps'.[97]) For the paradigmatic approach, this was a victory – a step

toward the human rights state. Then, in contrast to the perceived progress under the Obama administration, with a new
occupant of the White House, on 17 February 2017, the Army
Corps of Engineers terminated its environmental review
around DAPL. Newly installed North Dakota Governor Doug
Burgum set 22 February as the deadline for protestors to leave
camps on federal land. (With a view toward ending the police
blockades on Highway 1806, Archambault II had asked water
protectors to go home in December.) On 22 February, Morton
County Sherriff's deputies, North Dakota Highway Patrol officers and the Army Corps of Engineers joined together to evict
with dramatic force the water protectors who remained at
Oceti Sakowin camp. 'A Dine (Navajo) water protector asked
his elders back home what they should do about the traditional structures that they built in camp', the photographer
Larry Towell documented.[98] 'The elder said that because of
the previous behavior by law enforcement disposing of tipis
and ceremonial items in a disrespectful way in October, the
structures should be burned in a ceremony to protect them
from disrespect.'[99]

On 23 February, police with automatic weapons memorably
forced remaining water protectors onto the frozen Cannonball
River. On 10 March, the paradigmatic and critical approaches
came to a head when Archambault II gave a speech to the Native
Nations Rise march on Washington DC. For having previously
asked the water protectors to return to their homes, he was booed
during his speech and confronted by activists as he departed the
rally. On 24 March, the US State Department issued a presidential
permit approving the Keystone XL pipeline. Three years later, on
25 March, 2020, a US District Judge ordered a new environmental review of DAPL, demanding that the Army Corps of Engineers
examine further the environmental impact of the pipeline. This
order came in response to the Standing Rock Sioux's 2016
lawsuit to stop construction of the pipeline. It did not guarantee

that the construction of the pipeline would stop. Judge Boasberg ordered the tribe and the US government to submit briefings arguing that the pipeline either should or should not continue operating while the Army Corps conducted its environmental review.[100] Then, on 5 August 2020, the US Court of Appeals for the District of Columbia reversed the lower court's decision, in effect allowing oil to keep flowing. On 20 January 2021, the Biden administration revoked the Keystone XL permit, but in May, when a federal district court did not rule for stopping the flow of DAPL oil during the Army Corps of Engineer's environmental review, the Biden administration did not take action to stop the oil during the review. For the institutional aims of the paradigmatic approach, these actions, sanctioned by the state at every level, suggest a series of successes and failures. The organisational approach allows a different understanding.

In addition to, in some cases, making appeals to state and inter-state institutions, activism under the banner of human rights at Standing Rock served to build capacity among different communities within and beyond Standing Rock. The confluence of activists is crucial. As Magnum Photos notes in its distribution of Towell's photos at Standing Rock: '[E]nvironmental and human rights activists from both North and South America . . . had joined the protest to offer their solidarity.'[101] That is, human rights work at Standing Rock extended well beyond the site of contestation. Human Rights Watch's Acting Emergency Director Priyanka Motaparthy noted in a 2017 piece that '[t]he fight to protect indigenous rights – and all peoples' right to peaceful protest – doesn't end in North Dakota'.[102] In this way, I read Glissant's right to opacity as resonating with the Chilean singer Victor Jara's call to realise a universal 'right to live in peace' (*el derecho de vivir en paz*).

It is important here that I go further than citing the claims of NGOs. NGOs utilise the paradigmatic approach more than the organisational or critical approach. As Whyte reminds, 'Major human rights organizations like Amnesty International and Human Rights Watch have been deeply reluctant to factor questions of distribution and resources into their advocacy . . . and consequently, the deep structures that perpetuate such inequalities have been left untouched.'[103] What the politics at Standing Rock promises is a way of challenging questions of distribution, resources, and inequality – that is, questions of political economy and coloniality. Activists at Standing Rock directly called into question the actions of the pipeline companies, the banks that fund them and the state whose practices of dispossession create and maintain the conditions for extractive capitalism to flourish.

In a 2 November 2016 op-ed in *The Guardian*, Ladonna Bravebull Allard, a member of the Dakota Sioux, invoked rights in her appeal: '[W]e are fighting [for] our children's rights to clean drinking water.'[104] To some, this is heard as a call for the state to enable clean water, like the water that flows into suburban houses around Bismarck. But I think this line is better heard in a negative sense, naming the state as the violator – historically, at the time of her writing, and presently – of the human rights related to the waters and land of the Standing Rock Sioux. Understood this way, there is an element of self-determination in the call, reclaiming the sovereignty of the Sioux given the 1851 and 1868 Fort Laramie Treaties.

In a line that challenges paradigmatic suggestions to act through the 'persuasion' of the state, Allard writes, 'Our resistance has not been met with handshakes.' 'The national guard and state police', Allard continues, 'have been reinforced by forces from seven other states, to push corporate interest through our home.' After this condemnation of state forces working in conjunction with private capital, she appeals to organisation: 'We have always welcomed everyone to come stand with us against the injustices of the federal government.

Joining forces would be a source of great power.' If del Toro's case study of litigation exemplifies a rights maximalism in the vocabulary of the organisational approach, tending toward the paradigmatic approach, Allard's rights minimalism in her own claims tends toward the critical approach. As I read Allard's claims, they include the language of rights in a broader effort to bring activists together and build power. In this way, the organisational approach can be understood as a modification of the critical approach.

* * *

In sum, Standing Rock demonstrates that human rights claims, without a taken-for-granted orientation to the state, can become a shared language for protecting, imagining and realising alternative political communities, alternative self-authorised forms of social organisation. By citing human rights violations, activists call into question the legitimacy of the nation state that attempts to repress them. By highlighting how their efforts attend to human rights around food, healthcare and culture, activists affirm the legitimacy, as a political form, of the alternative community they are building. Thinking this way means allowing the content of human rights to be defined by the movement or community that invokes them. To allow for self-definition leads to clashes of values around human rights – both Palestinian and Israeli nationalists have invoked human rights to defend their projects.[105] To be clear, I see promise in the organisational approach to human rights discourse in the spirit of the Palestinian claims, which I understand under the decolonial rubric of what Walter Mignolo has called 'delinking', meaning separating themselves from the modern/colonial state as a legitimate form of political organisation.[106]

If human rights are to avoid a charity model, a model of endowment, then a strong first step is to avoid the paradigmatic presupposition of the state as the addressee of rights claims. More than an appeal for reform (the paradigmatic approach) or a tool for strategic litigation (the Left legalism side of the critical approach), a rights claim can be thought of as a rallying cry, a way of organising. Thus, human rights claims begin conversations that connect struggles and inform practices internationally. Claims documenting state-perpetrated human rights violations at Standing Rock were addressed to, and circulated among, activists in Puerto Rico, Ferguson and Palestine (and vice versa). They crossed territories and called into question states' claims to sovereignty and legitimacy. They were starting points to share strategies of survival, resistance and imagination. As gateways, organisational human rights claims are part of blueprints for alternative futures, which will always be made in particular and historical sites of contestation.

Here interlocutors would ask me to expand on the content of the organisational approach, on what human rights as a 'gateway' to politics leads to in concrete forms. But to say something general would be to betray my emphasis, which is that rights claims and their promises travel powerfully along lines drawn by actors participating in specific struggles, not theorists abstracting away from those struggles in an attempt to make claims with general applicability. Community and context condition content, or at least they should if the pseudo-universal and paternalistic lineages of human rights are to be avoided. The answers will always depend on the struggle that raises the questions in the first place.

Additional theoretical work remains to be done in order to speak to questions I have been unable to answer here, questions that are never abstract or universal, but rather that are always tied to particular conjunctures: not whether human rights discourse can be appropriated for liberatory ends, but in what cases human rights contribute to the larger work of delinking, how that functions specifically, and what paths these claims and practices open and foreclose for ethical actors in their own distinct, but often connectable, situations today. I return to these questions in the final chapter. Before doing so, I need to address a limitation of coalitional participation in rights-based movements.

Coalitions founded on what María Lugones calls an oppositional 'coincidence of interests' can be 'epistemically shallow'.[107] Deeper coalitions take as central not a target for critique but 'an openness to the interlocutors as real'.[108] That is, opposition and participation have their own pitfalls. Too often oppositional efforts lack a deeper sense of belonging. Too often participation is a one-time action: actors briefly joining the struggle at Standing Rock might attend a few protests but neglect their other secondary duties pursuant to the right to opacity. To paraphrase Walter Mignolo, resistance needs to be followed by re-existence.[109] A more sustained commitment, what Glissant would call a relational (as opposed to unvoiced) solidarity, is required for decolonial responsibility (DA 431/CD 142). The next chapter follows Glissant to offer a way to cultivate extended solidarity in terms of what I will call 'expansive belonging'.

Notes

1. Jack Donnelly, *Universal Human Rights in Theory and Practice* (Ithaca: Cornell University Press, 2013), p. 33.
2. Ibid. p. 34.
3. Ibid.
4. Ibid. pp. 257ff., 289ff.
5. Griffin, *On Human Rights*, p. 51.
6. Ibid. p. 202.
7. A. Dirk Moses, 'Empire, Resistance, and Security: International Law and the Transformative Occupation of Palestine', *Humanity: An International Journal of Human Rights, Humanitarianism, and Development* 8, no. 2 (2017): p. 382. Other scholarship avoids

the critical-reformist tension entirely by critiquing the state as a duty-bearer without prescribing reforms in turn. Mark Bray, for instance, has recently argued that anarchists 'were actually among the first to articulate a vision of human rights beyond the state', going as far as 'to develop a vision of human rights against the state' (Mark Bray, 'Beyond and Against the State: Anarchist Contributions to Human Rights History and Theory', *Humanity: An International Journal of Human Rights, Humanitarianism, and Development* 3, no. 3 (2019): p. 323).

8. For previous discussions of this tension, see for example Jean Drèze, 'Democracy and the Right to Food', in *Human Rights and Development*, ed. Philip Alston and Mary Robinson (Oxford: Oxford University Press, 2005), pp. 45–64.

9. My typology is partially inspired by Stephen Hopgood's illuminating distinction between (liberal, bureaucratic) Human Rights and (radical, grassroots) human rights. Hopgood's purpose is to present a decline in the import of human rights in order to argue for more localised, less professionalised practices (Stephen Hopgood, *The Endtimes of Human Rights* (Ithaca: Cornell University Press, 2013), pp. viii–ix).

10. Theodor Adorno, *Aspekte des neuen Rechtsradikalismus* (Berlin: Suhrkamp, 1967/2019), p. 41.

11. My metaphor of the path here might strike some as bourgeois, and such a comment would not be wrong given that I spent the time it took to conduct research for this chapter associated with prestigious universities, where many elites choose their level of engagement defending rights. I make this note to stress that, for many, utilising rights claims is not a choice but a necessity in negotiating colonial binds. That these individuals and collectives employ rights often reflects the repression they face more than their political imagination.

12. Jayan Nayar, 'The Non-Perplexity of Human Rights', *Theory & Event* 22, no. 2 (2019): p. 269.

13. Ayça Çubukçu, 'Thinking against humanity', *London Review of International Law* 5, no. 2 (2017): p. 258.

14. Ibid. pp. 258–9.

15. 'The numbers of people worldwide subject to the violence of their own states are staggering. More than a quarter of a million Kurds and Turks in Turkey have been beaten or tortured by the military, police, and prison guards since 1980; tens of thousands of indigenous peoples in Peru and Guatemala, street children in Brazil and Guatemala, Palestinians in Kuwait, Kurds in Iraq, and Muslim women and girls in Bosnia have been similarly treated. Mutilated bodies turn up somewhere every day' (Carole Nagengast, 'Violence, Terror, and the Crisis of the State', *Annual Review of Anthropology* 23 (1994): pp. 119–20).

16. Nayar, 'The Non-Perplexity', p. 269.

17. Kathryn Sikkink, *Evidence for Hope: Making Human Rights Work in the 21st Century* (Princeton: Princeton University Press, 2017), pp. 142, 179.

18. Ibid. p. 6.

19. Ibid. p. 142.

20. Ibid. p. 11.

21. Ibid. p. 142.

22. Ibid. p. 19; see p. 225ff.

23. Lindsey Kingston, *Fully Human: Personhood, Citizenship, and Rights* (Oxford: Oxford University Press, 2019), p. 32.

24. Ibid. p. 78.

25. Ibid. p. 240.

26. Ibid.

27. Ibid.

28. Ibid. pp. 231–2.

29. See Michele Alexander, *The New Jim Crow: Mass Incarceration in the Age of Colorblindness* (New York: The New Press, 2012).

30. Joy James, 'The Dead Zone: Stumbling at the Crossroads of Party Politics, Genocide, and Postracial Racism', *South Atlantic Quarterly* 108, no. 3 (2009): p. 474.

31. Fabian Klose, *Human Rights in the Shadow of Colonial Violence*, trans. Dona Geyer (Philadelphia: University of Pennsylvania Press, 2013), pp. 53–4.

32. Ibid. p. 56.

33. Ibid. p. 123.

34. Ibid.
35. See Saidiya Hartman, 'Wayward Lives, Beautiful Experiments, ft. Saidiya Hartman', <https://rustbeltradio.org/2019/04/24/ep28/>; John Crabtree and Francisco Durand, *Peru: Elite Power and Political Capture* (Chicago: Zed Books, 2017); Robert Nichols, *Theft is Property!: Dispossession and Critical Theory* (Durham, NC: Duke University Press, 2020). For a robust debate more specifically within the legal academy about the possibilities and limitations of rights discourse, see the work of, for example, Patricia Williams, Peter Gabel, Duncan Kennedy, Martha Minow, Richard Delgado, Mark Tushnet, Roberto Unger, Catherine MacKinnon and Kimberlé Crenshaw. I would like to thank Michael Sullivan for introducing me to these debates.
36. Joy James, 'Incarceration (Un)Interrupted: Reclaiming Bodies, Lands, and Communities', talk given at Macalester College, 10 October 2019; Nick Estes, *Our History is the Future: Standing Rock Versus the Dakota Access Pipeline, and the Long Tradition of Indigenous Resistance* (New York: Verso, 2019).
37. See Benjamin P. Davis, 'The Right to Have Rights in the Americas: Arendt, Monture, and the Problem of the State', *Arendt Studies* 6 (2022): pp. 43–57.
38. Glen Coulthard, *Red Skin, White Masks* (Minneapolis: University of Minnesota Press, 2014), p. 23.
39. Steven Ratner, 'International law and political philosophy: Uncovering new linkages', *Philosophy Compass* (2018): p. 4.
40. Ibid. p. 9.
41. Ibid. p. 3.
42. Robert Knox, 'Marxism, International Law, and Political Strategy', *Leiden Journal of International Law* 22 (2009): pp. 433, 434.
43. Benjamin Gregg, *The Human Rights State: Justice within and beyond Sovereign Nations* (Philadelphia: University of Pennsylvania Press, 2016), p. 24.
44. Ibid. p. 27.
45. Ibid. pp. 26, 45.
46. Ibid. p. 26.
47. Ibid. p. 33.

48. Ibid.

49. See Jessica Whyte, *The Morals of the Market*, p. 29; see also pp. 198–206.

50. Cf. Gregg, *The Human Rights State*, p. 36.

51. Ibid. p. 24.

52. Ibid. pp. 27, 24.

53. Ibid.

54. Ibid. p. 34.

55. See ibid. pp. 42, 52.

56. Ibid. p. 41.

57. Ibid. p. 42ff.

58. Ibid. p. 48.

59. Ibid.

60. Ibid.

61. Ibid. pp. 45, 55–6.

62. Wendy Brown and Janet Halley, 'Introduction', in *Left Legalism/ Left Critique*, ed. Wendy Brown and Janey Halley (Durham, NC: Duke University Press, 2002), p. 27.

63. Ibid. p. 5.

64. Ibid. p. 14. See Whyte, *The Morals of the Market*, p. 32.

65. Wendy Brown, '"The Most We Can Hope For . . .": Human Rights and The Politics of Fatalism', *The South Atlantic Quarterly* 103, no. 2 (2004): pp. 461–2.

66. Bernard Harcourt, *Critique & Praxis: A Critical Philosophy of Illusions, Values, and Action* (New York: Columbia University Press, 2020), p. 244.

67. Brown and Halley, 'Introduction', p. 25.

68. Harcourt, *Critique & Praxis*, p. 1; see also Chapter 1.

69. I borrow this phrase from Ayten Gündogdu, 'On the ambivalent politics of human rights', *Journal of International Political Theory* 14, no. 3 (2018): pp. 367–80.

70. Nelson Maldonado-Torres, 'On the Coloniality of Human Rights', p. 130.

71. Ibid. p. 129. Cf. Nelson Maldonado-Torres, *Against War: Views from the Underside of Modernity* (Durham, NC: Duke University Press, 2008).

72. I have presented a different decolonial vision of human rights in Benjamin P. Davis, 'What Could Human Rights Do? A Decolonial Inquiry', pp. 1–22.

73. Coulthard, *Red Skin, White Masks*, p. 179.

74. Valeria M. Pelet del Toro, 'Beyond the Critique of Rights: The Puerto Rico Legal Project and Civil Rights Litigation in America's Colony', *The Yale Law Journal* 128, no. 3 (2019): p. 800.

75. Ibid. p. 821.

76. Ibid. p. 829.

77. Ibid. pp. 831–2.

78. Ibid.

79. Ibid. p. 832.

80. Ibid. p. 833.

81. Ibid. p. 834.

82. For a theorisation of each of these communities as a 'reverso' of hegemonic models, see Eduardo Mendieta, 'Editor's Introduction', in *The Underside of Modernity: Apel, Ricoeur, Rorty, Taylor, and the Philosophy of Liberation*, ed. Eduardo Mendieta (Atlantic Highlands, NJ: Humanity Books International, 1996), p. xxii.

83. Mariana Ortega, 'Decolonial Woes and Practices of Unknowing', *The Journal of Speculative Philosophy* 31, no. 3 (2017): pp. 504–16.

84. See Patrick William Kelly, *Sovereign Emergencies: Latin America and The Making of Global Human Rights Politics* (Cambridge: Cambridge University Press, 2018).

85. Ibid. p. 6. For the formulation of 'in the wake', see also, of course, Christina Sharpe, *In the Wake: On Blackness and Being* (Durham, NC: Duke University Press, 2016).

86. Coulthard, *Red Skin, White Masks*, p. 6.

87. Rebecca Solnit, 'Standing Rock protests: this is only the beginning', *The Guardian*, 12 September 2016, <https://www.theguardian.com/us-news/2016/sep/12/north-dakota-standing-rock-protests-civil-rights>.

88. Amnesty International, 'Standing Rock', <https://www.amnestyusa.org/standing-rock/>.

89. Estes, *Our History is the Future*, p. 59.

90. Ortega, *In-Between*, p. 146. She later connects this concept to coalitional politics: 'Ultimately, coalitional politics can lead to *becoming-with* that involves not just understanding others but being transformed by them and with them' (ibid. p. 155). 'Becoming with amounts to becoming open to the interests of groups with whom I may not share identity markers; it means understanding these interests as being as important as my own interests' (ibid. p. 168). 'Despite our differences', she continues, 'we can struggle against oppression, not necessarily because I identify with your values or your identity markers but because our standpoints intersect in ways that lead us to recognize how we stand within relations of power and how working together with a good sense of our differences (of understanding the zones where contact is uncomfortable, challenging, and even hurtful) might provide avenues to undermine oppression' (ibid.).

91. Allar, 'The Case for Incomprehension', p. 42.

92. See 'About: LPLP History', <https://www.lakotalaw.org/about-us>.

93. See 'Dakota Access Pipeline: Standing Rock Sioux Issue Urgent Appeal to United Nations Human Rights Officials', *Indian Country Today*, <http://indiancountrytodaymedianetwork.com/2016/08/20/dakota-access-pipeline-standing-rock-sioux-issue-urgent-appeal-united-nations-human> (last accessed 17 March 2020).

94. See 'UN human rights expert calls on US to halt construction of North Dakota oil pipeline', <https://news.un.org/en/story/2016/09/541342-un-human-rights-expert-calls-us-halt-construction-north-dakota-oil-pipeline>.

95. Ibid.

96. At the same time, Archambault wrote a compelling op-ed in *The New York Times* that included historical context: 'When the Army Corps of Engineers dammed the Missouri River in 1958, it took our riverfront forests, fruit orchards and most fertile farm-land to create Lake Oahe . . . the tribes always pay the price for America's prosperity' (David Archambault II, 'Taking a Stand at Standing Rock', *The New York Times*, 24 August 2016, <https://www.nytimes.com/2016/08/25/opinion/taking-a-stand-at-standing-rock.html>.

97. Rebecca Solnit, 'The light from Standing Rock: beautiful struggle shows the power of protest', <https://www.theguardian.com/us-news/2016/dec/06/standing-rock-protest-success-demonstrations>.

98. See Larry Towell, 'The End of the Beginning: Closing Standing Rock', <https://www.magnumphotos.com/newsroom/environment/larry-towell-closing-of-standing-rock/>.

99. Ibid.

100. See Lisa Friedman, 'Standing Rock Sioux Tribe Wins a Victory in Dakota Access Pipeline Case', *The New York Times*, <https://www.nytimes.com/2020/03/25/climate/dakota-access-pipeline-sioux.html>.

101. See 'Magnum Distribution: Standing Rock', <https://shop.magnumphotos.com/products/magnum-distribution-standing-rock-larry-towell?variant=3238222266392>.

102. See 'Standing Rock's Last Stand: Fight to Protect Indigenous People's Rights in the US Continues', <https://www.hrw.org/news/2017/03/09/standing-rocks-next-stand#>.

103. Jessica Whyte, 'Human Rights and the Collateral Damage of Neoliberalism', *Theory & Event* 20, no. 1 (2017): p. 146.

104. Ladonna Bravebull Allard, 'Why do we punish Dakota pipeline protesters but exonerate the Bundys?', <https://www.theguardian.com/commentisfree/2016/nov/02/dakota-pipeline-protest-bundy-militia>.

105. See Perugini and Gordon, *The Human Right to Dominate*.

106. Walter D. Mignolo, 'Delinking: The rhetoric of modernity, the logic of coloniality and the grammar of de-coloniality', *Cultural Studies* 21, nos. 2–3 (2007): pp. 449–514.

107. María Lugones, 'On Complex Communication', *Hypatia* 21, no. 3 (2006): p. 76.

108. Ibid.

109. Walter D. Mignolo, 'On Decoloniality with Walter Mignolo', lecture given 10 February 2021. Transcript available at <https://thenewpolis.com/2021/02/10/critical-conversations-6/>.

3 Solidarity beyond Participation

Institutions and Imaginaries

In this chapter, in order to build on the political participation I described in Chapters 1 and 2, I consider the deeper demands of solidarity. Participation in coalitional action is necessary but not sufficient for a robust ethics that learns from decolonial movements. My inquiry here is partially inspired by Hannah Arendt's theorisation of 'the fleeting moment of action' that characterises a 'space of appearance', which 'does not survive the actuality of the movement which brought it into being'.[1] What is at stake in this inquiry is how an ethical turn could gain a sustained political edge. For this to happen, actors need to maintain political action beyond its initial appearance – not participating in a single march but making political responsibility a larger part of their lives, well beyond the start of the movement. Put differently, participation needs to be more than what Ortega has called 'political excursions', meaning 'a type of politically correct tourism – fleeting moments of experimenting with being political while not really being committed to effecting change'.[2] If we are to think of responsibility in terms of our most central commitments, then we must address the shift from coalitions to communities, from contacts to relations, in Glissant's terms. The oppositional action of demanding a right to opacity is important, but it says little about the 'meanwhile' present between connected instances of direct action. '[P]olitical resistance often begins in a meanwhile', novelist and artist John Berger writes.[3] Griffin's concept of 'secondary duties' speaks to this meanwhile, as does Lugones's concept of 'complex communication'. Lugones's starting point – not opposition but communication – introduces a sense of 'relational identity' that I will expand on in this chapter. It is in living out a relational identity that one moves from participation to solidarity.

In regard to the question of relational identity, we can immediately raise four concerns. The first is that a focus on the level of the individual and their identity presupposes a neoliberal subject of unlimited growth and change.[4] Yet even when we are discussing how global forces and movements affect cultures, actual interactions always occur on the level of individuals. As the anthropologist Richard Price puts it in an essay on creolisation in the Caribbean, 'Human beings meet and engage one another; cultures do not. Individuals who claim multiple identities interact with one another; ethnicities do not.'[5] I will maintain individuals and their identifications as my point of reference in this chapter, while all along attempting to account for the pressures and decisions, reception and activity – the heteronomy and the autonomy – that are part of the formation of individuals.

The second concern: any set of relations – however formed, intended or unexpected – risks an intolerant elevation of the identity of the collectivity. This is the problem of the totalising identity or root, such as when a nation state defines its members in ethnocentric terms. Glissant's concept of 'errancy' (*errance*) offers a way to respond to this concern. Errancy is a way to think about practices that divert or diffract attempts at identity-based totalisation. The 'err-' of *errance* suggests a move away from a fixed attachment to home, a detour away from the root identity of one group. Errancy guides a bearing practised by those in a non-totalitarian community, a community dynamically open and responsive to the interruptions and offerings of others. Glissant presents errancy not only as deviating from the progressive logic of the project of the West, but also, more concretely, as deviating from an identification with one's nation – 'this thinking of errancy, this errant thought, silently emerges from the destructuring of compact national entities that yesterday were still triumphant' and 'from difficult, uncertain births of new forms of identity that call to us' (PR 30/PO 18, translation modified).

A third concern is about how to practise relational identity. The habits that are part and parcel of identities, the philosopher Linda Martín Alcoff has argued, prove 'resistant to alteration or erasure'.[6] Why, then, take identity as a starting point for solidarities? With Alcoff, I want to avoid 'absolute determinism and thus pessimism' by noting that even when practices of perception are 'congealed into habit', there is still dynamism 'in various cultural productions and by the challenge of contradictory perceptions'.[7] 'To put it simply', she continues, 'people are capable of change.'[8] What is needed in turn is 'a more active and a more practical intervention'.[9] I will argue below that errant practices, in both their contestations and invitations, are such interventions.

A fourth and final concern notes a seeming contradiction: How could a group attain a sense of solidarity from an emphasis on errancy? How could a stress on nomadism lead to a feeling of home?[10] In the history of Western philosophy, the guiding metaphor for belonging has been the circle. Concentric circles symbolise ever-reaching spheres of obligations. Taken at face value, the concept of 'expansive belonging' I will advance here could suggest a similar idea of staring from one's already-held sense of responsibility and adding people to whom one feels obligated. But Glissant's concept of the expanse offers a different understanding (PR 59–75/ PO 47–62). Miguel Gualdrón Ramírez has argued that 'a Glissantian possibility of expanse' starts from 'the expansive characteristic of the Caribbean and its capacity to voice a cry, an echo, or a murmur'.[11] Gualdrón Ramírez's reading of Glissant allows us to hear in Glissant's concept an ethical valence, a call to give an account of oneself to this cry, echo or murmur. Read this way, expansive belonging begins from a self-critique, not an immediate spreading outward. The word itself gives this away: ex-, meaning 'out' or 'former', comes before what English has taken from the Old French *espandre*, which suggests to diffuse and scatter.[12] For implicated subjects, moving out of one's born-into norms needs to come before any self-satisfied expansion. Thought this way, expanse weaves itself in '[l]eap and variance' [*L'étendue se trame. Bond et variance, dans une autre poétique*], as Glissant puts it, marking 'another poetics . . . considerate of all the threatened and delicious things joining one another (without conjoining, that is, without merging) in the expanse of Relation' (PR 71, 74/ PO 58, 62). To expand is to move out of old habits before unfolding into, or becoming, the more responsible people we aim to be in relation to others. Such a relation requires a way of joining without merging, of standing-with and hearing others on their own terms – always a surprising, complicated, baroque endeavour (PR 91/PO 77).

Avoiding the metaphor of the circle starts ethical actors on a path to a non-linear way of thinking about responsibility. As implicated subjects, we are responsible for aspects of coloniality, including US slavery, not because of a linear, causal account (that is, if and only if my ancestors enslaved people), but to the extent that we continue to benefit from state-sanctioned practices of domination and racialised labour that are themselves still shifting. Just as these 'benefits' of domination are not linearly drawn, a sense of responsibility in the face of them must be at least as dynamic. For instance, many of us start by advocating for reparations and other modes of corrective justice through public policy. When state mechanisms kick in to prevent those reforms from occurring, we need to think more imaginatively about new angles to approach our responsibilities. Hence the need for errant concepts in the face of re-installed colonial models – 'what has been called neoco-lonialism has prospered almost everywhere', Glissant reflects poignantly in his late work (PhR 125). In the face of this 'pros-perity', expanded responsibility is a collective response.

It is worth repeating here my concern about audience underscored in the Introduction of this study: my normative endorsement of errancy and relational identity offers a way of life to established, settled citizens. I am not making a universal appeal, nor would I ask that (already) uprooted migrants, or other victims of centuries of colonial violence and state-based terrorism, deny further their cultural practices by adopting a sense of belonging different from what they understand as their own. For those on the dominant side of the colonial difference, however, the question of changing or diffracting practices of identification remains salient, even ethically neces-sary. But it is not easily done. Calling for Indigenous sovereignty in so-called Canada, Patricia Monture argues that '[s]elf-government requires the significant letting go of Canadian government power over the lives of Aboriginal citizens'.[13] She goes on: 'I do not doubt that the release of power is a difficult thing.'[14] One task for implicated subjects today remains the need to dwell with the idea of this 'release of power'. And, of course, to realise it.

But self-critique can become hyperbolic and ironic. Calls to 'become nomad', 'become refugee' or 'become indigenous' miss the physical displacement, political persecution and state enforcement that shape those conditions.[15] As Glissant taught us regarding solidarity and opacity, it is not necessary to become 'other' in order to stand in solidarity with others (PR 207/PO 193). Further, theories of ethics do well to take feelings of belonging seriously. Senses of belonging serve a need for orientation and purpose. This is a second reason to avoid the above 'become x' language. Such language risks overlooking what we may tentatively call a human 'need' for belonging, following what the mystic and philosopher Simone Weil calls a 'need for roots'.

The trajectory of this chapter is as follows: I begin from operative attachments to the state and other collectivities that place excessive emphasis on ready-made identities, such as one's ethnicity or nation. I start by looking to Weil's concept of 'roots' because it provides the strongest case for root identity and therefore one to consider carefully before dismissing it. It is also worth reading Weil because, like so many of us, she problematises the state but struggles to think beyond it. Her return to the state as a root-giving entity, prefiguring the recent reformist scholarship I discussed in the previous chapter, exemplifies a foreclosure of political creativity. I will then read what Glissant calls 'relational identity' as addressing the limitations of root identity. The root/relation distinction is helpful in that it provides a point of reference when thinking about practices and pursuits. Whereas root identity is based on origin, filiation and territory, relational identity is based on contacts, circulation and giving-with as opposed to claiming land (PR 157–8/PO 143–4).[16] With these distinguishing factors in mind, we can interrogate the presuppositions of political endeavours, from actual policies to imagined utopias: Does this imply an original claim to territory? Does the sense of identity at play here privilege a blood line, heritage or other filial lineage? Is this approach to land one of claiming or of yielding?

The above questions of identity are not only questions about the self-definition of a collectivity, but also questions about race and land. Glissant writes, 'In the Western tradition, filiation guarantees racial exclusivity, just as Genesis legitimises genealogy [*la filiation*]' (DA 428–9/CD 140, translation modified).

'Filiation and legitimacy have woven the canvas of duration', he continues in later writing (TTM 81). 'They guaranteed that no discontinuity would break certainty or corrupt belief. They established law on the territory' (TTM 81). Questions of identity and filiation, then, are not merely superficial inquires in service of an exclusive identity politics. They can refocus the attention of decolonial pursuits to country and territory – repatriation as part of redistribution. If decolonisation is not to be a metaphor, implicated subjects would do well to reconsider our identifications with 'roots', that is, with how we understand our heritage, tradition, and land we think of as our own.[17]

Today we witness within the United States a deeply held sense of root identity that delimits belonging not to original inhabitants but to lines of white settlers – a sense of 'America' as 'great'. This root identity informs logics of criminalisation that target racialised subjects in ways both juridically sanctioned and extra-legal. Root identity also marks as a problem people from other countries and culminates in a manic desire to build walls. Further, it is foundational for the current global rise of excessively nationalistic, ethnocentric and xenophobic political parties. Those who want to resist such developments are inquiring into forms of community and belonging that do not presuppose the nation state. This chapter aims to describe the types of root identity and their formations that subtend given political units, such as the nation state. It concludes by thinking with Glissant's errancy to suggest ways for communities to avoid the pitfalls of root identity and its specific manifestation as *excessive* nationalism.

As opposed to making a blanket condemnation of nationalism, I use here the modifier 'excessive' in regard to nationalism so as to leave outside of my critique nations that might be strategically demarcating a decolonial collectivity that resists oppressive forces. We can hear these strategic resonances when Derek

Walcott claims 'either I'm nobody, or I'm a nation' and when Mahmoud Darwish writes, '[W]henever I searched for myself I found others . . . There is no nation smaller than its poem.'[18] My terminological specification recognises not only my protected status as a citizen of the US as I theorise these concepts, but also the fact that my theoretical intervention comments on particular political contexts in which strategic nationalisms often compete with state-based, excessive nationalisms. For instance, in the waving of the Palestinian flag to commemorate the *Nakba* or in the marching of the Xukuru as a *povo* in the face of the Brazilian state, the collective unit of a 'nation' or 'people' is employed to challenge predominant state logics, even if, to continue the example, Darwish's poetry has inspired ways of thinking about belonging much more nuanced than a basic nationalism and even if the Xukuru think of their relation to their ancestral lands in ways more dynamic than the European sense of 'people' tied to territory suggests. I am not advising these nations. I am writing to those whose citizenship and class status is close to my own. 'One can reject the nation', Glissant writes, 'if one already has one' (DA 715/CD 218).[19] Yet the poet Dionne Brand adds: 'The right to nation. What we have to ask ourselves is, as everyone else in the nation should ask themselves also, nation predicated on what?'[20]

A final introductory note requires making explicit a distinction that is present in both the previous chapters and the present chapter. The hegemony of the state operates, David Lloyd and Paul Thomas explain, such that 'by definition and for all practical purposes' subjects 'accept the forms and precepts of the state at least to the extent that alternatives become literally and figuratively the state's unthinkable'.[21] If the conditions of globalisation/coloniality involve hegemony over both institutions and imaginaries, then a decolonial response to hegemonic colonial institutions and imaginaries involves challenges on both levels: rights claims brought together

Puerto Ricans in the wake of socially induced and exacerbated 'natural' disasters, Pablo Neruda's *Canto General* inspired anti-fascist protests, Darwish's 'ID Card' became a protest song, and Claudia Rankine's *Citizen* stirs protests today. Indeed, it might be argued that it is precisely the institutional changes gained by reclaiming the right to opacity – by defending third-generation rights through primary duties – that preserves the necessary conditions for the survival and cultivation of alternative imaginaries.

And yet, often a kind of existential (or strategic) choice is required. Chapter 2 investigated how activists can mobilise coalitions under the broad banner of human rights, but this struggle over institutions to some extent maintains the colonial imaginary. That is, the language of rights claims can imply the legitimacy of the institutional sites where such claims play out (courtrooms, bureaucratic offices, other state-based settings). '[C]ertain forms of rights', as Audra Simpson puts it, 'carry with them the residue of state imposition.'[22] Alternatively, poets and artists can mobilise coalitions through inventive verse and per-formance pieces, among other media, and this relayed mobili-sation can invite an alternative imaginary. Such imaginative efforts, however, often do little to challenge today's operative institutions.

One's emphasis on institutions or imaginaries is in part a question of conduct and of legibility: rights claims are legible to existing liberal governments and supra-national bodies, while performative assemblies or poetic associations, often lacking specific demands, make little sense to those immersed in official discourse. The latter forms of resistance, as Saidiya Hartman notes, no longer ask for recognition from 'predatory state forms' but instead turn attention to alternative forms of address so as 'to imagine an elsewhere . . . and mobilize other political imaginaries'.[23] In sum, in terms of daily pursuits or basic practical considerations, as we consider what it means to live in solidarity in a context of coloniality today, we face real choices about our divestments and attachments. We will, at different times and in the face of different issues, fall more on the side of institutions or imaginaries. Some go to law school or become professors. Others paint.

In our selective emphasis, we do well to keep in mind Glissant's reminder about living out 'a total logic of our comportment' (PR 166/PO 152). To repeat Glissant's line: 'You must choose your bearing' (PR 166/PO 152). He writes these words explicitly against an easy claim to both/and thinking. If we stay with Gilssant's errancy, then to err is to err on the side of the imaginary, lest we be too quick to adopt, and therefore to perpetuate, predominant colonial forms of living. Glissant teaches that 'the strategy of the system consists in placing the elite into a position where it must maintain dialogue with it in the name of the people' (DA 698/CD 206, translation modified). I make the institution/imaginary distinction explicit here because it guides some of the existing and existential tensions of actors who are sensitive to the questions I am raising.

Roots: Identity and Belonging

We can consider some questions of responsibility as questions of identification – what one takes oneself to be responsible for overlaps with what one identifies with: a coalition, a community or a country. A shorthand for these questions is found in the colloquial language of 'roots', such as when someone says they want to 'set down roots' in a given place, meaning that they desire to connect with others, make friends, join a recreational sports league, find a safe and welcoming place to worship, or otherwise participate in meaningful collective life. 'Rootedness', Christy Wampole writes in her recent study of the metaphor, 'is a primary organizing trope that accommodates the need to feel connected to something outside the self'.[24]

'Across cultures and through time', Wampole continues, 'the root surfaces again and again as a figure for filiation, cultural connectedness, regional or national allegiance, and symbiosis with the environment.'[25] By looking backward an individual learns more about herself. 'Our roots are where we sometimes look for explanations about our patterns of thinking and acting. We see them, perhaps erroneously, as sites for self-understanding.'[26] Reminding us of where we come from and pushing us to engage with others in the world, roots can function as both 'anchor' and 'vehicle'.[27] With this social, spiritual, psychological and communal importance in mind, in the early 1940s Simone Weil wrote that rootedness is a need of the soul. Weil also recognised that contemporary forces of abstraction, such as taking money and one's country as one's primary sources of meaning, militate against the setting of roots, such that the need for roots is difficult to acknowledge. 'To be rooted', Weil claims, 'is perhaps the most important and least recognized need of the human soul.'[28]

If this 'need for roots' claim sounds too conservative, territorial, or even – given Weil's language of the soul – too Platonically or theologically informed, then we can also hear in this phrase what Shannon Hoff has recently articulated as 'the political significance of belonging'.[29] 'What matters to human individuals is not simply their capacity for self-determination', Hoff writes, 'but the fact that other phenomena can appear as meaningful and important to them, demanding acknowledgement.'[30] Her list includes 'intimate others, the things they are involved in studying and learning, their family networks, their involvements in group activities, their religious commitments, [and] their opportunities for creative expression'.[31] Hoff's list allows us to hear questions of orientation less in Weil's Platonic sense and more as questions of politically contested contexts. 'We are oriented', Hoff continues, 'toward contexts that are oriented around us (such as families and, in a different way, nation-states), around particular ideas and interests (such as scholarly and artistic worlds)' and further 'around specific activities (such as sports and crafts), around specific beliefs and commitments (such as religious and activist communities), and so on.'[32] Whether we think in terms of 'roots' or 'belonging', the question remains how to evade an excessive elevation of the identity of the collectivity. After reading Weil's roots, I address this question in terms of errancy and expansion.

* * *

Weil wrote *The Need for Roots* in London from November 1942 to sometime in the spring of 1943. Living in exile and in a country whose language and customs were not her own, she was especially concerned with how her native France would take shape when it was no longer occupied by foreign soldiers. Persecuted for her Jewish heritage, and writing from England, she was not, then, articulating her concerns from a position of security or with the comforts of state protection. Rather, from a point of immediate precarity, she was trying to articulate a way for a people to move forward following immense destruction and military occupation.

Roots for Weil, as for many uprooted people, are not something that can be taken for granted and easily dismissed as unnecessary. They are essential to who she takes herself to be, and, when taken from her, became her central preoccupation. The human need for roots, Weil concedes, is one of the most difficult to define.[33] Nevertheless, she provides a few conditions for rootedness: 'A human being has roots by virtue of his real, active and natural participation in the life of a community which preserves in living shape certain particular treasures of the past and certain particular expectations for the future.'[34] There is, then, a material aspect informing Weil's roots. By 'real' she means the common, daily tasks of working physically with others, such as picking grapes together in a vineyard, as opposed to the abstractions she saw in the transactions of capitalism, the jargon of intellectualism, and the hierarchies and calculations of bureaucracy. She diagnosed a sense of alienation in all three of these phenomena, noting that the modern world around her was, as Wampole comments, 'becoming ever more remote from itself, replacing the real with empty figures'.[35] There is also a communal aspect to roots: they are shared through participation. Roots require a community in which this active sharing-with occurs. Finally, roots contain and carry time within them: they are both retrospective and prospective, both preservative and expectative. In a figurative sense, then, roots move both backward and forward in time, in memories and dreams, legacies and hopes.

The form of roots is dynamic. Their shape is not static, which is to say dead. Rather, the shape of roots is changing in that they are 'living', being woven and performed in encounters both reiterated and unexpected. Importantly, to be rooted is to attend to particularities of the past and the future – to both historical 'particular treasures' and expectations. When one is rooted, one looks in both directions, having both histories and hopes. Roots are also culturally specific. Finally, Weil's term is not 'root' but 'roots', in the plural. She writes, 'Every human being needs to have multiple roots.'[36] In a line resonant with Glissant's concept of contacts as I read it in Chapter 1, she adds: 'We must also keep . . . some arrangement whereby human beings may once more be able to recover their roots. This doesn't mean they should be fenced in . . . Rooting in and the multiplying of contacts are complementary to one another.'[37] In sum, Weil gives us a sketch of roots in a specific sense: roots are material, active, communal, participatory, temporal, living, particular and plural – 'a certain terrestrial poetry'.[38]

In *The Need for Roots*, Weil applies her key concept to the context of France in the early 1940s. She develops a sense of compassion that she suggests the French citizen adopt toward France, but which, unlike national pride, is universal, meaning that it is able to cross borders and foster tenderness ardently expressed, she writes, 'over all countries in misfortune, over all countries without exception'.[39] Here I want to suggest a slightly different angle, not among nation states but within them. This lens poses questions such as: What psychological boundaries are built within a national identity, and how do these boundaries buttress and contest that identity? Within the geopolitical and psychological boundaries of the state, what does Weil's compassion look like for the marginal, the deviant, the rebel, the Indigenous, the immigrant? Is a state a suitable form of collectivity to respond to these others? We should read her on her own terms.

For Weil idolatry is the obdurate obstacle to the compassionate sensibility she advances in her conceptualisation of roots.[40] As she explains, 'Idolatry is the name of the error which attributes a sacred character to the collectivity; and it is the commonest of crimes, at all times, at all places.'[41] Idolatry, then, is a problem of nationalism in that 'one's country is something limited whose demands are unlimited'.[42] This socially endowed 'sacred' character, taking what are in fact means to be ends, she also sees operating in 'money, power, the state, national pride, economic production, universities', and political parties.[43] Focusing on the latter, she claims that each political party advances idolatry through the 'collective pressure' it exerts on its members while seeking 'its own growth, without limit', and for this reason she issues a condemnation of political parties per se. '[E]very party is totalitarian – potentially, and by aspiration.'[44] An important ethical and political question becomes: How would a community concretely cultivate its needed roots with a view toward compassion while avoiding idolatry, including taking the nation state as an idol? But this is not exactly the question

Weil takes up. In her extended commentary on roots, she moves in a different direction.

Despite her major claim in *The Need for Roots* – that the state is an agent of uprooting – Weil makes a minor claim that complicates following her as a political guide, namely, that it is the duty of the state to make a 'new patriotism' a reality, such that the country becomes 'a life-giving agent', 'turned into good, root-fixing ground'.[45] Her minor claim proceeds in a few parts. First, in a discussion of territory-based collectivities, she describes the nation and the state as synonymous, noting critically that 'in our age, money and the State have come to replace all other bonds of attachment'.[46] In the modern world, as Weil has it, the state maintains the temporal links within the collectivity, a decidedly root-giving activity and a check against an important feature of uprooting, namely, destroying links with the past. In a later passage, Weil uses synonymously 'country' and 'nation'. 'Country is merely another name for nation [*La patrie est un autre nom de la nation*] . . . The nation is a fact [*un fait*], and a fact is not an absolute.'[47] By this point in the text, nation, state and country are functioning synonymously. In this quotation, we also see her concern about idolatry. She is arguing against any idolatrous claim that the state is absolute, noting instead that it has been made. In English, in translating *fait* we hear *fac-*, the all-too-human or creaturely prefix of making, seen in words like 'fact' and 'factory'. Ultimately, Weil sees the state as natural and contingent – created by chance and by creatures (as opposed to by the Creator, for her at this point in her spiritual development).

A third passage is crucial in understanding Weil's position in *The Need for Roots*. 'The State's most obvious duty', she writes, 'is to keep efficient watch at all times over the security of the national territory'; and more than that, 'The State's duty is to make the country, in the highest possible degree, a reality . . . it must really become, in fact, a life-giving agent, really be turned into good, root-fixing ground.'[48] If the state's duty is to make the homeland (*la patrie*) a reality, and if that requires both possession and that the country become root-fixing ground (*un terrain d'enracinement*), and further if we have established a kind of synonymous and mutually informing usage in Weil in regard to the nation, state and country, then here we can see Weil as suggesting that the state militate toward becoming a supplier or provider of collective life – a mechanism for rooting. For Weil the state is ultimately a frame for other kinds of expression, a *milieu* for other *milieux*, notwithstanding her critiques of the state and her anarchism both in earlier writings and even in *The Need for Roots* itself.

I have spent so much time reading the relationship between Weil's roots and the state because she makes a mistake so many of us do. She was not immune to the disease she herself diagnosed in 1934: 'It seems fairly clear that contemporary humanity tends pretty well everywhere to a totalitarian form of social organization', she writes, 'that is to say, towards a system in which the state power comes to exercise sovereign sway in all spheres, even, indeed, above all, in that of thought.'[49] In our considerations of contemporary belonging, political theorists often fall into positions similar to hers: we return to the state, and we offer compassion as the proper ethical mode. We understand the problems of excessive nationalism, of the exclusions of the state vis-à-vis its non-citizens and those outside of its self-declared root identity. And yet, so powerful is the hegemony of state-based thinking that theorists end up arguing for little more than a more tolerant country. 'That the nation-state as an entity itself has continually failed African and Black people is almost never *the* story we hear', Rinaldo Walcott observes.[50] 'The nation-state as an entity', he goes on, 'takes its imprimatur and its practices from the plantation economies and logics that foreclosed Black subjecthood in the first instance.'[51]

'Therefore, the forces propelling movement (poverty, wars, environmental disasters, trade imbalances, coups, etc.) cannot be singularly understood as failure, but rather as having achieved the intended effects of how the organism that is the nation-state conditions the lives of Black people.'[52] When we cannot think about belonging beyond the state, we return to its familiarity, and in asking for a state that is open, welcoming and hospitable, we are asking for a resolution to an irresoluble contradiction. We are asking the uprooting force *par excellence* to be rooting. We are asking the modern/colonial political form to be decolonial.[53]

* * *

Reading Weil has drawn our attention to three elements important to a study of responsibility: (1) that in a context of modern/colonial uprooting, there is a felt or stated 'need' for belonging; (2) that the state is an idol essentially totalitarian in organisation; and (3) that the hegemony of the state extends to the sphere of thought such that we often fail to imagine an alternative. That Weil herself falls into the trap of (3) does not mean we have to dismiss her insights. We can read her against herself, noting that her conception of the state as rooting is not any less susceptible to idolatry than the political parties, bureaucracies and other collectivities she criticised previously in her work for uprooting ordinary, organic and real relations. Reading Weil brings into relief the overall argument in this chapter: while expanding responsibilities requires a community serving as a *cadre* toward other *milieux* (in Weil's terms), the state is not one of these communities. To refuse the state the status of a root-generating community recognises that the modern/colonial state is not organically developing from below (anarchy) but fabricated, imposed and imagined from on high (bureaucracy). The history and ongoing actions of the state as a force of violence against Indigenous and other made-precarious people within it demonstrate that the state, as the modern/colonial way of organising political power, re-installs deeply unjust hierarchies of gender, race and labour.

It is on this point – regarding the space bounded by root identity that appeals to the state – that Weil's conceptualisation of roots can be criticised immanently. On her own terms, the state as a generator of 'root-fixing ground' is at variance with the universality of compassion. As Walcott asks us to keep in mind, the emergence and continuation of the nation state in the Americas involves its attempted genocide of Indigenous nations and ongoing anti-Black violence, including in forms of imprisonment and forced labour. If violent exclusions and oppressions emerge at the same time as the nation state's identity, then treating the nation state as a mechanism of rootedness will perpetuate racialised violence as well as other forces of uprootedness. The shared stories of strangers continue to be erased as the history of those with force endures.

If there are to be organically unfolding, decentralised and mutually hospitable communities in a given territorial aggregate, as Weil advances, then a mechanism of compassion must emphasise the plurality and particularity of roots – growing in multiple directions, queerly crossing borders – over and against elements of origin and universality, such as taking the nation state, with its single language and clear-cut territory, as root-fixing ground. This follows Weil's central claim in *The Need for Roots*, namely, that the state destroys roots by demanding absolute (and thus idolatrous) loyalty to itself. Despite or because of this immanent critique, however, rootedness in Weil's sense is worth tarrying with in that it stresses a human 'need' for communal, participatory, particular and pluralistic engagement in community life – a need for a sense of belonging.

Showing the limits of thinking with Weil, some theorists have recently argued that compassion and critique are not the best modes to challenge the reality of the rights-denying state today. Didier Fassin has asked humanitarian actors to dwell with 'the problems posed by the mobilization of empathy rather than the recognition of rights'.[54] Humanitarians 'prefer to speak about suffering and compassion than about interests or justice', Fassin goes on, resulting in a situation where 'those at the receiving end of humanitarian attention know quite well that they are expected to show the humility of the beholden rather than express demands for rights'.[55] In these conditions, immense suffering can quickly become grounds for invoking a state of emergency. A security imperative, Fassin shows, can take over easily from where humanitarianism left off.[56]

For its part, critique calls into being a crisis, which in turn requires more critique. Indeed, the words *critique* and *crisis* share a Greek root related to both judgement and decision. But if Walcott is right, then the state is not just a form that institutes a crisis, but itself a catastrophe. An empirical field saturated with violence leads us to the conclusion that the state is essential to the ordinary catastrophe that Glissant notes *is* colonial power (DA 802/CD 255). Maldonado-Torres recently writes about the social (not 'natural') disasters of hurricanes in the Caribbean: 'While there is something to gain by referring to Hurricane María as a disaster instead of merely as a crisis, the most adequate term for it may be *catastrophe*.'[57] 'Catastrophe', he continues, 'is not about a decision or about fate, but about a dramatic turn of events.'[58] If the more precise description of the state is catastrophe and not crisis, then what would be a mode of response more robust than critique? Glissant's concept of errancy invites practices that diverge from an exile's appeal to a territorial origin of a collectivity. Errancy is not just a judging but a turning of practices that offers responses aiming to prevent further catastrophe.

Relations: Solidarity, Anarchy and Generosity

Given the technological mediations present in our modern/colonial context, as I discussed in Chapter 1, an individual's identity is constantly challenged. In other words, one is frequently invited to diverge in their practices of belonging. The constitution of the modern/colonial subject, Celia Britton comments, reading Glissant, occurs 'within this fluid and multiple, "relayed" circulation of identifications'.[59] This means that through daily contacts modern subjects are invited into a more relational identity. While a person does not have to give up the sense of belonging that made one into who one takes oneself to be, a person also has the feeling that her upbringing does not have the final hold on her. One always has other points of reference by which one could orient oneself – points, as Marisa Parham puts it, of 'social configurations and cultural productions that offer insight into [her] sense of rootedness in them, even as these configurations clearly grow, thrive and transform'.[60]

The vicissitudes of daily life, in addition to the political forces that frame one's perceptions, belie any previously linear and self-guided narrative of one's own development. Work of re-identification begins with a recognition of one's 'capacity of variation', to use Britton's phrase.[61] The beginning of relational living is a passing, Britton continues, '[t]hrough a succession of different mediations, temporary stylistic constructs that serve a strategic purpose rather than being the expressive incarnation of a permanent individual identity'.[62] What I call 'expansive belonging' involves a capacity of variation not in the sense of a postmodern flattening of difference, but in the sense of 'strategic purpose' at play here.[63] Just as one's identity is not permanent, so too is it not free-floating, simply amorphous or somehow borderless. Rather, while relational identity includes a capacity for variation, it also involves passing through different identifications *strategically* – that is, for the purposes of further solidarities.

We should therefore not romanticise the fluidity of relational identification. The specific promises of relational identity lie less in the formation of a free-floating individual and more in how the individual can work with others. Again, I need to repeat my concern about audience. Exile is a forced position, occurring when an individual becomes a victim of what Weil calls uprooting. Errancy, as I endorse it, is something that could be taken up voluntarily as one responds to a call – a 'vocation of errancy', as Glissant puts it (PR 32/PO 20, translation modified). Errancy is the relevant term to the implicated subjects I am addressing. He goes on: 'In contrast to arrowlike nomadism (discovery or conquest), in contrast to the situation of exile, errancy gives-on-and-with [*l'errance donne avec*] the negation of every pole and every metropolis' (PR 31/PO 19).

What precisely is this gives-on-and-with, the keystone to understanding how errancy is relational, as opposed to individual and isolated, as in certain forms of Stoic or neoliberal ethics? First, the term itself suggests generosity (the giving). Here we can return to Weil to issue a caution. 'Generosity', Weil noted in writing on colonialism, 'hardly ever extends in any people as far as making an effort to discover the injustices committed in their name.'[64] A decolonial sense of generosity, then, is an examined one, meaning that it calls its own rhetoric into question in order to inquire into the injustices of those claiming to be generous. This form of generosity is clearly an 'error' according to the account of responsibility that predominates today in the US, where generosity, seen in philanthropy and development, aims to celebrate, not interrogate, reigning institutional forms.[65]

Second, Glissant's gives-on-and-with also suggests community (the with). It could thus outline a political valence beyond an ethics of hospitality and toward what Drabinski calls an 'ethics of building-with and solidarity'.[66] We can think of this as a move from Levinas's hospitality and welcoming to a stronger political position. The gives-on-and-with of errancy does not share Levinas's concern about community doing violence to singularity so much as it places its hopes precisely in that community.[67] Errancy can also be read as 'anarchic' when that term is understood in its etymological relation to the Greek *arché*, meaning 'origin', 'rule' or 'empire' and related to hierarchy. The *err-* of errancy carries an everyday sense of travelling away from an established centre, such as the state as an intellectual 'centre' or hegemon of thinking. An errant individual understands that the state is not the only possible political form, as it is according liberals who adopt an implicitly end-of-history position. To consider errancy is to ask what it looks like to refuse, to distance oneself from, the centring cities, capitals, texts, styles and imaginaries that decide projects and projections, such as the 'Washington Consensus'.

In this way errancy is anti-imperial. It is different from an appeal to a pure root, essential origin, or any hierarchy as such. Glissant's sense of creolisation suggests mixing from the beginning and emphasises horizontal entanglements. It also prescribes relational practices.

In a memorable line, Glissant writes, 'What Relation gives us to imagine, creolization has given us to live out' (TTM 25). To think of errancy this way is to read it as a critique of the monolingual nation with its origin story of filiation. Errancy offers a different story, one that is more ambiguous, fragile and derivative (TTM 31). Errancy, as Drabinski has suggested, is '[e]*xile without the thought of origin*'.[68] It 'transforms exile into an archipelagic thinking – and therefore an aesthetics of fragmentation'.[69] Without the thought of a single origin, and without harkening back to Africa or Europe as essential, Glissant moves away from both the (retrophilic) root and exile as key concepts. Instead, he turns toward new beginnings, new methods, here and now. 'Let's invent new products, fruits of new methods', Glissant says in an invitation (TTM 232). 'Our responsibility in the matter is collective, and so should be our action' (TTM 232). Errancy, then, moves not to solitude but toward solidarities. One powerful example of errancy is found in the individuals who raided Harper's Ferry with John Brown. 'They were not men of culture or great education', W. E. B Du Bois writes of these deviant individuals, but '[t]hey were intellectually bold and inquiring . . . nearly all were skeptical of the world's social conventions'.[70] Errant in their scepticism and practice, they broke social bonds with a view toward building new ones.

In addition to 'giving' solidarity and anarchy, the gives-on-and-with of errancy can be read in yet another way. Errant political forms would not seek the eternity of empire, as seen in the postage stamp of the United States, guaranteed 'Forever'. Rather, errant work knows that political forms will fade in time. This temporal expectation can be learned from the world, learned from landscape and seascape, and errancy can be tied to an ecopolitics, when it is understood as yielding, in Valérie Loichot's beautiful phrase, 'as if under the constant palimpsests and erasures of writing on sand under a wave'.[71] In sum, I have read the gives-on-and-with of errancy in three senses – as a way to think about building with others (solidarity), calling into question hierarchies and origins (anarchy), and understanding the impermanence of any community (temporality).

Practices of errancy work to challenge the trajectory of elite actors' root identifications, which inform ties to a territory and usually assume a predatory state form. The modern state form is uprooting in its claims to and conquering of land, seen for instance in the patterns of *uti possidetis* on which land was demarcated following decolonisation in much of the world. In turn, errant individuals place their roots not in territories but in relation to other actors amidst struggles. Belonging is a matter not of filiation but of politics.[72] Glissant writes in a paradox: 'Errancy allows us to moor ourselves' (TTM 63). 'Sometimes, by taking up the problems of the Other', he says elsewhere, 'it is possible to find oneself' (PR 31/PO 18).

Root Identity and Relation Identity

In reading Weil and Glissant so far, I have presented a distinction between root and relational identity. The criteria that inform this distinction allow us to see whether or not a given form of identification, as well as the sense of responsibility that follows from identifying in certain ways, falls prey to the concerns about fixity and territory I noted in introducing this chapter. For Glissant, root identity is founded on a creation myth. What follows this vision is 'the hidden violence of a filiation', the exclusions inherent in the founding episode (PR 158/PO 143). Root identity also comprises a claim to legitimacy that entitles the community to the possession of land, of territory. To preserve this identity, it is projected onto other territories in a further violent imposition – a conquest that includes 'the project of a discursive knowledge' (PR 158/PO 144). In this way, root identity features a 'masked colonisation' (PR 159/PO 144). 'The story that settler-colonial nation-states tend to tell about themselves', Simpson explains, 'is that they are new; they are beneficent; they have successfully "settled" all issues prior to their beginning.'[73] Even if 'they acknowledge having complicated beginnings, forceful beginnings, what was there before that process occupies a shadowy space of reflection'.[74]

Glissant elaborates on the link between root identity and colonisation in a later essay co-written with Patrick Chamoiseau: '[T]he colonial nation imposes its values and claims to be an identity preserved from any outside infringement . . . a singular root identity.'[75] '[T]hough any colonization is primarily about economic exploitation', they continue, 'no colonization can forego the overvaluation of identity that justifies exploitation.'[76] That is, the narrative of the singular root, which subtends many nation states today, leverages self-preservation as a means to achieve an exclusion of the strange, a territorial conquest and an epistemological imposition. Tendrilled in place, myth, and fixed identity, root identity consequently condemns the immigrant, who struggles to reconcile their past belonging with their present, hostile context, and whose very displacement state practices likely caused. In sum, the problem is not with identity per se, but rather comes when identity is lived, as Clevis Headley puts it, 'as root, as unique, which is the same as thinking identity as sameness or as One'.[77]

Relational identity, by contrast, emerges with 'the conscious and contradictory experience of contacts among cultures' (PR 158/PO 144). Those who identify relationally view the land not as territory, and thus as a base for projection and conquest but, rather, as a place 'where one gives-on-and-with' as presented above – that is, a place of errancy, giving and building solidarity as opposed to grasping, comprehending and needing knowledge. Like a gift circle among islands instead of an IMF loan between nations, relational identity circulates without circumscribing. Instead of returning to roots, relational identity imagines alternative routes, new beginnings precisely from feelings of alienation and disorientation. Such a beginning, Drabinski explains, 'refuses to re-root according to an atavistic logic of origins or the oblique version of the same in the form of ruins and remnants, but instead re-routes', and does so with a view toward more complicated relations.[78] It is this refusal to re-root that I see as opening space for alternative modes of belonging.

An example shows how relational identity contests the presuppositions of root identity. Root identity informs how states respond to migrants. In 2007, in response to France's establishment of the Ministry of Immigration, Integration, National Identity and Co-Development, Glissant and Chamoiseau called into question not only the desirability of such an excessively nationalistic project, but also its possibility. They articulate a clear thesis: never fixed, identity is 'continuously developed and reinforced', such that 'it can neither be established nor safeguarded by rules, edicts, or laws that would imperiously establish its nature or forcibly guarantee its durability'.[79] That is, no identity can be determined ahead of time. Worse, to the extent that this pre-determination is fixed, 'the life of a community would become mechanical, its future sterile, rendered infertile by a static command center, as in a laboratory experiment'.[80] Their point can be summarised as follows: to emphasise a fixed, territorial identity is to limit relation, which is a concept of change and mobility with a strategic view toward solidarities.

These Caribbean thinkers made a public stance to remind the French people of a point Glissant had articulated previously: 'Relation lives in coming to fruition, that is, in achieving itself in a common place [*La Relation vit de se réaliser, c'est-à-dire de s'achever en lieu commun*]' (PR 219/PO 203, translation modified). In other words, relation exists in being realised, not as realised. The aspect of the verb is progressive, not completed. Relation is both already underway and continually ongoing. It cannot be achieved in any final sense. To live in relation is to live as part of this realising (not this realisation, itself a kind of fixation). Before expanding on relational identity found in expansive belonging, it is worth addressing a point about the vocabulary of ethics I am articulating.

* * *

While my trajectory is from Weil to Glissant, learning from the former but ultimately siding closer to the latter, there is an additional concept worth adding from Weil's vocabulary. Like Levinas, at times Glissant invokes 'the Other', even when he is describing grounded relationships (e.g. PR 28/PO 16). In relational thinking, he writes in a promising phrase with a limited term, 'each and every identity is extended through a relationship with the Other [*un rapport à l'Autre*]' (PR 23/PO 11). It is surprising that Glissant would use this capitalised term in *Poetics* given that he arguably claimed, in *Caribbean Discourse*, that the inflated, capitalised 'Other' is the term invoked by dominant classes in colonial impositions. There Glissant writes: 'When I say *relative*, I mean the Diverse, the opaque necessity to consent to the other's difference [*consentir à la différence de l'autre*]'; and 'when I say *absolute*', he continues, 'I refer to the dramatic endeavour to impose a truth on the Other [*imposition d'une vérité à l'Autre*]' (DA 440/ CD 147–8, translation modified). To return again to Weil: her description of the neighbour makes a practical advance on the language of the Other.

The neighbour is the one to whom, Weil claims, one must be able to ask: 'What are you going through?'[81] In a very concrete sense, to be able to ask this question of another, one must have already placed oneself alongside others through participation and, over time, in solidarity. Like how errancy is actively taken up and therefore different from enforced conditions of exile, the neighbour is not pre-given but involves acts undertaken. 'The neighbor', the liberation theologian Gustavo Gutiérrez writes, 'is not the one whom I find in my path, but rather the one in whose path I place myself, the one whom I approach and actively seek.'[82] In this way, the neighbour is not found. Neighbours are always made. It is only after this approaching and seeking, only after building with others – a pursuit that often takes a long time, so a pursuit not just of participation but of solidarity – that one can ask, as one would of a friend, 'What are you going through?' Weil's ethical question, therefore, presupposes the solidarity that is the result of living out an active bearing of relational identity with others.

Expansive Belonging

Glissant's term 'rooted errancy' (*errance enracinée*) presents the main, productive tension of this chapter: the settling stability of belonging and the unsettling motion of expansion (PR 49/ PO 37, translation modified; see also DA 754/CD 232). Rooted errancy aims to guide identity formation within, through, and perhaps beyond the constraints of law and order, possessive attachments and made-sacred institutions.[83] But the term might suggest something other than what it intends.

In its traditional usage, the metaphor of the root manifests a desire for comfort and a kind of retrophilia.[84] Whatever the term 'roots' promises to allow in organic growth and developing life, it also threatens to disallow in territorial grasping and conserving the past. Here we think of the 'roots' of the US – not only, quite literally, the crops that allowed for the growth of the nascent state, but also, relatedly and figuratively, how those roots are predicated on dispossession, namely, the country's twin foundations of genocide of Indigenous nations and enslavement of African peoples.[85] Neal Allar documents how the metaphor of roots can cover over what Glissant identified as already mixed from the beginning: 'America was built on a foundation of racial mixing, but its dominant narrative constantly struggles to recuperate its pure "roots" in the Old World.'[86] We can also think of the roots of the state of Israel at the expense of the lives of Palestinians. The state's 'roots' continue to uproot not only memories and livelihoods, but also, through its settlements, the physical roots of olive trees.[87] In her final analysis of the metaphor, Wampole goes as far saying that '[t]he most evil acts in twentieth-century Europe were precipitated by root thinking'.[88]

Instead of beginning from the roots of 'rooted errancy', then, in cultivating a vocabulary for ethics today, I want to think more with Hoff's phenomenological 'belonging' than with Weil's quasi-theological 'roots'. Expansion maintains the deviance and experimentation of errancy. To begin from or to foreground expansion calls upon settled elites to think first about a moving toward alternative forms of belonging. It is only from that motion, away from any taken-as-natural sense of belonging, that expansion serves as a route to an alternative sense of community and relation.

Expansive belonging is neither a reversal of nor a reform to the functional responses that Glissant demands we reject in our bearings – it is not a new patriotism (Weil), an incremental integration (liberal reform), or a muted tolerance (liberal multiculturalism). Indeed, 'integration' for Glissant is ultimately against the interests of a community. Integration is 'a vertical pride', he writes with Chamoiseau, 'that haughtily requires the preliminary disintegration of what comes to encounter us, leading to our impoverishment'.[89] The rhetoric of tolerance, while itself an improvement upon the hateful rhetoric that dominates contemporary US politics, tends to presuppose that another needs to be tolerated. As Wendy Brown has shown, tolerance regulates aversion and fixes hierarchies of subordination and oppression.[90] The question becomes: For implicated subjects, what might expanding our most central commitments, our senses of belonging – indeed our responsibilities – allow or disallow? Put differently, what are the political threats and promises, precisely, of newly imagined practices of responsibility?[91]

In Glissant's terms, expansion is characterised by detour more than opacity. Britton brings out this distinction, noting that 'the detour overlaps with opacity, but whereas opacity is above all an ethical value and a political right, the detour is more tactical and ambiguous'.[92] Detour, she continues, is 'an indirect mode of resistance that "gets around" obstacles rather than confronting them head on, and it arises as a response to a situation of disguised rather than overt oppression and struggle'.[93] '[I]tself marked with the alienation it is trying to combat', Britton continues, the detour is a bearing of self-estranging that moves away via a track. It is less a re-rooting and more a re-routing, and it can thus be understood as 'both an evasion of the real situation and an obstinate effort to find a way round it'.[94]

Expansion is not only shaped by its affective charge, its feeling of alienation, but also by its provinciality, its locality. Avoiding an impossible abstraction to no-place from the beginning, as if relations were not connected to locations, expansive belonging starts from the affective practices in which the alienated and potentially errant actors find ourselves. Expansive belonging and reclaiming a right to opacity can work together. Indeed, expansive belonging can be understood as a summary term for the secondary duties around the right to opacity, as duties to defend countries in the Global South, the peoples of its diasporas, and Indigenous nations everywhere so that they can cultivate their cultures on their own terms and thus enrich the beauty and knowledge of what Glissant calls the *tout-monde*, the world-entire. Thinking of belonging in this way may seem indirect or overly abstract to those accustomed to thinking about duties in terms of institutional channels. What does expansive belonging look like in practice?

The individual who expands her practices of belonging is different from her colleagues who adopt only the pseudo-relational identity of the plane-travelling 'cosmopolitan' or withdraw into idyllic spaces on expensive yoga and mindfulness retreats. Expansive belonging suggests, in Britton's terms, 'the unheroic, multiple, *interstitial* resistance of the present day, in the city rather than in the forest'.[95] While relational identity is internationalist, relational actors work on local levels.

To become a neighbour is not to gentrify, but to break with one's elite affiliations in the first place. Emerging and expanding markets, which always violate opacity in order to dictate and fulfil cultural needs, are always tied to individual actors who want to look, eat and otherwise live a certain way. Competition over the materials that make up flashy lifestyles in the US leads to what Michael Klare calls 'low-intensity conflicts', such as proxy wars and now a so-called Global War on Terror.[96] Low-intensity conflicts allow elite actors 'to go on buying condominiums, wearing chic designer clothes, eating expensive meals at posh restaurants, and generally living in style without risking their own lives'.[97] To begin by expansion means first renouncing elite practices and affiliations – to cease to desire that way of life.[98] Liberation theology is helpful once again because of its emphasis on class. 'We have to break with our mental categories, with the way we relate to others, with our way of identifying with the Lord, with our cultural milieu, with our social class', Gutiérrez continues, 'in other words, with all that can stand in the way of a real, profound solidarity with those who suffer'.[99] These breaks with social class are what I mean, first and foremost, by expansion.

* * *

Expansive belonging understood first as a break with an elite position has several implications for contemporary human rights practice. In brief, it calls for a shift from a model of advocacy to a model of activism. These terms are often understood synonymously in literature on human rights. For instance, in their 1998 *Activists beyond Borders: Advocacy Networks in International Politics*, Margaret Keck and Kathryn Sikkink open by comparing the fictional state violence against banana workers in Gabriel García Márquez's 1967 novel *One Hundred Years of Solitude* to the actual state violence against students in Mexico City in 1968 and against dissidents in Argentina in the 1970s.[100] While there was not justice for the banana workers in the novel, they write, the real-life story has a happier ending because military actors took responsibility and offered condolences. 'A key part of the explanation' of the differences between the fictional and real-life events, they argue, 'is the work of a network of domestic and international human rights activists who provided crucial information on events in Argentina and lobbied governments and international organizations to express concern, investigate, and bring pressure for change'.[101] In this important text for defining how activism is understood in political science today, activists are informants who *lobby* and *bring pressure* to states. Too often elite actors maintain their positions of power while perhaps briefly considering 'empowering' others, a phrase that can sound insulting to its recipient. In other words, despite its good intentions – and so often a strong advocate is all that one accused of a crime or facing repression has – advocacy, viewed in terms of the systems it works through, faces a built-in ethical limitation: it represents more than it stands-with. It is a model of political mediation instead of political participation. It tends toward charity instead of solidarity.

The advocate's charity is a result of their professional class position. From the 1970s onward, Stephen Hopgood documents, neoliberal policies contributed to 'a humanitarian marketplace' in which permanent NGOs meant 'a widening class of professional activists and advocates'.[102] Hopgood's use of 'professional' is critical in its tone. His concern is that many human rights NGOs are so large, 'with large staffs who have significant salary and pension entitlements, that they are locked in to this model'.[103] As a result, acquiring funding from donors, not standing with the downtrodden, becomes the means of what gets called 'activism'.[104] Amnesty International's 2012 appointment of Suzanne Nossel as its director exemplifies the hyper-professionalism of contemporary human rights practice. Nossel's previous employment included the US State Department, McKinsey and Co., and *The Wall Street Journal*.[105] She is someone who knows how to negotiate with, not resist, dominant systems. While 'cultural resistance by negotiation', to use Stuart Hall's phrase, is a key skill for dominated populations – and today there remains a number of colonial binds in which precarious populations often have no option besides appealing to the state, even when they desire protection from the state – elite actors do not need to perform such negotiation to ensure their survival.[106] Most elite actors are not under the kind of persecution or living in a state of exile that caused Weil to appeal to the state. So then, what is going on in elite calls for professional negotiation in predominant institutional channels?

An advocacy model of human rights raises questions of belonging because advocates often think of themselves as part of larger struggles, despite the class divisions between them and those for whom they speak. Advocates often live in wealthy neighbourhoods and send their kids to the best schools while their clients remain poor. '[L]egal struggles are almost of necessity mediated through a professional class of lawyers', Robert Knox writes in an echo of Critical Legal Studies' attention to class and community.[107] This social location is problematic not only because 'access to lawyers tends to be mediated by access to money' but also because 'the necessity for a professionalized, specialized, bureaucratic, and ultimately alienated mediation in this respect is profoundly disempowering and demobilizing'.[108] The point I am trying to bring home in this chapter is best put by the Native American and Indigenous Studies Association: 'Belonging does not arise simply from individual feelings – it is not simply who you claim to be, but also who claims you.'[109] Justice-oriented actors who belong to cycle clubs in their cities, for instance, belong to elite circles, not resistant ones. The professionalisation of human rights 'activism' evidences that while people invested in human rights are willing to challenge nation states, corporations, and the leaders of both in their jobs, say through arguing cases or crafting publicity campaigns, many of these people are not willing to break from their social class in a larger sense of what it means to live a good life. Fassin calls this 'the inequality between benefactors and victims'.[110] And once again it is Weil who makes this point most poignantly. Although '[t]heir motives are generous', she writes about elite proponents of human rights in her time, they do not 'see the mass of people as anything but mere anonymous human matter. But it is hard to find this out, because they have no contact with the mass of people.'[111]

Describing models of 'resistance' that structures of domination themselves foster, Glissant makes the following observation: '[D]omination . . . produces the worst kind of change, which is that it provides, on its own, models of resistance to the stranglehold it has imposed, thus short-circuiting resistance while making it possible' (DA 42/CD 15). Advocacy is often a model of 'resistance' provided by dominant structures. Consequently, human rights advocacy is easily 'short-circuited' as state power reabsorbs challenges into is structures. Elite 'resistance' tends to prescribe the same models (especially voting). It promotes, as Joy James documents, 'only those avenues delineated within legal strategies: no protests, civil disobedience, or lawbreaking in their various social and political forms'.[112] Expansive belonging breaks with the models of social change suggested by dominant structures and actors. Often justice-oriented actors today make false starts because they have not felt the hegemony of the state. In turn, they not only fail to make possible alternative forms of political belonging, but they also hinder that making, that *poiesis*, by maintaining dominant forms. In Chapter 4, I consider a learning process that allows elite actors to see the professional culture of humanitarianism for what it too often is: a set of practices of domination, many of which are disguised as resistance.

Notes

1. Hannah Arendt, *The Human Condition* (Chicago: University of Chicago Press, 1998), pp. 201, 199. I thank Sophie Bourgault for noticing that this book can be read as a response to the fleetingness of political movements and the need to sustain them. For a reading of Arendt that explains the political potential of such fleeting movements in a way different from what I understand my inquiry to be doing in this chapter, see Judith Butler, *Notes Toward a Performative Theory of Assembly* (Cambridge, MA: Harvard University Press, 2015).
2. Ortega, *In-Between*, p. 141.
3. John Berger, 'Terrain', in *Landscapes: John Berger on Art*, ed. Tom Overton (New York: Verso, 2016), p. 224.
4. For neoliberalism's problematisation of politics (and proposed solutions of laws and markets), see Jessica Whyte, *The Morals of the Market*.
5. Richard Price, '*Créolisation*, Creolization, and *Créolité*', *Small Axe* 21, no. 1 (2017): p. 216.
6. Linda Martín Alcoff, *Visible Identities: Race, Gender, and the Self* (New York: Oxford University Press, 2006), p. 188.
7. Ibid. p. 189.
8. Ibid.
9. Ibid. p. 243.
10. For an imaginative rethinking of the nation, see Kris F. Sealey, *Creolizing the Nation* (Evanston, IL: Northwestern University Press, 2020). See esp. the Introduction, 'Setting the Stage', and Chapter 1, pp. 3–44.
11. Miguel Gualdrón Ramírez, 'Resistance and Expanse in *Nuestra América*: José Martí, with Édouard Glissant and Gloria Anzaldúa', *Diacritics* 46, no. 2 (2018): p. 19.
12. See 'expand, v.'. *OED* Online. Oxford University Press.

13. Patricia Monture-Okanee, 'Thinking about Aboriginal Justice: Myths and Revolution', in *Continuing Poundmaker and Riel's Quest: Presentations Made at a Conference on Aboriginal Peoples and Justice*, ed. Richard Gosse (Saskatoon, SK: Purich, 1994), p. 230.

14. Ibid.

15. The subtitle of James Clifford's recent book is indicative: *Returns: Becoming Indigenous in the Twenty-First Century* (Cambridge, MA: Harvard University Press, 2013). Clifford, a careful and nuanced thinker, invokes 'becoming indigenous' only twice in the text, and in those cases loosely; much more important to his analysis is the idea of 'indigenous becoming', which he claims to be a key organising principle and invokes thematically throughout the text (see ibid. p. 8). The fact that 'becoming indigenous' is selected for the subtitle likely illustrates a marketing ploy more than Clifford's sense of decolonial practice.

16. We can compare Glissant's relational identity to what the anthropologist David Graeber describes as 'open reciprocity', a form of reciprocity that 'keeps no accounts, because it implies a relation of permanent mutual commitment' (David Graeber, *Toward an Anthropological Theory of Value: The False Coin of Our Own Dreams* (New York: Palgrave, 2001), p. 220). My reading is that, like Graeber's 'open reciprocity', Glissant's 'relational identity' involves ongoing commitment, but it would keep accounts in order to demand accountability, or what I am calling in this book decolonial responsibility.

17. See Eve Tuck and K. Wayne Yang, 'Decolonization is not a metaphor', *Decolonization: Indigeneity, Education & Society* 1, no. 1 (2012): pp. 1–40.

18. Derek Walcott, *The Poetry of Derek Walcott 1948–2013* (New York: Farrar, Straus and Giroux, 2014), p. 237; Mahmoud Darwish, *Mural*, trans. Rema Hammami and John Berger (New York: Verso, 2009), pp. 15, 20.

19. There is a second reason to consider modifying, and not rejecting, the language of nationalism: secondary duties around the right to opacity should inform a life not of cosmopolitanism,

but of internationalism. In her study of the World Tribunal on Iraq, *For the Love of Humanity*, Ayça Çubukçu notes that 'the self offended by the war on Iraq was a "human self," rather than a "national self" acting in solidarity with another nation. This cosmopolitan understanding marks a significant shift away from the affects of international solidarity' (Ayça Çubukçu, *For the Love of Humanity: The World Tribunal on Iraq* (Philadelphia: University of Pennsylvania Press, 2018), p. 40). Çubukçu explains the distinction between cosmopolitan understanding and international solidarity in the following claim: 'I insist that this is what Habermas, Bartholomew, and other cosmopolitan theorists lamented in the occupation in Iraq: the displacement of a supranational empire by an American empire. They mourned the alleged displacement of a *universal* "law's empire" by an *American* "empire's law"' (ibid. pp. 150–1). If, with Çubukçu, and 'contrary to most cosmopolitans', we understand 'law's empire' as 'not an alternative to, but an articulation of "empire's law"', then we would do well to place ourselves in a tradition of radical internationalism, not liberal cosmopolitanism (ibid. p. 14). After all, 'socialist internationalism' since its inception formed a 'counter-politics to colonialism', Robert J. C. Young summarises (Young, *Postcolonialism*, p. 115).

20. Dionne Brand, *A Map to the Door of No Return: Notes to Belonging* (Toronto: Vintage Canada, 2011), p. 68.
21. David Lloyd and Paul Thomas, *Culture and the State* (New York: Routledge, 1998), p. 21.
22. Audra Simpson, *Mohawk Interruptus: Political Life across the Borders of Settler States* (Durham, NC: Duke University Press, 2014), p. 190.
23. See 'Wayward Lives, Beautiful Experiments, ft. Saidiya Hartman', Rustbelt Abolition Radio, <https://rustbeltradio.org/2019/04/24/ep28/>.
24. Christy Wampole, *Rootedness: The Ramifications of a Metaphor* (Chicago: University of Chicago Press, 2016), p. 2.
25. Ibid.
26. Ibid. p. 4.
27. Ibid. p. 18.

28. Simone Weil, *The Need for Roots: Prelude to a Declaration of Duties Toward Mankind*, trans. Arthur Wills (London: Routledge, 2010), p. 40.
29. Shannon Hoff, 'Rights and Worlds: On the Political Significance of Belonging', *Philosophical Forum* 45, no. 4 (2014): pp. 355–73.
30. Ibid. p. 356.
31. Ibid.
32. Ibid. p. 362.
33. Weil, *Need for Roots*, p. 40.
34. Ibid. p. 43.
35. Wampole, *Rootedness*, p. 132.
36. Weil, *Need for Roots*, p. 43.
37. Ibid. pp. 48–9.
38. Simone Weil, *Waiting for God*, trans. Emma Craufurd (New York: HarperCollins, 2009), p. 116.
39. Weil, *Need for Roots*, pp. 172–3.
40. Cf. Walter Benjamin's, 'Capitalism as Religion', in *Walter Benjamin: Selected Writings 1, 1913–1926*, ed. Marcus Bullock and Michael W. Jennings (Cambridge, MA: The Belknap Press of Harvard University Press, 2004), p. 288.
41. Simone Weil, 'Human Personality', in *Simone Weil: An Anthology*, ed. Siân Miles (New York: Penguin, 2005), p. 76.
42. Weil, *Need for Roots*, p. 155.
43. Simone Weil, *On the Abolition of all Political Parties*, trans. Simon Leys (New York: New York Review of Books, 2013), p. 12.
44. Ibid. p. 11.
45. Weil, *Need for Roots*, pp. 142, 163.
46. Ibid. p. 99.
47. Ibid. p. 130. Translation modified. See Weil, *L'enracinement: Prélude à une déclaration des devoirs envers l'être humain* (Paris: Les Éditions Gallimard, 1949), pp. 90–1.
48. Weil, *Need for Roots*, pp. 160–1.
49. Simone Weil, 'Reflections concerning the Causes of Liberty and Social Oppression', in *Oppression and Liberty*, trans. Arthur Wills and John Petrie (New York: Routledge, 2001), p. 109.
50. Rinaldo Walcott, *The Long Emancipation: Moving toward Black Freedom* (Durham, NC: Duke University Press, 2021), p. 47.

51. Ibid. p. 48.

52. Ibid.

53. For a history of the exclusions of the nation state, see Eric D. Weitz, *A World Divided: The Global Struggle for Human Rights in the Age of Nation-States* (Princeton: Princeton University Press, 2019). For a discussion of a radical understanding of one's country, see Gary Wilder's engaging and tremendously helpful reading of Césaire and Senghor in *Freedom Time: Negritude, Decolonization, and the Future of the World* (Durham, NC: Duke University Press, 2015).

54. Didier Fassin, *Humanitarian Reason: A Moral History of the Present*, trans. Rachel Gomme (Berkeley: University of California Press, 2011), p. x.

55. Ibid. pp. 3, 4.

56. Ibid. p. 43. Cf. Eyal Weizman, *The Least of All Possible Evils: Humanitarian Violence from Arendt to Gaza* (New York: Verso, 2011), p. 4.

57. Nelson Maldonado-Torres, 'Afterword: Critique and Decoloniality in the Face of Crisis, Disaster, and Catastrophe', in *Aftershocks of the Disaster: Puerto Rico Before and After the Storm*, ed. Yarimar Bonilla and Merison LeBrón (Haymarket Books: Chicago, 2019), p. 335.

58. Ibid.

59. Celia M. Britton, *Edouard Glissant and Postcolonial Theory: Strategies of Language and Resistance* (Charlottesville: University of Virginia Press), p. 171.

60. Marisa Parham, 'Breadfruit, Time and Again: Glissant Reads Faulkner in the World Relation', in *Theorizing Glissant: Sites and Citations*, ed. John E. Drabinski and Marisa Parham (London: Rowman & Littlefield International, 2015), p. 132. Henceforth TG.

61. Britton, *Edouard Glissant*, p. 171.

62. Ibid. p. 175. It is important here to distinguish what I think Glissant offers those I am addressing in my study from both Rosa Braidotti's and An Yountae's positions. Yountae criticises Braidotti for presenting her European/American readers with a version of Glissant that is too sanitised. Braidotti's language

of 'overcoming' loss and fragmentation, Yountae writes, misses the fact that 'for Glissant loss involves a different level of magnitude and intensity that derives from the "weight" of colonial history and the devastated socioeconomic reality created by it' (Yountae, *Decolonial Abyss*, p. 104). Thus, it would be a false equivalence to present the European/American readers' taking up Glissant as similar to those of 'racialized/colonized subjects who have experienced slavery, displacement, and diasporization' (ibid.). The former do not have to live with the weight that bears on the latter. I am writing more to Braidotti's intended readership than to Yountae's. I attempt to avoid what Yountae calls Braidotti's 'ethical unaccountability' by avoiding her 'affirmation of movement and her model of the all-transcending and unlocatable subject' (ibid. p. 105). The errancy I am advancing in different registers begins with located subjects and everyday situations. Such errancy would occur in connection to labour and decolonial movements in cities. It is errant because elite actors tend to maintain their class positions.

63. This concept of 'expansive belonging' relies on Miguel Gualdrón Ramírez's theorisation of Glissant's concept of the expanse in 'Resistance and Expanse in *Nuestra América*'.

64. Simone Weil, 'New Facts about the Colonial Problem in the French Empire', in *Simone Weil on Colonialism: An Ethic of the Other*, ed. and trans. J. P. Little (Lanham, MD: Rowman & Littlefield, 2003), p. 68.

65. Didier Fassin writes regarding Western aid to tsunami victims: 'We lamented their dead but celebrated our generosity. The power of this event resides in the rare combination of the tragedy of ruination and the pathos of assistance. Such disasters now form part of our experience of this-worldliness, just as do aid organizations, relief operations, and humanitarian interventions' (Fassin, *Humanitarian Reason*, p. ix).

66. Drabinski, *Levinas and the Postcolonial*, p. 174.

67. Ibid. pp. 174, 191.

68. Drabinski, 'Aesthetics and the Abyss' in TG pp. 161, 162.

69. Ibid.

70. W. E. B. Du Bois, *John Brown* (New York: Routledge, 2015), p. 144.

71. Valérie Loichot, 'Renaming the Name: Glissant and Walcott's Reconstruction of the Caribbean Self', *Journal of Caribbean Literature* 3, no. 2 (2002): p. 2.

72. Cf. how Stuart Hall ends his memoir: 'I had to find a modus vivendi with the world I had entered and indeed with myself. Surprisingly, this turned out to be partly through politics. Establishing, as I had, a foothold in British radicalism and inhabiting a necessary distance from England and its values meant that I never came to be seduced by the old imperial metropole. It allowed me to maintain a space I felt I needed. I wanted to change British society, not adopt it. This commitment enabled me not to have to live my life as a disappointed suitor, or as a disgruntled stranger. I found an outlet for my energies, interests and commitments without giving my soul away. And I had found a new family' (Stuart Hall, *Familiar Stranger: A Life between Two Islands* (Durham, NC: Duke University Press, 2017), p. 271).

73. Simpson, *Mohawk Interruptus*, p. 177.

74. Ibid.

75. Patrick Chamoiseau and Édouard Glissant, 'When the Walls Fall: Is National Identity an Outlaw?', trans. Jeffrey Landon Allen and Charly Verstraet, *Contemporary French and Francophone Studies* 22, no. 2 (2018): p. 260.

76. Ibid.

77. Clevis Headley, 'Glissant's Existential Ontology of Difference', in TG p. 81.

78. Drabinski, *Levinas and the Postcolonial*, p. 149.

79. Chamoiseau and Glissant, 'When the Walls Fall', p. 260.

80. Ibid.

81. Simone Weil, 'School Studies', in *Waiting for God*, p. 64.

82. Gustavo Gutiérrez, *A Theology of Liberation: History, Politics, and Salvation*, trans. Sister Caridad Inda and John Eagleson (Maryknoll, NY: Orbis, 1973), p. 113.

83. 'Beyond philosophy', Eduardo Mendieta writes, 'means to go beyond . . . academicized, professionalized, domesticated, and "civilized" philosophy by taking recourse to all that demystifies

the autonomy of philosophy and that at the same time turns our attention to its sources . . . This realization takes form primarily through the transformation of a social situation in which the living human agent is enslaved and dehumanized' (Eduardo Mendieta, 'Introduction', in Enrique Dussel, *Beyond Philosophy: Ethics, History, Marxism, and Liberation Theology*, ed. Eduardo Mendieta [Lanham, MD: Rowman & Littlefield: 2003], p. 2).

84. Wampole, *Rootedness*, pp. 7–8.
85. See Nichols, *Theft is Property!*
86. Allar, 'The Case for Incomprehension', p. 49.
87. 'The earth is closing in on us . . . Here and here our blood will plant its olive tree' (Mahmoud Darwish, 'The Earth is Closing in on Us', in Adonis, Mahmud Darwish and Samih al-Qasim, *Victims of a Map: A Bilingual Anthology of Arabic Poetry*, ed. Abdullah al-Udhari (London: Saqi Books, 2005), p. 13).
88. Wampole, *Rootedness*, p. 123.
89. Chamoiseau and Glissant, 'When the Walls Fall', p. 268.
90. See Wendy Brown, *Regulating Aversion: Tolerance in the Age of Identity and Empire* (Princeton: Princeton University Press, 2006).
91. The phrase 'threats and promises' is from Monique Roelofs, *The Cultural Promise of the Aesthetic* (London: Bloomsbury, 2014), p. 207.
92. Britton, *Edouard Glissant*, p. 25.
93. Ibid.
94. Ibid. p. 16.
95. Ibid. p. 132.
96. Michael Klare, 'Low-Intensity Conflict: The War of the "Haves" against the "Have-nots"', *Christianity and Crisis* (1998): p. 12.
97. Ibid.
98. Aijaz Ahmad: 'The pain of any ethical life is that all fundamental bondings, affiliations, stable political positions, require that one ceases to desire, voraciously, everything that is available in this world; that one learns to deny oneself some of the pleasures, rewards, consumptions, even affiliations of certain sorts' (Aijaz Ahmad, *In Theory: Classes, Nations, Literatures* (New York: Verso, 1992), p. 219).

99. James B. Nickoloff, ed., *Gustavo Gutiérrez: Essential Writings* (Maryknoll, NY: Orbis Books, 1996), p. 289.

100. Margaret E. Keck and Kathryn Sikkink, *Activists beyond Borders: Advocacy Networks in International Politics* (Ithaca, NY: Cornell University Press, 1998), pp. vii–viii.

101. Ibid. p. viii.

102. Hopgood, *The Endtimes of Human Rights*, p. 110.

103. Ibid. p. 105.

104. Ibid.

105. Ibid. p. 15.

106. Stuart Hall, 'Culture, Resistance, and Struggle', in *Cultural Studies 1983*, p. 198; Judith Butler, *Frames of War: When Is Life Grievable?* (New York: Verso, 2009), p. 26.

107. Robert Knox, 'Marxism, International Law, and Political Strategy', p. 432.

108. Ibid. pp. 432–3.

109. Native American and Indigenous Studies Association, 'NAISA Council Statement on Indigenous Identity Fraud', quoted in Nancy Mithlo, *Knowing Native Arts*, p. 201.

110. Fassin, *Humanitarian Reason*, p. 242.

111. Simone Weil, 'Human Personality', p. 78. For a poignant reflection on Weil and human rights in our time, see Lyndsey Stonebridge, *Placeless People: Writing, Rights, and Refugees* (Oxford: Oxford University Press, 2018).

112. James, 'The Dead Zone', p. 469.

4 The Feasibility of Ethical Pursuits

Feasibility

So far this study has argued for a shift in the vocabulary of decolonial ethics: from alterity to opacity, from exile to errancy, from root identity to relational identity ('expansive belonging'), and from hospitality to solidarity – where solidarity allows a reconsideration of politics, as Nitzan Lebovic puts it, 'not as a binary relation between friend and enemy, but as a network . . . united against abuse and coercive power'.[1] In arguing for this shift, this study has advanced a politicised sense of responsibility that works to demand opacity against state and market forces as well as to break from familiar identifications, such as one's nation and class. The promise of re-description is that it re-presents 'responsibility', suggesting different associations with the term, different ways of hearing it and thinking about it. An alternative understanding leads to aberrant actions. In other words, the promise of our shift in linguistic practices lies in our non-linguistic practices, our bearings of engagement with the world. If this is right, then it would be instructive to elaborate on what makes possible relational politics as well as to describe already ongoing practices that exemplify such relational work. Such an elaboration is the task of this chapter.[2]

Among the francophone Left of his generation, Glissant was famous for saying we must 'put the poetic back into the heart of the political'.³ To some this sounds like a superficial aesthetic statement, a fundamental misunderstanding of materialist politics, or perhaps, at best, a call for richer language in slogans and speeches. Even if these were the only ways to hear Glissant's point, it should not be underestimated. As Martin Puchner's scholarship shows, Marx's *Manifesto* was successful as a political provocation in part because of its reinvention of a genre.⁴ Of course, there are other ways to hear Glissant's saying.⁵ As Loichot has commented, 'Poetry, for Glissant, is not just the art of accommodating words in a lyrical mode by the use of sound, rhythm, or metaphorical language.'⁶ 'Poetry also means "making" in a material way', she continues: '*Poétrie*, the seeming neologism that Glissant uses in French, evokes simultaneously the poem, inhabited by the English word "poetry", and the verb *pétrir*, to knead dough or to give shape to clay.'⁷ This is a poetics of everyday acts – as kneading and sculpting suggest domestic scenes of eating, drinking and gathering that are in touch with the rhythms of the earth, such as the milling of flour or the making of clay. With this in mind, while Loichot acknowledges Peter Hallward's and Nick Nesbitt's claims that Glissant's early 'anticolonial ideology' is not present in his later work, she also makes an important counterclaim, namely, that late Glissant 'takes not an apolitical turn, but rather a new political turn, an ecopoetic turn'.⁸

The work that Glissant's call to poeticise politics demands, when read through Loichot's attention to the quotidian, is an orientation to politics less as something of elite procedures and more as something of daily processes. Because he consistently described his work in terms of poetics and not simply poetry, Glissant offered a specific kind of call, a call for making imaginative political goals actual. We can consider Glissant's famous saying in terms of a call to 'make possible', noting the etymological resonance between poetics and what Dussel calls *factibilidad* ('feasibility').[9] Both terms suggest the importance of making – not of the made, where the aspect of the verb is completed, but of continual processes of making, where the aspect is ongoing. This chapter focuses on feasibility, shifting slightly the outline of this study from the negative defence of particular practices (reclaiming a right to opacity) and divestment from attachments as part of rerouting (expansive belonging) to a question of positive pursuits. Some of the positive practices I treat below, such as kinship relations, might initially seem too far abstracted from the secondary duties around a right to opacity. But I maintain that they are rather its widest implications, linked through a decolonial responsibility that includes what Joy James calls 'risk-taking commitments' amidst 'the intimidations of political marginalization, despair, and the factionalism of coalition cross fire'.[10]

I contend that feasibility is not simply a judgement concerning a design or project. Dussel's *factibilidad* implies more than a judgement concerning whether or not a goal can be carried out, whether or not it is possible or practicable. As I read it, feasibility is a fruit of participation and solidarity. What becomes practicable is made so through what has been practised. In this sense, practicability does not precede practice. The point is not to act based on some overarching judgement ('Is this possible?') but to act in ways with a view toward desired outcomes ('Let's make this possible'). Ethical actors make alternative futures possible through risk-taking actions. In turn, these actions are linked with one another, relaying a politics of resistance in basic ways. How this works requires further discussion.[11]

In his *Epistemologies of Resistance*, José Medina has argued that resistance is performed through 'chained actions'. 'Acts of resistance are not simply isolated instances without repercussions', he writes.[12] Rather, 'Chained actions are actions that echo or resonate with one another, actions that overlap and share a conceptual space or joint significance, actions that can be aligned and have a (more or less) clear trajectory.'[13] Showing up to a march, supporting local and co-operative organisations, and raising a child in a communal way are all basic examples of chained actions. As Medina emphasises, these actions can be engaged in *before* a movement exists. The metaphor of the chain suggests a 'middle ground between notions of individual and collective action'.[14] When social change is understood as a process, the implicated subject understands that smaller acts start to carry greater importance. Like opacity, feasibility is not a given. Feasibility is always achieved or made – 'fashioned through the act', as Dussel puts it.[15]

Following Dussel's *factibilidad* involves recognising that each actor is not a metaphysical, time-out-of-mind Subject of History but rather that 'they are *subjects or actors*' – plural in that they are acting in concert with others – 'who emerge "historically" in the "diagrams" of power'.[16] As I discussed in the previous chapter, in the errancy of these actors there is a certain temporality and generosity. For Dussel, they 'emerge in certain moments and disappear after having accomplished their concrete function in a certain historical epoch', thus creating the 'possibility for other emerging critical movements'.[17] These are key reminders for elite actors who want to avoid reproducing practices of domination within coalitional efforts.[18] Such reminders stress that actors need to know when to listen to emerging approaches to struggle. For example, in contrast to some Left efforts in US history, today's Movement for Black Lives (M4BL) has argued that 'anti-racism needs to be central, rather than an afterthought, to anti-capitalist politics', as the political theorist Siddhant Issar summarises.[19] Thinking race and class together is only one part of how M4BL 'names the pursuit of another world altogether', as Christopher Paul Harris puts it, a naming that involves 'a temporal experience that is simultaneously now, before, and not yet'.[20]

In turning to positive practices to conceptualise feasibility, I am guided by Drabinski's claim that the postcolonial crisis is an aesthetic crisis. Drabinski poses the following question: 'How can and ought affects of alienation, exile and hope be transmitted, represented and brought to palpable affective presence?'[21] That is, how can and ought already palpable affects of alienation, exile and hope be received, heard and responded to while we are up against the walls elite actors build to secure ourselves from such affects? This question of feeling a palpable presence, and of affectively manifesting in turn, is the question of the activist (protester, manifester). The activist asks in turn: What work is required for a critical arrest? What affects are present in contacts among cultures? How are we to practise what Glissant would call a 'critical approach' (DA 16–17/CD 3)? And what is made possible through its practice?

Glissant makes a distinction similar to Dussel's critical/functional distinction, but in different terms.[22] What Dussel calls functional efforts represent a model of what Glissant calls 'thought of the Other', while critical work is closer to a mode of 'the Other of thought'. Building on this distinction, I will argue that what leads from a functional or establishment position to a critical or oppositional approach is a cultivation of what Gloria Anzaldúa calls *la facultad* ('the faculty'), a capability to sense, understand, and imagine. Like the critical approach of *factibilidad*, *la facultad* is not merely procedural but processual. Understanding *la facultad* asks us to reimagine language and kinship. This imaginative conceptual work is foundational for additional practices of decolonial responsibility.

The Other of Thought

In a setting where the natural attitude is colonial, it is ethically insufficient – it is simply not enough – to think of others, or to try to change the habits of oneself, one's family, one's community, one's country, or to make an effort of living differ-ently.[23] Work must be done, moving must be realised in active, participatory ways. Glissant makes this point in his distinction between 'Thought of the Other' and 'The Other of thought' (PR 169/PO 154). Understanding this distinction prevents an easy politics of charity or a passive, logocentric accountability to another that is not realised in actions. Embodied responses change the actors who undertake them.

One of the functions of aesthetics is to concretise imaginar-ies (PR 220/PO 203). Aesthetic inquiry concretises imaginaries when the questions it asks are less ontological or categorical – 'Is this literature or philosophy, art or something else?' – and more political and invitational, as in 'What follows, in prac-tice and with others, from my experience with this art?' John Berger writes with respect to what happens in engaging tradi-tional forms of art, 'Painting and sculpture are clearly not the most suitable means for putting pressure on the government to nationalize the land.'[24] Nevertheless, in engaging such artwork there is an occurrence 'less direct and more comprehensive'.[25] 'After we have responded to a work of art, we leave it, car-rying away in our consciousness something which we didn't have before.'[26] The question is how this 'which we didn't have before' moves us in turn. This is a question of an experience that precludes an easy return, leaving us wondering about altering our routes. Through his distinction between 'thought of the Other' and 'the Other of thought', Glissant presents an ethical counterpart to Berger's aesthetic point.

Mere 'thought of the Other', Glissant writes, 'is sterile with-out the Other of thought' (PR 169/PO 154). His own words merit attention:

The thought of the Other is the moral generosity disposing me [*m'in-clinerait*] to accept the principle of alterity, to conceive of the world as not simple and straightforward, with only one truth – mine. But thought of the Other can dwell within me without making me alter course [*peut m'habiter sans qu'elle me bouge sur mon erre*], without 'prizing me open' [*m'écarte*], without changing me within myself. An ethical principle, it is enough that I not violate it. The Other of thought is precisely this altering [*ce bougement même*]. Then I have to act. That is the moment I change my thought, without renouncing its contribution. I change, and I exchange. This is an aesthetics of turbulence whose corresponding ethics is not given in advance. If, thus, we allow that an aesthetics is an art of conceiving, imaging and acting, the Other of thought is the aesthetics implemented [*mise en oeuvre*] by me and by you to join the dynamics to which we are to contribute. This is the part fallen to me in an aesthetics of chaos, the work I am to undertake, the path I am to travel [*le travail à entreprendre, le chemin à parcourir*]. The thought of the Other is occasionally presupposed by dominant populations, but with an utterly sovereign power, or proposed until it hurts by those under them, who set themselves free. The Other of thought is always set in motion by its confluences, in which each is changed by and changes the other. (PR 169/PO 154–5, translation modified)

We notice first that the 'moral generosity' with which Glissant describes thought of the Other is close to – perhaps a slight, but only slight, improvement upon – 'giving' in a standard sense, where a politics of charity renders humanitarian development the primary global expression of responsibility today, as Spivak has argued.[27] At the very least, to some extent thought of the Other disposes or inclines the individual away from the position of familiar, settled patterns. And many of us, after all, start from thought of the Other: this is the well-intentioned outreach of humanitarian responsibility, the reformist approach of professional NGOs. But such an inclination is not itself sufficient in light of political and economic catastrophes today. Inclination, disposition or account should not be equated with response. Indeed, there is a certain comfort to thought of the Other – to simply donating some of one's income each month or adding another figure to a syllabus. There can be dwelling without altering. One's route does not have to shift. One can maintain one's habits, one's day-to-day life. Others are tolerated. Sovereignty is maintained.

The key distinction between thought of the Other and the Other of thought turns on the point of maintenance. The Other of thought is a non-maintaining of particular patterns, an altering course. In fact, it is a making of alternative routes. The Other of thought is an interrogation of actions, practices and pursuits. It is a shift in actions in turn. It requires moving and work. Thus, the Other of thought is not a question of temperament. Nor is it merely a one-time choice ('today, yes, I will change and exchange!'). To make such a choice would be to act based on the standards of that time and of one's position. Glissant teaches, by contrast, that a decolonial ethics cannot be decided in advance not only because it is not pre-given or ready-made, but also because it is an ethics of the future, one that is in the process of being imagined (and thus not yet realised) as well as one that is responsible to posterity.

If one falls habitually into thought of the Other, then how does one achieve the Other of thought? If, in Dussel's terms, one is taught to adopt a functional and not a critical approach, then how does one alter course? If implicated subjects begin from the establishment, then how do they move to the opposition? The line of argumentation I have been articulating suggests that – in a context of coloniality – conceiving, imagining and acting will in effect proceed according to the dominant terms. Therefore, to imagine differently is not first a question of (individual) creativity, but of a way of life that precedes and makes possible community. I have described that way – what Glissant called above *le chemin à parcourir* – in terms of participation and solidarity. For those socialised into the coloniality of responsibility, participation and solidarity precede a decolonial imaginary. A first step toward the Other of thought is a kind of becoming-with or participation, 'join[ing] the dynamics toward which we are to contribute'. A second step remains there through solidarity 'in which each is changed by and changes the other'. Only from this non-maintenance of sovereignty that is participation and solidarity, felt initially as disorienting and chaotic, can a fruitful, imaginative reorientation occur.

Here an interlocutor might raise an objection following Ortega's claim in 'Decolonial Woes', namely, that an attention to imagination – to the future that is not yet present – can serve to overlook ongoing work.[28] According to this objection, looking to some future 'beyond' the present performs an erasure of historical and continued labour. Ortega draws attention to the fact that methodological orientation determines conceptual orientation, meaning where one looks for ethical insight determines the insights one finds. By arguing that a decolonial imaginary is secondary to participation and solidarity, I am siding with Ortega.[29] It is only through attention to and support of the decolonial work already underway that a responsible reimagining is conducted.

La Facultad

Participation and solidarity cultivate a required ethical and imaginative capability, what Gloria Anzaldúa calls *la facultad*, meaning most basically 'the faculty' or 'the capacity'. I suggest that Anzaldúa's *facultad* is the 'how' of *factibilidad*. Cultivated with others, it is the hinge between thought of the Other and the Other of thought. It is the capability to move from a politics of charity (false generosity and tolerance) to a politics of participation (errancy and solidarity). Many of us are initially disposed to what Levinas calls the Same. He writes, 'The possibility of possessing, that is, of suspending the very alterity of what is only at first other, and other relative to me, is the *way* of the same.'[30] The Same is a helpful concept because it summarises habits and practices that deny difference or lack receptivity. Segregation, racially discriminatory lending and zoning, calls for closing national borders, and elite international travel all proceed through the way of the Same.[31] Through the becoming-with of participation and the expansive belonging of solidarity, we cultivate our *facultades* and begin to live out modes alternative to standardised models. This also answers the question of the 'when' of feasibility. Understood as more than just the judgement of possibility ('Can I afford to give up my corporate job?'), feasibility comes after participation and solidarity. This is why I discuss feasibility here, in the fourth chapter, only after discussions of participation and solidarity.

Anzaldúa's *facultad* is not a phenomenological bracketing, a kind of *epoché*. That is, *la facultad* is not an accomplishment of the 'I', a certain suspension the philosopher achieves (often by a corn stove or at a writing desk). It is an interruption or a suspension of the 'I' not because one wills it, but in an indirect or expansive way: will is involved, yes, but only because one places oneself with others and works with them, such that, over time, one's previous 'I' is challenged as a new 'I' is cultivated. It is only thorough and thereby after this work that we can imagine alternatively – that we can deem what we are working toward responsible in the face of coloniality.

On Anzaldúa's own terms, '*La facultad* is the capacity to see in surface phenomena the meaning of deeper realities, to see the deep structure below the surface.'[32] 'The one possessing this sensitivity is excruciatingly alive to the world.'[33] *La facultad* is a capability to see from a different place and to see beyond an ideological surface, and thus it is a kind of here-and-now rupture, what she goes on to describe as a 'break in one's defenses and resistance, anything that takes one from one's habitual grounding, causes the depths to open up, causes a shift in perception'.[34] 'This shift in perception', she continues, 'deepens the way we see concrete objects and people.'[35] As I read it, this 'deepening' is less spatial and more relational.

Like Glissant directing us to 'those on the margins, the rebels, the deviants, all specialists in distancing' (PR 170/PO 156), Anzaldúa writes: 'Let's look toward our nepantleras (poetas, artistas, queer, youth, and differently abled) who have a tolerance for ambiguity and difference, la facultad to maintain numerous conflicting positions and affinity with those unlike themselves.'[36] What exactly this 'looking' amounts to requires further explanation, lest *la facultad* be read as merely a gaze toward Others. While *la facultad* is most often a practice of those 'pushed out of the tribe for being different', as Anzaldúa writes, or 'most often developed by those who have been disempowered', as AnaLouise Keating comments, *la facultad* is, Keating goes on to say, 'latent in everyone'.[37] Ortega draws out how, while marginalisation is important to Anzaldúa's concept of *la facultad*, this does not mean there is an essentialism at play: '[T]he epistemic privilege conferred to the new *mestiza* should not be seen as automatically deriving from the experience of liminality or from sharing an indigenous heritage.'[38] Instead of saying that *la facultad* is ontological, that its very existence is derived from a filiation (race, heritage), it can be read as normative. My reading here follows Chela Sandoval, who notes that *la facultad* is 'the learned capacity to read, renovate, and make signs *on behalf of* the dispossessed'.[39] That *la facultad* is a learned capacity also suggests that it is not natural but achieved. Sandoval emphasises this point in a footnote that serves to ground *la facultad* less as an individual practice and more as a capacity cultivated with others amidst struggle – signs made on behalf of the dispossessed not through advocacy but through activism. 'The consciousness that typifies *la facultad* is not naïve to the motives of power', she writes.[40] 'Often dismissed as "intuition"', she continues, 'this kind of "perceptiveness," "sensitivity," consciousness, if you will, is not determined by race, sex, or any other genetic status; neither does its activity belong solely to the "proletariat," the "feminist," or the oppressed.'[41] The consciousness of *la facultad*, she concludes, 'is a learned emotional and intellectual skill that is developed amid hegemonic powers'.[42]

To be sure, Sandoval's claim that *la facultad* is not determined by one's standpoint is not to say that *la facultad* is not conditioned by standpoint. But the concept leaves room for a learning process. Like Glissant's point that errancy is not a renunciation (PR 31/PO 18) – that errancy is not an individualistic withdrawal into some 'pure' realm of contemplation or *theoria* – Sandoval emphasises that *la facultad* is cultivated with others in challenging domination. This is not some kind of wilderness period of learning, nor is it a type of 'study abroad' or tourism, voyaging far away in order to gain some sort of exotic skill. It is, rather, a here-and-now study as well as a breaking-away and a standing-with. From this embodied and embedded situation, perspectival and material shifts are cultivated relationally. Anzaldúa writes:

Seeing through your culture separates you from the herd, exiles you from the tribe, wounds you psychologically and spiritually. Cada arrebatamiento is an awakening that causes you to question who you are, what the world is about. The urgency to know what you're experiencing awakens la facultad, the ability to shift attention and see through the surface of things and situations.[43]

Made through the perceptual shifts of becoming-with and the expansion of belonging, *la facultad* is achieved as a capability to feel with those around us. For those of us on the dominant side of the colonial difference, it is important to note that this is not a kind of metaphysical or new-age sense of interconnection while walking down the street.[44] It requires an active displacement, a shift in places, loyalties, ties and orientations – a break with one's class, with one's previous desires to live like actors in an American Express commercial and then to declare that, yes, 'life is good'. As Anzaldúa puts it, 'When we shift geographical or social positions, another identity may spring into being. Roots grow and ground us in a particular moment or reality *if we're available* to the emotional currents among those present.'[45] Like how elite theorists often misread Lugones's concept of 'world-travelling' to suggest a kind of cosmopolitan, plane-travelling nomadism, it would be easy to misread Anzaldúa's 'shift . . . positions' as a similar endorsement of constant travel and superficial empathy. Importantly, Anzaldúa grounds *la facultad* in seeing through precisely these superficialities. What she is actually pointing to is much more radical – both more grounded and more political. To understand this distinction, we can consider further her sense of 'if we're available'.

Participation and solidarity distinguish what Anzaldúa calls availability from a non-availability in the context of affective standardisation – where certain emotional currents are hegemonic, threatening to render some calls and currents unheard or impalpable. A functional approach, responsible to bureaucrats and other elite figures, is not available. It is able to incline, but not respond. Those who perform a functional practice belong to – are claimed by – those on the dominant side of what Glissant calls 'History [*l'Histoire*]' (PR 37/ PO 25). They have not shifted or renounced their social position, and therefore they have not cultivated the capability to grow amidst alternative (his)stories. The World Bank officer counts Paris as home and stays in four-star hotels when she is on projects in Senegal. Likewise the Georgetown development economist, *mutatis mutandis*. In this functional approach ('thought of the Other'), there has not been what is an initial promise of *la facultad*, what Ortega beautifully calls 'a more reflective everyday existence due to these everyday tears or ruptures of norms and practices'.[46] In the functional model, there is at best reflection, but not rupture – and indeed there can be hyper-reflection at the expense of rupture, as seen in the elite positions 'I just don't know enough yet' or 'this is more complicated than you present it!' – both of which recall that *complicated* and *complicity* share an etymological root.[47]

What is at stake in varying levels of 'availability' is that it is precisely from these potential positions, what we might call receptivity, that we imagine. Presupposing a becoming-with and building-with position, *la facultad* works to imagine from a situation of solidarity. In the 'decolonizing reality' section of *Light in the Dark/Luz en Lo Oscuro*, Anzaldúa explains how this works. 'You must interrupt or suspend the conscious "I" that reminds you of your history and your beliefs because these reminders tie you to certain notions of reality and behavior', she begins.[48] 'Imagination opens the road to both personal and societal change – transformation of self, consciousness, community, culture, society.'[49] Someone who imagines alternatives to colonial models from an elite position maintains patterns of domination, because one has not yet suspended one's sense of what is real. The elite actor keeps his ties to a reality of coloniality. He might be in favour of Indigenous sovereignty, but he still throws on his Ray-Bans and goes on road-trips without asking Indigenous nations if he may pass through their land. In Anzaldúa's language, he is not available.

If imagination is less a matter of innovation and instead more a question of position and practices, then an ethics of *la facultad* severely calls into question standard (functional) approaches to social reform. Thought this way, ethics is less about 'doing the right thing' or aligning oneself with what is proper or respectable, and more about beginning a responsive, dynamic learning process with others. Just as many poets suggest that the aspiring change-agent patiently cultivate their craft as opposed to getting an MFA, studying Anzaldúa might inspire the activist, in certain cases, to cultivate their *facultad* in community service instead of getting a law degree or an applied master's degree.[50] This critical, unprofessional sensibility of *la facultad* is in line with what Edward Said has designated, in regard to speaking truth to power, as 'amateurism', namely,

the desire to be moved not by profit or reward but by love for and unquenchable interest in the larger picture, in making connections across lines and barriers, in refusing to be tied down to a specialty, in caring for ideas and values despite the restrictions of a profession.[51]

La facultad eschews professionalism, which is already caught in the unavailability of busy, and ultimately irresponsible, standardised middle-class living.[52] 'The will to keep one's distance from any form (whatever the distance may be) produced by the system', Glissant states without equivocation, 'is therefore one of the most useful ways to prepare for true creativity' (DA 706–7/ CD 212). 'Any artist who does not abide by this rule', he continues, 'is condemned to neutralise his creativity (consciously or not) in the "business as usual" colonial scheme of things' (DA 707/CD 212).

Deslenguada

An example helps to concretise what is at stake in *la facultad*. We can consider what it means to alter social practices regarding language. A thought-of-the-Other approach would look like allowing for other languages to be spoken in public. It would tolerate non-dominant discourses. By contrast, an Other-of-thought approach would learn other languages and be challenged by them. In his poem 'Las Ciudades Perdidas', the liberation theologian and political radical Ernesto Cardenal writes, 'La palabra "señor" era extraña en su lengua. / Y la palabra "muralla". No amurallaban sus ciudades.'[53] We can read this line in what is perhaps its most obvious translation: that the words 'master' or 'mister' or 'sir', as well as the word 'wall', were foreign to their (Mayan) language, such that they did not wall their cities. 'Señor' here also carries a religious connotation, meaning 'Lord' (with all of its feudal connotations maintained). Cardenal's line, then, makes a point of contrast between Christianity's complicity in colonial domination and Maya ways of life. A more literal reading of his lines highlights how this particular form of domination is foreign to the promise of Maya ethics he draws out: 'The word "master" was strange on their tongue, / as was the word "wall". They did not wall their cities.'

How might Cardenal's description becomes a prescription – how could we read this line receptively in order to sense how it invites a different mode of ethical life today? In my view, Cardenal's description offers one of the most important ethical calls of our time: to estrange ourselves from the *lengua* of masters (hierarchy, especially patriarchy given the gendered 'señor') and walls (such as border walls in the US). Cultivating *la facultad* is the pursuit of this estrangement. To understand the work of ethics this way, we must think of language as one step removed from spoken or written words. We must consider everything that is implied and required such that certain terms can feel foreign on our tongues. For in a society constituted by gender and state violence – as Joy James observes, 'Domestic violence and state violence are so routinely practiced and deployed on the American landscape that they are normalized' – and in a country that continually attempts to wall itself in, perhaps no words are more familiar on our tongues than 'master' and 'wall'.[54]

Glissant's distinction between language used (*langue*) and linguistic bearing (*langage*) explains a useful first step. *Langue* is the 'what' and *langage* is the 'how' with respect to a given language and how it is used (see DA 401–4/CD 120–1; TTM

86, 112, 122). For instance, while Glissant and Walcott do not write in the same *langue*, they can share resonant *langages* in that they are attempting to use their inherited languages to call into question the colonial impositions of that inheritance. The *langage* both Glissant and Walcott practise resonates with what Anzaldúa calls 'deslenguada' – literally meaning something like tongueless and therefore speechless or language-less. But this is not a lack of language in a sense of deficiency. It might be translated more fruitfully as un-languaged, emphasising an intentional way of departing. '*Deslenguadas. Somos los del español deficiente*. We are your linguistic nightmare, your linguistic aberration, your linguistic *mestizaje*, the subject of your *burla*', she writes.[55] *Deslenguada* suggests not the realisation of (career or social) success in its present forms, not achieving the so-called American Dream, but an orienting alternative, an opposition, a failure, a 'nightmare'. She goes on: 'Because we speak with tongues of fire we are culturally crucified. Racially, culturally and linguistically *somos huérfanos* – we speak an orphan tongue.'[56] As opposed to the violent lineages of root identity and its filiation, *deslenguada* is an 'orphan' comportment. Anzaldúa's robust conceptualisation of 'orphan' informs practices of secondary duties around estranging oneself form born-into, biological ties.[57]

Anzaldúa is describing first and foremost 'Chicanas who grew up speaking Chicano Spanish'.[58] Here I abstract from Anzaldúa's specific situation in order to consider *deslenguada* not only as a description of a particular group but as a prescription for others, a bearing to learn from – and thus part of the learning or pedagogy of *la facultad*. In her 'linguistic aberration', the 'err' of errancy is echoed. *Deslenguada* is another way to say a motion of estranging, a work of ethics, which I have endorsed in this study. In a prescriptive register, it is more accurate to say that *deslenguada* is also the goal or result of estranging, a mark of character that is achieved, or something like a regulative ideal. And already in the feminine gender, *deslenguada* is different from what Cardenal so evocatively describes as the *señor* of domination. *Deslenguada*, then, is a bearing or *langage* against the predominant *langue* when that *langue* is understood not only linguistically but also culturally.

In a second step of abstraction, we can read Anzaldúa as presenting a description not only linguistic but also cultural in its scope. Language here is a stand-in for related processes of socialisation. The 'lengua' or 'tongue' is present in the bearing of *deslenguada*. 'The tongue', Loichot observes with subtlety, is 'the target of a double colonization, a double civilization: that of eating and that of speech'.[59] The away-from-*langue* stance that *deslenguada* suggests is helpful in that it suggests taking up a mode that resists both colonisations.

A third colonisation of the tongue – following Lugones in regard to the coloniality of gender – is found in what is expected in terms of sexual practices. What *deslenguada* invites is diffracting these practices. One way of doing so is challenging the operative sense of filial kinship. This challenge attempts to make kin instead of drawing on pre-given bloodlines, and thus it is a kind of orphan practice. Making kin is fundamental to *factibilidad*, to the feasibility of a decolonial responsibility. It provides a relational basis for other decolonial pursuits to be taken up. I address making kin after revisiting Glissant's concept of entanglement, a final concept for the vocabulary of responsibility I am offering.

Entanglements

Glissant's 'entanglements of global relation' is not only a way to describe a phenomenon in the contemporary world but also something to be realised (PR 44/PO 31, translation modified).[60] As I argued in Chapter 1, 'entanglements' can be read in both descriptive and prescriptive senses. To reiterate, now diffracting the concept through the previous and present chapters, it is true that entanglements describe the interconnections – always weighed differentially and informed historically, and therefore never neutral – of our world today. But we can also think of entanglement as something to be made actual, lived toward and demanded. This is the prescriptive sense of entanglement, which is informed by active relays, the right to opacity, and the duties that follow from that right. Pursuits of resistance and relations, through relays, become planetary in scope against forces of globalisation/coloniality. Those resisting coloniality in Palestine engage and inspire those doing the same in Ferguson, in Puerto Rico, in sites where Mexico borders the US, and vice versa.

To endorse 'entanglement' in this chapter is to make it vulnerable to the critique that it obfuscates the violence it describes. Why keep the term, then, much less endorse it? Reading Glissant, the theologian Catherine Keller writes in regard to these objections: 'This is another version of the problem of all relational thought: it is not that relation itself is good or responsible. It is *mindfulness* of relation that plies the ethical.'[61] This is a mindfulness, she writes, opposed to 'the corporate *mindlessness* of entanglement'.[62] For me and for Keller, neither relation nor entanglement themselves present responsible bearings. As I have argued, responsibility is a particular kind of work – it must be taken up, must be achieved actively, communally and continually. I would ask Keller here, then, to go further. The plying – the steady work, travel and unfolding – of the ethical is much more than mindfulness, a word that resonates more with the passivity of a bourgeois yoga class than with the politics of a resistant community.[63] What challenges corporate mindlessness is not mindfulness but politics, as seen in the Xukuru *retomadas* in Brazil.

The ethical import of our entanglements lies in its suggestion of widening and deepening our obligations, our responsibilities.

In this one respect, the Levinasian and my own conceptualisation of responsibility align to some extent: as demands of others
and shared *facultades* gain their respective senses that every
here is an elsewhere, the individual can no longer live responsibly if their actions are not conditioned by those others and
elsewheres. As Keller asks, '[M]ight our planetary entanglement itself ironically expose the violence of the *pax economica*,
the coloniality of its free markets and the hopelessness of its
triumph?'[64] Here Keller is in line with a number of thinkers
important to this study, all of whom have damning criticisms of
what is called 'peace' by the powerful. Levinas is clear-eyed on
this point from the beginning of *Totality and Infinity*: 'The peace
of empires issued from war rests on war.'[65] In an essay on war,
Weil warns about 'a peace which in itself is a new catastrophe'.[66]
And Du Bois worried in the 1940s that a post-war order that did
not shift away from colonisation would create simply 'a peace
resting on force'.[67] But what follows from understanding this
peace as false? Would not such understanding lead to excessive
fatigue, which Simon Critchley calls 'ethical overload', a valo-
risation of passivity that comes at the expense of political pursuits?[68] Indeed, the scope and depth of interconnections might
weigh us down. It is daunting to think of how to begin amidst a
dense web of deeply unjust global entanglements.

One positive practice resonant with the 'making' we hear
in *factibilidad* as well as with Anzaldúa's *facultad*, is that of
making kin. Making kin is a way to think about pursuing
entanglements. Echoing Fanon in his prayer at the end of
Black Skin, White Masks, in concluding her study *Poetics of the
Flesh*, Mayra Rivera calls for an understanding of the entangled
reality of life on this planet today: 'We pray that our bodies
may keep us open to others, to sense the entanglements of
our carnal relations.'[69] Such a sense of entanglement adds
new resonances to Glissant's line: 'Consider that the West
itself has produced the variables to contradict its impressive

trajectory every time. This is the way in which the West is not monolithic, and this is why it is surely necessary that it move toward entanglement' (PR 205/PO 191). Making kin is one example of this moving toward, a *bougement* in the style of the Other of thought.

Making Kin

I borrow the language of making kin from Donna Haraway. Making kin is not a utopian ideal.[70] 'Kin', Haraway asserts, 'must be reconfigured in the contact zones, not on the fantastic right or wrong sides of these immense, complicated matters.'[71] This is to say that there is no pure, unapologetic space for ethical relations on our entangled planet. To affirm someone or something in this context risks the accusation of theodicy or apology – that what we are calling beautiful obfuscates the violence that led to it. On this account, to celebrate the excitement of hearing multiple languages while walking down Bloor Street in Toronto is also to defend the historical events that led to those contacts: the Middle Passage, the colonisation of the Americas, the attempted genocide of Indigenous peoples, and so on.[72] But Haraway's point – and Glissant's – is that this violence is the inherited condition of our modern/colonial present. Despite, or indeed because of this history, only in such contacts can relations be configured. Glissant teaches us to understand ethics in terms of entanglements and weaves much more than withdrawal or purity. It is only from contacts that we move through and toward a poetics of relation.

The reason elite actors need to make kin is simple: implicated subjects cause excessive stresses on the planet, destroying human and non-human ways of living.[73] What is required in response are what Haraway and Adele Clarke call 'new kin inventions', meaning new ways of relating to non-biological ties as well as heightened attention to already occurring radical kin practices.[74] Implicated subjects need to re-describe ways of thinking about our most obvious obligations, our most basic bonds – our responsibilities to others and to a shared planet. Re-description requires 'legitimating vocabularies' for making non-filial bonds.[75] The change in vocabulary is crucial because 'family' in the US context indicates nuclear and biological ties at the expense of wider non-biological relations.

Haraway offers 'making kin' as an alternative to the form of the family. Such a shift does not stigmatise existing children – all children should be cared for and cherished. The goal is to ensure 'that babies are rare, nurtured, and precious and that kin be abundant, surprising, enduring, and treasured'.[76] But how to call for making kin in a way that does not proceed according to the Same, that does not repeat previously coercive methods of a white elite's denying others by various means, including genocide and eugenics?[77] In Haraway's words, 'How to build solidarities with people who need more babies, even while most peoples and communities must learn to flourish with many fewer new babies?'[78]

Haraway and Clarke present making kin in a way that resonates strongly with the shared epistemological practices that guide Glissant's sense of relation: '[P]eople become kin largely by sharing experiences and generating a sense of belonging . . . Kinfolk are parts of one another to the extent that what happens to one is *felt* by the other.'[79] Macro-level forces, such as state residential schools, demand by force only a certain conception of the family. The family is the micro-level that perpetuates those models, models that include how we understand ourselves and how we consider others.

The nuclear family remains the predominant model of relation in the US today. It is a form feminists have long called into question without necessarily challenging its ideal content. In other words, while many feminists agree that the relational content of love, affection and intimacy are goods and perhaps needs of human life, it is not clear that the nuclear family is the ideal form to achieve these social goods.[80] A more open weave also requires work to be done to unravel the binds of constraining ways of understanding families, sexualities and species, and thus to expand responsibilities in a planetary sense.[81]

It is through 'the prepolitics of the family', Keller adds, that many of us learned 'the affective force' of opposing a common enemy, and where, often, 'a fragile harmony would be instantly restored by assent to a common enmity, often racialized'.[82] Thus, the family asserts a friend-enemy distinction as opposed to what Lebovic calls 'a network of solidarity, united against abuse and coercive power'.[83] It is often the case that the response to this friend-enemy distinction is to produce more of your own kind, a protection through filial reproduction. The demand of a kinship weave is different. Haraway's 'weave' – 'a strong regional, integrated environmental and social justice movement led by indigenous communities' – resonates with Glissant's *trame*, with his emphasis on resistance (through a right to opacity) and plurality (through humanities) (see PR 54, 107, 136, 204/PO 42, 93, 122, 190).

The premise underlying the above call – to shift from practices of the family to practices of making kin – is that the form of responsibility determines the content. That is, the form of the traditional family delimits responsibility to a localised unit and often no further. Given such a politics of the family, maintaining the nuclear family reproduces colonial patterns. As Kim TallBear writes, 'If pronatalism involves reproducing the middle-class settler family structure, *no matter* the race or sexual orientation of the middle-class family, I lament it.'[84] This is once again more of a normative than an ontological treatment. TallBear reminds us that responses to the coloniality of kinship are at best communal practices. She writes, 'Decolonization is not an individual choice'.[85] Opposing 'settler sexuality' includes 'opposing norms and policies that reward normative kinship ties (e.g. monogamous legal marriage, nuclear bio-logical family) over other forms of kinship obligation', and it includes 'supporting others in living within nonmonogamous and more-than-coupled bonds'.[86]

Resonant with Glissant's calls to the political and the poetic in resisting integration, TallBear calls ethical actors to both pol-itics and poetics (as making) with a view toward connections beyond the standard family. 'Recognizing possibilities of other kinds of intimacies – not focused on biological reproduction and making population, but caretaking precious kin that come to us in diverse ways – is an important step to unsettling settler sex and family.'[87] Here we can think about the importance of the body (as opposed to the face) in a vocabulary of planetary responsibility, where the overall pursuit is to 'decolonize the ways in which we engage other bodies intimately – whether those are human bodies, bodies of water or land, the bodies of other living beings'.[88] The bodies we deem our kin are those to whom we take ourselves to be responsible. The making involved here, the poetics, involves a remaking or revaluation, a twofold action, as Rivera puts it, both of 'rejecting the pro-jection of flesh conceived as depravity or weakness on certain bodies – bodies of women, peoples of color, nonnormative sex-ualities, persons with disabilities' and of 'revaluing the affec-tive charge of flesh and beauty of the bodies on which it has been projected'.[89] In this way, making kin is not only an ethical but also an aesthetic pursuit, a question of value and revaluing in different ways.

It is important to note that in many cases additional knowl-edge or resources is not necessary to motivate action. 'It is no longer news that corporations, farms, clinics, labs, homes, sciences, technologies, and multispecies lives are entangled', Haraway reminds her readers.[90] Experiments are more impor-tant than over-extended research. If analysis aids imagination, as Glissant writes that it should (PR 184/PO 170), then once the alternative can be imagined, the task is more practical (realising it) than it is theoretical (dwelling with additional potential pitfalls, which, in any case, can only be understood in practice and experience). This is partly why Haraway concludes *Staying with the Trouble* with a story of speculative fiction, a thought experiment, where children have multiple parents, where individuals practise multiple genders, where most people modify their bodies in different ways, and where kin relations are formed and re-formed throughout a life cycle (not just given at birth).[91] Having a baby becomes not something individuals chose to do (a standard couple's 'Should we try for a baby now?') but rather a collective decision emerging from a community.[92]

Some might argue that there is a great distance between practices of making kin and actions that might more properly be called political. But feminists have long asserted the connection of kinship and politics. In an interview regarding resistance to the Line 3 pipeline running through Indigenous land across what is now called Canada and the United States, writer and activist Winona LaDuke connects feelings of belonging and conceptions of kinship to the politics of land:

Marchese: My question is, What do you want white people to be thinking about Native people?

LaDuke: What I want is, I want white people to quit being white people. White is a social construct. I want them to know who the hell they are, and I want them to be not a patriot to a flag but a patriot to a land. That's what I want. The transience of white people has put us in this situation where they don't even know who they are, where they come from; the idea that I'm just going to keep moving to greener pastures. What happened to community and place? I want people to find something and take care of it. I want them to let go of their white privilege and be good humans. We need to address these things, and some people are not going to get it. I'm hoping those people still get that they want to be able to drink the water. Even if you're a Proud Boy, you need the water.

Marchese: Rather than a lack of a sense of community, isn't the bigger problem that too many people's ideas about community and place are not expansive enough?

LaDuke: Yeah, I do think that Americanization is about being insular – the nuclear family, the slightly extended nuclear family. I'm not a nuclear-family person. I live in my community, but my extended family – I feel responsible for hundreds of people in our community. Some people only take care of themselves. That's sad, and it's part of the reason we're in the mess we're in now. Instead of, 'Let's make sure everybody has enough food', we're busy hoarding toilet paper.

Marchese: You've criticized Enbridge for 'paying' the local police. But isn't what's happening that the company is reimbursing law enforcement for expenses that they wouldn't have otherwise incurred? Maybe it's just doublespeak, but that is a slightly different thing than funding them, right?

LaDuke: They've incentivized oppression where cops can get extra money if they take more patrols. So a lot of people are stopped – no reason to stop them but to rack it up. And you know, a couple days ago I was on the river facing a bunch of cops, and I said the corporation violated the law. They had a spill. It's called a frac-out. I said, 'You're here to arrest us, but they're the ones who committed the crime'. It's this betrayal of what you think your officers are for. You assume that 'to serve' would mean to serve you. The other thing is, I can feel the body-burden of hatred. There's this hating on water protectors and Indians that they've incentivized by trying to criminalize us. I really feel it some days.[93]

LaDuke teaches that making kin alerts us to more than constructive possibilities of different futures. It also obligates us to a negative or critical function at present, in which, as TallBear puts it, 'responsibility to ongoing violences' includes 'the responsibility to not only build alter-relations, but also the responsibility to dismantle and shutdown'.[94] Indeed, if Haraway is right to connect the standard family to an 'ongoing daily assent in practice to this thing called capitalism', then in considering erring from the standard family, we are beginning to practise modes of daily dissent from capitalism and coloniality.[95] As Joy James reads Fanon's *Wretched of the Earth*, 'He applauds the restoration of a vocabulary of kinship as a form of resistance: "Brother, sister, friend – these are words outlawed by the colonialist bourgeoisie, because for him my brother is my purse, my friend is part of my scheme for getting on".'[96] But, she reminds us, there has to be a solidarity to this vocabulary. Non-discursive practices follow from the discursive ones: 'The life or death of that expansive kinship is determined by the willingness of its members to share the same body, that is, to suffer its common vulnerabilities and victories as the moving target of colonial and racist repression.'[97] Making kin sees through the connections of the settler family and of elite advocacy that never suffers common vulnerabilities. Brothers, sisters and friends in newly made kin relations work and endure together in a world held in common.

Notes

1. Lebovic, 'Introduction: Complicity and Dissent', p. 8.
2. I would like to thank Andrea Pitts for reading and commenting on this chapter, and thus greatly informing its shape and tone.
3. Mike Watson, 'An Interview with François Maspero: "A Few Misunderstandings"', trans. David Broder, Verso Blog, <https://www.versobooks.com/blogs/1937-an-interview-with-francois-maspero-a-few-misunderstandings>.

4. Martin Puchner, *Poetry of the Revolution: Marx, Manifestos, and the Avant-Gardes* (Princeton: Princeton University Press, 2006).

5. One other way is that poetics, in its many forms of making-with, is a kind of aesthetic training for a new decolonial and planetary politics. See Nikolas Kompridis, 'Introduction' in *The Aesthetic Turn in Political Thought*, ed. Nikolas Kompridis (New York: Bloomsbury, 2014). Kompridis writes: 'If politics is also about what can appear and how it appears to sense, about what can be seen and heard and what can't be seen and heard; if it is about what we are able to see and hear and about what we are unable to see and hear, then *democratic* politics is about letting what could not be seen and heard *be* seen and heard by cultivating new ways of seeing and hearing' (ibid. pp. xvii–xviii).

6. Valérie Loichot, *Water Graves: The Art of the Unritual in the Greater Caribbean* (Charlottesville: University of Virginia Press, 2020), p. 46.

7. Ibid.

8. Ibid. p. 61. See Peter Hallward, *Absolutely Postcolonial: Writing between the Singular and the Specific* (Manchester: Manchester University Press, 2002), p. 105. See also Nick Nesbitt, *Caribbean Critique: Antillean Critical Theory from Toussaint to Glissant* (Liverpool: Liverpool University Press, 2013), p. 184.

9. Dussel, *Ética de la Liberación*, pp. 201, 235–94.

10. James, *Resisting State Violence*, p. 243.

11. For Dussel, *factibilidad* comes after 'practical truth' and 'intersubjective validity', the two other foundations of his ethics. For an introduction to these terms, see Frederick B. Mills, *Enrique Dussel's Ethics of Liberation: An Introduction* (London: Palgrave Macmillan, 2018). '[T]he *feasibility principle* limits the outcome of deliberation to achievable policies and practices', Mills explains (ibid. p. ix). 'None of these universal ethical principles is reducible to one only principle, nor can any one principle guide a liberatory project unless it conditions and is conditioned by the others' (ibid.).

12. José Medina, *The Epistemology of Resistance: Gender and Racial Oppression, Epistemic Injustice, and Resistant Imaginations* (Oxford: Oxford University Press, 2012), p. 225.

13. Ibid.

14. Ibid. p. 226.

15. Dussel, *Ethics*, p. 159, table 6.
16. Ibid. p. 354.
17. Ibid.
18. See Derrick A. Bell Jr., 'Brown v. Board of Education and the Interest-Convergence Dilemma', *Harvard Law Review* 93, no. 3 (1980): pp. 518–533.
19. Siddhant Issar, 'Listening to Black lives matter: racial capitalism and the critique of neoliberalism', *Contemporary Political Theory* (2020): p. 66.
20. Christopher Paul Harris, 'For the Culture: #BlackLives Matter and the Future Yet to Come', *The South Atlantic Quarterly* 121, no. 3 (2022): p. 493. Harris goes on: 'Black culture, and performance – an unapologetic Black joy – were centered at and central to the aesthetics of the uprisings . . . The critical and world-making disposition of Black culture is not for Black people alone' (ibid. p. 494).
21. Drabinski, *Levinas and the Postcolonial*, pp. 154–5.
22. For this distinction, see Dussel, *Ethics*, pp. 331, 326.
23. For the language of a colonial natural attitude, see Lisa Guenther, 'A Critical Phenomenology of Solidarity and Resistance in the 2013 California Prison Hunger Strikes', in *Body/Self/Other: A Phenomenology of Social Encounters*, ed. Luna Dolezal and Danielle Petherbridge (Albany: State University of New York Press, 2017), p. 55.
24. John Berger, 'Redrawing the Maps', in *Landscapes*, p. 96.
25. Ibid.
26. Ibid.
27. Spivak, 'Responsibility', p. 21.
28. See Ortega, 'Decolonial Woes'.
29. Cf. Emma Pérez, *The Decolonial Imaginary: Writing Chicanas into History* (Bloomington: Indiana University Press, 1999).
30. See TI 27/EE 38.
31. Hence Levinas describes the work of ethics as follows: 'A work conceived radically is a movement of the Same toward the Other which never returns to the Same' (Emmanuel Levinas, 'Meaning and Sense', in *Collected Philosophical Papers* (Dordrecht: Martinus Nijhoff, 1987), p. 91).

32. Gloria Anzaldúa, *Borderlands/La Frontera: The New Mestiza* (San Francisco: Aunt Lute Books, 1987), p. 38

33. Ibid.

34. Ibid. p. 39.

35. Ibid.

36. Ibid. p. 94.

37. AnaLouise Keating, ed., *The Gloria Anzaldúa Reader* (Durham, NC: Duke University Press, 2009), p. 321. Mariana Ortega puts it this way: *La facultad* is 'a survival tactic that according to Anzaldúa is latent in all of us but that is particularly honed by border dwellers that constantly face difficult situations or those who do not feel psychologically or physically safe in the world. It constitutes what Anzaldúa calls a shift in perception that deepens our awareness and vision of everyday objects and people' (Ortega, *In-Between*, p. 37). Paula Moya disagrees strongly with what she calls Sandoval's postmodern reading of *la facultad*, and by extension with Keating's reading of latency; Moya contends that the pain of the development of *la facultad* is missed when it is opened up to everyone (Paula Moya, *Learning from Experience* (Berkeley: University of California Press, 2002), pp. 86–91). In my view, Cynthia Paccacerqua's take on *la facultad*, taking into account both potentiality and actuality, honours some of Moya's concerns while staying closest to the invitational sense I read in Anzaldúa's text: 'Although *la facultad* is a potential within all subjects, it is clearly evidenced in peoples subjected to violent cycles of shifting hierarchies of power and symbolic orders. They are thus painfully well adjusted to undergo the critical labor of individuation' (Cynthia M. Paccacerqua, 'Gloria Anzaldúa's Affective Logic of *Volverse Una*', *Hypatia: A Journal of Feminist Philosophy* 31, no. 2 (2016): p. 344).

38. Ortega, *In-Between*, p. 34.

39. Chela Sandoval, *Methodologies of the Oppressed* (Minneapolis: University of Minnesota Press, 2000), p. 60. Emphasis mine. I would like to thank Sandoval for related conversations at the 2019 Philosophies of Liberation Encuentro.

40. Ibid. p. 195, n. 52.

41. Ibid.

42. Ibid.

43. Anzaldúa, *Light in the Dark/Luz en lo Oscuro: Rewriting Identity, Spirituality, Reality* (Durham NC: Duke University Press, 2015), p. 125. These lines resonate with how Stuart Hall thinks about shifts in culture: 'Culture is not just a voyage of rediscovery, a return journey. It is not an "archaeology". Culture is a production . . . It is therefore not a question of what our traditions make of us so much as what we make of our traditions. Paradoxically, our cultural identities, in any finished form, lie ahead of us. We are always in the process of cultural formation. Culture is not a matter of ontology, of being, but of becoming' (Stuart Hall, 'Thinking the Diaspora: Home-Thoughts from Abroad', in *Essential Essays Vol. 2: Identity and Diaspora*, ed. David Morley (Durham, NC: Duke University Press, 2019), pp. 221–2).

44. For the notion of 'colonial difference', see Walter D. Mignolo, 'The Geopolitics of Knowledge and the Colonial Difference', *The South Atlantic Quarterly* 101, no. 1 (2002): pp. 57–96.

45. Anzaldúa, *Light in the Dark/Luz en lo Oscuro*, p. 83, emphasis mine.

46. Ortega, *In-Between*, p. 59. It is important to note, especially as I will describe *deslenguada* as a bearing, that Ortega distinguishes between two kinds of ruptures: '[T]here are different senses of not being-at-ease, including what I regard as a *thin* sense of not being-at-ease, the experience of minimal ruptures of everyday practices, and a *thick* sense of not being-at-ease, the experience of a deeper sense of not being familiar with norms, practices, and the resulting contradictory feelings about who we are given our experience in the different worlds we inhabit and whether those worlds are welcoming or threatening' (ibid. p. 61). I am presenting the cultivation of *la facultad* as a becoming-available to the thick sense of not being-at-ease.

47. As you would guess by now, I find liberation theology's language of 'break' with one's class more fruitful than the Levinasian 'rupture'.

48. Anzaldúa, *Light in the Dark/Luz en Lo Oscuro*, p. 44.

49. Ibid.

50. Anzaldúa writes, 'A university is a private space that's been made public so that it offers a kind of safety and containment to draw in students . . . In reality, this space is only secure and safe and comfortable for people complicit in the system. But if you're a resister, a challenger, if you're an activist it's a very uncomfortable place, an alienating place' (Gloria Anzaldúa, 'Doing Gigs' in *Interviews/Entrevistas*, ed. AnaLouise Keating (Routledge, New York: 2000), p. 231). She says in a separate interview: 'But does the school listen to its undergraduates, to its community people who don't have a standing in their community? No, it tries to win them over, seduce them into mainstream ways of thinking'; and she continues, speaking to students: 'Will they change in ways that the group in power wants them to, or will they seek out their new identity and follow their own direction?' ('Making Alliances', in ibid. p. 199).

51. Edward W. Said, *Representations of the Intellectual* (New York: Vintage, 1994), p. 76.

52. Authors in Critical Legal Studies put the experience of deprofessionalisation this way: 'For the lawyer, the experience of deprofessionalization can be equally significant, because it requires giving up the pseudo-power that the State has bestowed upon her in exchange for the actual power of discovering a way of working that is expressive of her true political being. The notions held by many lawyers that one should feel guilty about being a professional, that political change must be brought about by others, that lawyers "can't do anything" – all of these are mere expressions of a false consciousness resulting from a sense of powerlessness' (Peter Gabel and Paul Harris, 'Building Power and Breaking Images: Critical Legal Theory and the Practice of Law', *N.Y.U. Review of Law & Social Change* XI:369 (1982–3): p. 410).

53. Ernesto Cardenal, 'Las Ciudades Perdidas', in *Nueva Antología Poética* (Mexico DF: Siglo XXI Editores, 2006), p. 141.

54. Joy James, 'Sorrow: The Good Soldier and the Good Woman', in *Warfare in the American Homeland: Policing and Prison in a Penal Democracy*, ed. Joy James (Durham, NC: Duke University Press, 2007), p. 70.

55. Anzaldúa, *Borderlands/La Frontera*, p. 58.
56. Ibid.
57. Cf. Eduardo Mendieta, 'The Jargon of Ontology and the Critique of Language', *The Aesthetic Ground of Critical Theory: New Readings of Benjamin and Adorno*, ed. Nathan Ross (Lanham, MC: Rowman & Littlefield, 2015), p. 62.
58. Ibid.
59. Loichot, 'Between Breadfruit and Masala: Food Politics in Glissant's Martinique'. *Callaloo* 30, no. 1 (2007): p. 126.
60. Paul Gilroy provides an example of a reading of Glissant's concept of relation aligned with how I read it. 'His creative use of [relation]', Gilroy writes, 'brings a concern with what has been relayed together with a critical interest in relative and comparative approaches to history and culture and attention to what has been related in both senses of that word: kinship and narration. Approaching the issue of relation in this spirit requires a sharp departure from all currently fashionable obligations to celebrate incommensurability and cheerlead for absolute identity' (Paul Gilroy, *Against Race: Imagining Political Culture beyond the Color Line* (Cambridge, MA: The Belknap Press of Harvard University Press, 2000), p. 7).
61. Keller, *Cloud of the Impossible*, p. 255.
62. Ibid.
63. When the Harvard Business Review writes a self-help book on a concept or practice, we wonder about its political valence. See *Mindfulness* (Boston: Harvard Business Review Press, 2017). That said, the question of mental health amidst participation in decolonial movements remains a very important one, and one I attend to insufficiently in this study. I look forward to learning from the work of others regarding this topic. Thanks to Bukky Gbadegesin for related questions.
64. Keller, *Cloud of the Impossible*, p. 255.
65. TI 6/EE 22.
66. Simone Weil, 'Cold War Policy in 1939', in *Selected Essays*, trans. Richard Rees (Eugene, OR: Wipf & Stock, 1962), p. 180. Cf. Murad Idris, *War for Peace: Genealogies of a Violent Ideal in Western and Islamic Thought* (Oxford: Oxford University Press, 2018).

67. Du Bois, *Color and Democracy*, p. 246. He went on: 'So long as colonial imperialism exists, there can be neither peace on earth nor goodwill toward men' (ibid. p. 304).

68. Simon Critchley, *Infinitely Demanding: Ethics of Commitment, Politics of Resistance* (New York: Verso, 2007), p. 68.

69. Mayra Rivera, *Poetics of the Flesh* (Durham, NC: Duke University Press, 2015), p. 158.

70. Social theory and anthropology have stressed the point of treating kin as made and not given. Pierre Bourdieu writes, 'To treat kin relationships as something people *make*, and with which they do something, is not merely to substitute a "functionalist" for a "structuralist" interpretation, as current taxonomies believe; it is radically to question the implicit theory of practice which causes the anthropological tradition to see kin relationships "in the form of an object or an intuition", as Marx puts is, rather than in the form of the practices which produce, reproduce, and use them by reference to necessarily practical functions' (Pierre Bourdieu, *Outline of a Theory of Practice* (Cambridge: Cambridge University Press, 1977), pp. 35–6).

71. Donna Haraway, 'Making Kin in the Chthulucene: Reproducing Multispecies Justice', in MKNP, p. 87. Italics removed for ease of reading.

72. Cf. Glissant's critique of *métissage*, which can celebrate beauty while obfuscating the original violence (PR 46/PO 34).

73. See MKNP, p. 1. It is important to note here that this is a recent 'crisis' only among dominant populations. Indigenous people in the US, for example, already know too well what it means to have land taken from them. Black people are too familiar with being robbed of body and knowledge, language, and relations. It is cultural elites and primarily white people, then, for whom there is a sort of shock about the potential of loss of life (Michele Murphy, 'Against Population, Towards Alterlife', in MKNP, p. 117). To respond again to the question of audience: in advancing making kin, I am speaking only to dominant populations.

74. Clarke, 'Introducing *Making Kin Not Population*', in MKNP, pp. 2–3.

75. Ibid. p. 31.

76. Donna Haraway, 'Making Kin', in MKNP, p. 91. Italics removed.

77. As Ruha Benjamin notes about Black women's having their fallopian tubes tied without their consent, 'Eugenic sensibilities and practices are alive and well' (Ruha Benjamin, 'Black AfterLives Matter: Cultivating Kinfulness as Reproductive Justice', in MKNP p. 56).

78. Haraway, 'Making Kin', in MKNP p. 98.

79. Ibid. pp. 2–3.

80. '[A]ffection, security, intimacy, sexual love, parenthood and so on', Michèle Barrett and Mary McIntosh acknowledge in their classic critique of the promises of the nuclear heterosexual family, 'are not artificial' (Michèle Barrett and Mary McIntosh, *The Anti-Social Family* (New York: Verso, 2015), p. 133). They go on to present the family's affective content 'as human needs, not pathological constructs', but the form in which these needs are currently met 'we regard as both unsatisfying and anti-social' (ibid.).

81. Donna J. Haraway, *Staying with the Trouble: Making Kin in the Chthulucene* (Durham, NC: Duke University Press, 2016), p. 102. Cf. Allison Weir, *Identities and Freedom: Feminist Theory between Power and Connection* (Oxford: Oxford University Press, 2013).

82. Catherine Keller, *Political Theology of the Earth: Our Planetary Emergency and the Struggle for a New Public* (New York: Columbia University Press, 2018), p. 24.

83. Lebovic, 'Introduction: Complicity and Dissent', p. 8.

84. Kim TallBear, 'Making Love and Relations Beyond Settler Sex and Family', in MKNP, p. 152.

85. Ibid. Italics removed.

86. Ibid.

87. Ibid. p. 154.

88. Ibid. p. 161. In regard to what these insights offer Continental ethics, we can consider also how Jean-Luc Marion concludes his discussion of humanitarian donation in *Being Given*. '[T]he gift can be given *without regard for the face of the Other*; and if one admits that ethics is governed by the silent injunction of the face of the Other, by definition transcendent because Other,

then', he concludes, 'the gift does not fall strictly within ethics' (Jean-Luc Marion, *Being Given: Toward a Phenomenology of
Givenness*, trans. Jeffrey L. Kosky (Stanford: Stanford University
Press, 2002), p. 88). Marion's claim that humanitarian giving
proceeds 'without regard for the face of the Other' only makes
sense if he erases the existence of the face soliciting money
in the first place ('because he perhaps does not exist'). Thus,
we find another 'blanched' encounter, here under the guise
of being 'bracketed'. Further, it is clear in that section of *Being
Given* that the humanitarian operation Marion endorses still
relies on the face understood as, in Levinas's terms, a 'moral
summons' (TI 213/EE 196). For the limits of the metaphor of
the face in response ethics, see also Kelly Oliver, 'Witnessing,
Recognition, and Response Ethics', *Philosophy & Rhetoric* 48, no.
4 (2015): p. 474.

89. Rivera, *Poetics*, p. 119.
90. Haraway, *Staying with the Trouble*, p. 115.
91. Ibid. p. 138.
92. Ibid. p. 139.
93. David Marchese, 'Winona LaDuke Feels That President Biden
    Has Betrayed Native Americans', *New York Times*, 6 August 2021,
    <https://www.nytimes.com/interactive/2021/08/09/magazine/
    winona-laduke-interview.html>.
94. TallBear, 'Making Love', in MKNP, p. 123.
95. Haraway, *Staying with the Trouble*, p. 50.
96. Joy James, '"Concerning Violence": Frantz Fanon's Rebel Intel-
    lectual in Search of a Black Cyborg', *South Atlantic Quarterly* 112,
    no. 1 (2013): p. 58.
97. Ibid.

5 The Limits of Ethics and the Question of Political Commitment

Summary of Study

Today many humanitarian and human rights organisations project their ethical ideals through colonial models of development and protection. A more critical strand of human rights discourse responds to acknowledged global injustices with minimal demands that are simply not enough to challenge capitalism and coloniality.[1] In light of this context, *Choose Your Bearing* has argued that if theorists of rights discourse are to take decolonial concerns seriously, we will both recognise the nation state as a generally predatory entity (against minorities and immigrants) and move from a model of minimal advocacy for the downtrodden to a model of maximal activism. In this way, we would make demands on the institutions and actors that keep a majority of people across the world down in the first place. Conversely, this book has also suggested that decolonial theory should reconsider its critique of human rights. The primary and secondary duties that third-generation (solidarity) rights claims entail provide a way for people to connect to decolonial work through the terms that are already the most important to them. More specifically, the duties of Glissant's right to opacity fall on elite actors in the West. Standing with others is a primary duty that supports the right to opacity in an age of colonial resource extraction and blatant violations of land rights across the planet. Enacting the secondary duties around the right to opacity could look like attending to what we purchase or boycott, where we live, to what we belong, whom we consider kin, and what risks we are willing to take in our personal and professional lives. As opposed to the position- and career-maintaining efforts of professional reforms, this is ethical work found in much more banal, much less prestigious disengagements from professional spaces as they are. But this is not a withdrawal in the sense of denying the world. Like a boycott, this is an action verified by a community, and this community can be organised by rights claims made in different parts of the world. Its collective actions aim to uphold political, economic and cultural rights internationally. In this way, the local mode of engagement that lives out the primary and secondary duties of a right to opacity embodies a provincial bearing that does not become a provincialism, but that instead participates in a radical internationalism (DA 438/CD 146). The larger point here is that colonisation is not just a question of states and economies; it is a question of everyday life. In other words, by reading Glissant, Coulthard, Weil, Anzaldúa, Hall and Du Bois in this book, I am trying to raise questions for ethical theory that Jeanne Morefield, by reading Edward Said, has raised for political theory.[2]

The Limits of Ethics

It is worthwhile, in closing, to consider the limits of this study. 'Participation' can function to compartmentalise spheres of life: someone might participate in a protest but still vacation as if the land is their own, purchase seasonal and imported clothing items made in conditions of slavery, and vote for politicians who start wars. For these reasons, participation requires a wider sense of solidarity, one that asks elite actors to find spaces of belonging different from the options they are often born into, especially the jingoistic nation state, the professional career path and the patriarchal family. But even when elite actors negate their socialisation, they risk colonising other communities. For instance, today we witness elites gentrifying neighbourhoods as much as they are arrogating leadership to themselves in coalitional settings, an arrogation which betrays the radical potential of the coalition. Anzaldúa offers a way for actors to work together attentively through her concept of *la facultad*, a faculty developed over a long, humble apprenticeship. But my reading of cultivating *la facultad* comes close to setting the goal of ethics as yet another kind of self-improvement project, where elite actors once again try to purify their soul more than to challenge repressive structures. And perhaps the kind of poetic making-with I have called for in local settings and daily life is really another iteration of, more than a departure from, Levinas's ideal ethical relation as bearing witness, which I criticised in Chapter 1. Is there a bearing witness that could be political?[3] Or is witnessing the mark of political failure – is it all we have left when pipelines are still being built and trees are still understood as commodities?[4] Another limitation of my inquiry into decolonial responsibility is that, in the terms of the philosopher Nikolas Kompridis's wonderful book *Critique and Disclosure*, I have promoted critical practices more than an openness to how the world discloses itself.[5] *Choose Your Bearing* has emphasised learning from under-studied traditions, but it has not stayed with the deeply human need to learn from the land and the water themselves. Where do these limitations leave justice-oriented actors today?

* * *

When actors in the West respond to ethical appeals only through interpersonal ethics, ethics proceeds through a conceit: it attempts, without revolutionary force, to get the powerful to cede power. Such an ethics tends to treat political problems in non-political ways. For instance, Oxfam addresses global gaps in standards of living through donations. Charity: Water looks to increase access to clean water without challenging the companies that extract and contaminate water in the first place. Scholars at university-based ethics centres rarely raise questions about the corporations and philanthropists who fund their centres. Overall, neoliberal charities and many ethicists prefer to pose problems in ethical terms. It is easier to gain funding and maintain institutional respectability that way. Thus, we are not yet outside of the problematic that the journalist José Carlos Mariátegui diagnosed in his 1920s Marxist writings on Indigenous people and land in Peru, namely, the tendency to see all social problems as ethical ones – the 'liberal, humanitarian, enlightened nineteenth-century attitude that in the political sphere of the Western world inspires and motivates the "leagues of human rights"'.[6] 'Humanitarian teachings', Mariátegui continues, 'have not halted or hampered European imperialism, nor have they reformed its methods.'[7] This is why, as a socialist, he wants to start by 'declaring the complete obsolescence of the humanitarian and philanthropic points of view'.[8] In other words, having made this diagnosis, he moves from ethics to politics: 'The struggle against imperialism now relies only on the solidarity and strength of the liberation movement of the colonial masses.'[9]

In the US context at our present conjuncture, the moral or humanitarian point of view is not obsolete. But we ethical theorists would do well to acknowledge our own limitations, including those of ethical inquiry itself. Philosophising with the hammer of ethics may lead not to figuring out whether old ethical ideas are hollow, but only to believing all practical problems are ethical nails. Humanitarian sentiment is a point of departure. The work of ethics is valuable to the extent that it contributes to the strength of contemporary anti-capitalist and decolonial movements. Sometimes the framing of a problem as a moral one is only a step on the way to understanding it as a political one. Any ethics worth its salt offers not just a critique but a construction, not just a provocation but a path.[10] In the face of massive environmental and cultural destruction today, justice-oriented actors would do well to return to the post-World War II decolonial spirit of making maximal demands – and we need to make these demands not only on the repressive states in which we live, but also on each other, calling those around us to live up to the commitments we claim to hold. Such political and ethical demands follow an old Marxist point: a worthwhile 'ethical project', as Aijaz Ahmad puts it, should be 'materialized as the *praxis* of a revolutionary transformation of an ethically intolerable world'.[11]

The Question of Political Commitment

The final question for this book to consider, then, is one of political commitment. The term is Stuart Hall's. Hall opens his 1966 essay 'Political Commitment' by arguing that such commitment is less about taking a position ('I'm against corporations!') and more about consciousness, meaning one's knowledge of and holistic stance in the political context of one's time. This kind of consciousness, he notes, has declined in his time. Quite simply, Hall says, 'A giving of the whole self to politics, the harnessing and orchestrating of one's life around a political commitment, is a stance adopted by fewer and fewer people . . . it is a personal style which runs against the grain of contemporary feelings and attitudes'.[12] His essay, then, is less about the political commitment of his time and more about its absence, which occurs for three reasons.

The first is that influential media outlets and leading politicians of various parties all describe politics as 'middle-ranged, the art of the possible'.[13] Joe Biden's victory in the 2020 Democratic primary, fuelled by his reputation as the 'avatar of normalcy' and his call for bi-partisanship, exemplifies this tendency in our time.[14] Biden's politics, operating through the status quo, provides yet another example of the ultimately conservative, minimally reformist model of politics that has come, as Hall puts it, 'to be the dominant model of political action among both conservative and radical groupings in society (and especially in the political parties)'.[15]

The second reason Hall diagnoses for the absence of political commitment is that teachers and mentors funnel the political energies of students into formal studies, effectively making politics 'degutted' as it is transmuted into mere social inquiry.[16] Hall's essays tarried with this transmutation across his intellectual life. For instance, in the fifth of the lectures that became *Cultural Studies 1983*, he extended this criticism to French theory: 'By reducing theory to a question of internal conceptual coherence and textual privilege', some post-structural theory 'opened the door to theoreticism which privileges a logical and epistemological rigor at the expense of the extremely difficult question of how thought is articulated to social relations'.[17] Critical theorists who would position themselves on the Left despite divergent views, from Ahmad in the 1990s to Bernard Harcourt in 2020, have shared Hall's criticism of theory as too self-referential, such that theory too often fails to contest predominant forms of life on the terrain where those forms gain strength, such as in public schools and across new forms of media.

Hall's third explanation for a lack of political commitment is that mass media has penetrated society such that political values are diluted into 'consumption values'.[18] Reading articles on humanitarian crises and human rights violations in *The New York Times* or *The Economist* also means exposing oneself to advertisements of luxurious watches, jewellery and clothing – the making of which, in mining and production, fuels the environmental devastation that causes the humanitarian crises in the first place. We start reading an article; with a click, we might end up buying a bracelet whose production abets the crises. Political inquiry can, in our computerised age, become ironically transmuted into consumption.

What these three ways of minimising true political commitment share is a placement of class-based conflict in the background. Political issues, such as enduring economic inequality, seem to recede as mainstream candidates declare they will bring us all together, academics lose sleep over the coherence of their essays, and students face advertising of shoes, sunglasses and bracelets claiming to help refugees or plant trees with every purchase. If politics, as Hall teaches, is 'the *form* in which the connexions are made between lived experience and the demands made upon the system', then the above 'Left' forms, as ultimately capitalist and individualised, are neoliberal: endorse the candidate who won't make healthcare a right for all, publish your way to the upper-middle class, and look good while on the hustle.[19]

Hall's corrective steers Left actors away from directly siding with the political party that gets the most votes and has considerable institutional power. One of his concerns is that simply stating a position serves as an evasion of a more total sense of commitment, the now largely absent 'giving of the whole self to politics' that he diagnosed in opening the essay.[20] Against simply taking a position in this sense of self-presentation, he reiterates the need for social movements 'to develop forms, structures, and relationships which represent real alternatives to those which belong, typically, to the dominant social system'.[21] The social movements he has in mind are the related New Left and anti-nuclear movements that emerged in response to political events in 1956, when Israel, Britain and France invaded Egypt to take control of the Suez Canal and when Soviet troops invaded Hungary to quash democratic resistance.

The question of this final chapter becomes: What is the relationship between rights claims and political commitment? This is a reiteration of the book's guiding question. Once again, we will find that there is no necessary or guaranteed relation. For that reason, rather than prescribe a fixed and universal orientation to rights, I will examine W. E. B. Du Bois's strategic use, and subsequent abandonment, of the language of human rights in the late 1940s. From this example, contemporary readers will gain a sense of the strengths and limitations of rights discourse for motivating or foreclosing wider practices of political commitment, because the tensions between capitalism and socialism that Du Bois navigated in the late 1940s remain central to human rights advocacy today.

W. E. B. Du Bois's Critique of Elite Human Rights Discourse

W. E. B. Du Bois exemplifies political commitment. His lifelong struggle on behalf of Black people, other minorities, and dispossessed people more broadly includes several shifts in position and strategy. Following Black Studies scholar Charisse Burden-Stelly, instead of understanding Du Bois's strategic shifts as 'inconsistency, contradiction, and backpedaling', I think it makes the most sense to acknowledge his 'flexibility and experimentation, deep attunement to the problems of the time, consistent self-reflection, and an abiding dedication to liberation and equality'.[22] Perhaps none of his flexible and experimental strategies better reflects his political commitment than his brief use of, and then departure from, the discourse of human rights in the late 1940s.

Du Bois had long advocated in favour of expanding political rights in order to achieve true democracy in the United States. Although political rights are part of human rights, it is worth maintaining the distinction here in order to allow his critique of the latter to emerge. Further, while an exhaustive examination of his relationship to civil, economic and cultural rights is beyond the scope of this chapter, understanding his promotion of and departure from human rights claims in the 1940s requires a sense of his previous advocacy for other rights. Hearing his own voice making such claims remains inspirational.

In a 1906 meeting associated with the Niagara Movement, Du Bois leveraged rights claims to call for federal enforcement of the Fourteenth Amendment, one of the Reconstruction amendments.[23] 'We claim for ourselves every single right that belongs to a freeborn American political, civil, and social', he said.[24] '[A]nd until we get these rights we will never cease to protest and to assail the ears of America. The battle we wage is not for ourselves alone but for all true Americans.'[25] He was also known for connecting the struggle of gaining civil rights for Black people to that of gaining civil rights for women. At the February 1919 Pan-African Congress, for instance, he noted that no one more than women appreciates 'the struggle for broader rights and liberties'.[26] His advocacy for rights across struggles means that his defence of civil rights can be described as part of his 'militant liberalism', to use Burden-Stelly's term.[27] 'Militant liberalism', she continues, 'was one framework through which Du Bois advocated political and juridical freedom for African descendants, enjoined the best and brightest class of Black leaders to use their skills and resources to serve and uplift the race, positioned culture emanating from Africa and its diaspora as the special provenance and gift of Black people, and encouraged personal and group responsibility.'[28] It makes sense to talk about Du Bois's rights claims in the first few decades of the 1900s through liberalism because he was not yet a Marxist.

It was not until 1933 that Du Bois studied Marx intensively. As his biographer David Levering Lewis describes, he was 'self-instructed' in Marxism: it was 'Marx in months, not years'.[29] Informed by this self-guided turn, at Atlanta University he taught 'Karl Marx and the Negro Problem' and 'The Economic History of the Negro'. The course on Marx specifically included studies of *Capital* and *The Communist Manifesto*.[30] Importantly, Du Bois's most substantial engagement with human rights discourse came after his engagement with Marx, meaning that he did not see Marxist and human rights projects as incompatible, or at least not in theory. Now, it is true that prior to the 1940s, he had made some political claims through the language of human rights. For instance, having joined the Socialist party in 1911, he wrote in *The Crisis* in 1912 regarding Socialist presidential candidate Eugene V. Debs that, out of Woodrow Wilson, Teddy Roosevelt, Howard Taft and Debs, '[Debs] alone, by word and deed, stands squarely on a platform of human rights regardless of race or class.'[31] This early usage notwithstanding, the 1940s remains the period in which Du Bois's now-Marxist claims to human rights are the most instructive for the question of political commitment today.

Through the course of the 1940s, human rights discourse became a substitute for the 1941 Atlantic Charter, which was a formal expression and not a treaty – it was not even signed. But it did include the promise of self-government, which would allow nations to define their own statehood and political form. 'Self-government' was a hint at self-determination, meaning the independence of colonies. In part with this line about self-government in mind, in his 1945 *Color and Democracy*, to which I will return in more detail below, Du Bois writes, 'The Atlantic Charter brought a new examination of the colonial question.'[32] The Atlantic Charter's allusion to self-determination contrasts with the 1948 Universal Declaration of Human Rights (UDHR). The UDHR lacked a line about self-determination. This lack clearly demonstrated that after the war, France, Britain and the US desired to maintain their empires. In the wake of World War II, then, human rights and decolonisation became two separate ideas of international organisation. These two distinct traditions at the United Nations (UN) were eventually brought together through decades of anti-colonial organising around the right to self-determination.[33] Ultimately, however, as an elite and individualistic version of human rights discourse gained traction in international institutions, the separation between human rights discourse and a decolonial world-making imaginary would lead Du Bois to depart from human rights discourse after only a few years of leveraging it strategically.

In 1944 Du Bois, now in his seventies, said of colonisation, 'This is the problem to which I propose to devote the remaining years of my life.'[34] He would make good on this proposal. Also in 1944, he left Atlanta University to start his second period at the NAACP. Walter White, the NAACP's executive secretary, asked him to come back to the organisation to give advice to the US government about colonialism in allied territories around World War II. Back in New York, Du Bois aimed to push the NAACP from pursuing mainly questions of national courts and civil rights to raising questions of international courts and human rights. This was a continuation of the trajectory of his study and practice: during his final days at Atlanta University, he worked to secure sponsors for the Fifth Pan-African Congress. One response to this work that interested him was from Amy Jacques Garvey, who asked him to draft an African Freedom Charter to complement the Atlantic Charter.[35] Then, when Riverside Church's eminent pastor Harry Emerson Fosdick responded to Du Bois's invitation for a workshop on developing the Pan-African Congress by questioning his label of an international colonial conference, Du Bois reminded the pastor that 'seven hundred and fifty million people on this earth live in colonies and have rights to which no white nation is bound to respect'.[36] In late 1944 he criticised the American Jewish Committee's 'Declaration of Human Rights' for failing to mention the general rights deprivation of people living in colonies in Africa and Asia.[37] Du Bois's attunement to the rights of colonised peoples in late 1944, coupled with his increasing sense of the insufficiencies of liberal rights claims, illustrates steps in his shift from militant liberalism, refracted through his readings of Marx, to what the scholar of American Studies Bill Mullen calls his 'revolutionary optimism'.[38]

Du Bois would press his critique of colonisation further in 1945. In March of that year, at a briefing in Washington on the Bretton Woods Conference, he attempted, we could say, to stop the nascent International Monetary Fund before it took its first steps. 'Seven hundred and fifty million people, a third of mankind, live in colonies', he said to assistants of the US Secretary of the Treasury.[39] 'Cheap colonial labor and materials are basic to post-war industry and finance. Was this matter mentioned in any form in Bretton Woods?'[40] In April 1945 he attended the United Nations conference in San Francisco, where the UN Charter was signed and the organisation was formed. There he was disappointed that the US government did not press questions of ongoing colonialism with its European allies – that it departed from the promise of the Atlantic Charter. One month into the conference, Du Bois's *Color and Democracy: Colonies and Peace* appeared.

Color and Democracy can be read as an extension of his 1915 *Atlantic* essay 'The African Roots of War', where he claimed that competing colonial claims across Africa caused World War I.[41] Colonialism causes war in two ways, he explains in the 1945 book: 'It encourages war within the colonies themselves and between the powers which possess them.'[42] It would be a step too far to say that *Color and Democracy* is about human rights per se. The book's central claim is that no country that colonises other nations has a rightful claim to democracy. At the same time, the fact that colonisation denies rights is more than a motif of the book, and how Du Bois employs the language of human rights reflects his continual strategic experimentation with rights discourse.

The 'Preface' immediately sets the book's critical tone:

Henceforth the majority of the inhabitants of the earth, who happen for the most part to be colored, must be regarded as having the right and the capacity to share in human progress and to become copartners in that democracy which alone can ensure peace among men, by the abolition of poverty, the education of the masses, protection from disease, and the scientific treatment of crime.[43]

What he means by 'progress' is important to the normative claim he is making. Having already supported Debs, learned from Marx and underscored the injustice of colonialism, Du Bois here anticipates his clear definition of progress to Howard University students in 1958: 'Today, the United States is fighting world progress, progress which must be towards socialism and against colonialism.'[44] In other words, by 1945, progress for Du Bois is tied to socialism and decolonisation. In *Color and Democracy* he goes on to criticise the Dumbarton Oaks Conference, foundational for the United Nations, as claiming to work toward peace while in fact preserving imperial power, thus failing to address a leading cause of war.[45] In addition to causing war, colonisation denies rights, including human rights, which he places in scare quotes in his first mention of the term in the book.[46] The 'broadest ground' for criticising Dumbarton Oaks, he contends, lies in the fact that there are

at least 750,000,000 colored and black folk inhabiting colonies owned by white nations, who will have no rights that the white people of the world are bound to respect. Revolt on their part can be put down by military force; they will have no right of appeal to the Council or the Assembly; they will have no standing before the International Court of Justice.[47]

In other words, under the world order proposed at Dumbarton Oaks, 'between one-fourth and one-half the inhabitants of the world will have no part in it – no power of democratic control and scarcely an organized right of petition'.[48] Attending to the denial of cultural rights in addition to political rights, he adds later that 'the colonial system', in '[p]erhaps the greatest disaster', has meant for peoples across the world 'the ruthless and ignorant destruction of their cultural patterns'.[49] Overall, he concludes, one element of empire is always 'slave trade in human rights'.[50]

One of Du Bois's still-applicable claims in *Color and Democracy* is his critique of professionalised institutions claiming to advance human rights. He observes that without true democracy and guaranteed rights, paths to justice narrow until what is left is only the halls of philanthropy. In practice, this means that 'reform and social uplift will depend upon the free states and the empires'.[51] This is no path to justice, Du Bois concludes as Mariátegui did, because to rely on philanthropy is to rely on 'masters who have historical and strong interest in preserving their present power and income'.[52] He also anticipates objections to his claims. Critics of Dumbarton Oaks, he notes, have been told 'not to rock the boat in these difficult times'.[53] 'First we want peace and security', he summarises what he and other critics are told, 'then we will have a chance to pursue political rebuilding and social uplift.'[54] In response to these objections, he makes a diagnosis that echoes into the present: 'Many organizations that in the early stages of the discussion of postwar difficulties had stressed problems of colonies in the matter of human rights are today hesitating' – hesitating, that is, to make maximal demands for decolonisation that would disrupt the capitalist and colonial programmes that supply the wealth of the philanthropic organisations in the first place.[55]

Du Bois's frustration at the hesitations of human rights discourse came to the fore during his work to organise and present the historic petition *An Appeal to the World: A Statement of Denial of Human Rights to Minorities in the Case of Citizens of Negro Descent in the United States of America and an Appeal to the United Nations for Redress*. In 1946 Du Bois had pitched the NAACP board of directors to write a petition to the UN challenging US human rights violations against Black people. 'At a time when Washington was seeking to indict Moscow on similar charges', the historian Gerald Horne comments, 'this petition was not accepted with equanimity in the Oval Office – or in the inner sanctums of the NAACP.'[56] In the introduction to this petition, Du Bois describes the 'restricted legal rights' of Black people in the United States. He covers patterns still central to conservative political organising in North America today – such as that propertied interests use a false logic of racial inferiority to divide working-class Black and white people. He also argues that disenfranchising Black people is part of a larger effort to discourage large numbers of white people from voting.[57] '[W]hile this nation is trying to carry on the government of the United States by democratic methods', he says, 'it is not succeeding because of the premium which we put on the disfranchisement of the voters of the South.'[58] He underscores that, because it disenfranchises Black people and that white women are not yet used to voting, the United States remains more aristocratic than democratic. Given these threats to democracy, the enemies of the US are not external but internal: 'It is not Russia that threatens the United States', he says, 'so much as Mississippi.'[59]

Highlighting violations of the right to vote and the right to enter public spaces based on skin colour, Du Bois goes on to argue that 'the United States is today in danger of encroaching upon the rights and privileges of its fellow nations'.[60] '[A] discrimination practiced in the United States against her own citizens and to a large extent a contravention of her own laws', he writes, 'cannot be persisted in, without infringing upon the rights of the peoples of the world and especially upon the ideals and the work of the United Nations.'[61] He addresses his petition not to his own nation state, but to the UN. He acknowledges that many people say it should be addressed to the US, but concludes that appealing to one's country has been tried 'decade by decade' and had some success but 'not enough'.[62]

As the historian Manfred Berg puts it, Du Bois's petition would ask the UN 'to step to the very edge of its authority' – meaning that it would request the multi-state organisation to call into question the practices of one of its strongest members, and by doing so, imply an ability to challenge sovereignty.[63] Horne adds that the petition received great support in Africa and the Caribbean, because such an indictment 'gave momentum to their own anticolonial efforts and raised severe questions about whether millions would align with Washington or Moscow as Cold War tensions waxed'.[64] But leading the NAACP, Walter White hindered the opportune release of the petition by penning his own introduction.[65] The US also encouraged any delay of the petition's release at the UN. Still, at this time Du Bois's maintained his strategic use of human rights claims.

On 29 April 1947, he gave a speech called 'Human Rights for All Minorities' at the Town Hall of New York City. His title is important. It is not 'Human Rights *of* all minorities', suggesting that minorities already have human rights. Instead, he uses 'for'. This usage predates Hannah Arendt's critique of a natural rights understanding of human rights in *Origins of Totalitarianism*. It suggests that for Du Bois, human rights are not a natural possession but something that have to be demanded and achieved. Du Bois's title and speech, then, can be read alongside Glissant's 'For Opacity' title and chapter in *Poetics*.

I also suggest that 'Human Rights for All Minorities' develops further the 'new conception of human responsibility' Du Bois offered in *Color and Democracy*.[66] Du Bois's speech begins by making the point that taken together, minorities in the world's nation states – he specifically names Catholics, Muslims and Jews in the US; minorities in India; and Indigenous people in South America, among others – in fact form a majority of human beings. What unites the minorities of the world – cultural, religious and racial minorities within each nation state – is 'that repeatedly and in various ways their rights have been denied'.[67] That he begins from this claim sheds light on his strategy here: naming rights violations could be a starting point for organising across places and histories. The political problem is that, in many countries across the globe, 'the dominant majority [in any one country] calls itself the world'.[68] There are several roadblocks to organising against this false claim: 'it is not at first clear that there is any inter-minority unity' and, he observes sociologically, 'there seems no logical nor functional unity among these minorities'.[69] Instead, there is often friction between them. Further, whenever there is social mobilisation in the face of the powerful, there is 'immediately violence, hate and intolerance', which leads to 'increased denial to men of basic human rights'.[70] Poverty and repression are problems that persist beyond formal decolonisation: '[E]ven though [some] unjustly treated minorities do not actually occupy colonial status, often they occupy quasi-colonial status, segregated in the slums of a large and prosperous nation which is leading civilization.'[71]

Following this discussion of the denial of minority rights, Du Bois's next sociological observation is damning not only for those of us who grew up in the middle classes of countries of the West but also for the implicated elite anywhere on the planet:

Remember today that we depend upon colonial and quasi-colonial workers for coffee, tea and cocoa; for sugar, rubber, and the increasingly valuable vegetable oils; for minerals like gold, diamonds, uranium, copper and tin; for fibers like cotton, hemp and silk; for rice, spices, quinine and gum Arabic. Indeed for a mass of material which are so inextricably part of our modern life that it would practically be impossible for us to get on without them. Yet all of these materials are raised by labor which does not receive in return enough income to keep it healthy, trained or effective, or even physically to reproduce itself. In order to force this labor to work it is systematically deprived of ownership of land and of a share in the free bounty of nature. It is kept in ignorance, first because intelligence would bring active or passive revolt against these conditions; and secondly because the cost of education would reduce the profits which are pouring into the coffers of the investors and into the mounts and on our backs. This means that every civilized man is part and parcel of the colonial system and is depending for his welfare and convenience, not to mention his luxury, upon the degradation of the majority of man.[72]

Two elements of this passage immediately stand out. First, Du Bois asserts that colonial conditions remain because of how land is distributed, namely, how the victorious great powers in the 1940s continue to claim ownership of land that they gained through colonisation, thus continuing to deprive Indigenous peoples in Africa, Asia, Australia and the Americas of their ancestral land, which Du Bois describes as a deprivation of their ability to receive from the 'free bounty of nature'. Second, rather than praise 'civilisation', Du Bois demonstrates the proximity of civilisation and colonisation, showing that the project of Western civilisation relies on colonisation.

The result of the patterns of resource extraction Du Bois names, coupled with racial antipathy and religious intolerance (the conceptual tools undergirding the resource extraction), is 'wide-spread denial of human rights' caused in part by everyday life in the West.[73] Du Bois's bringing human rights down to everyday life presents a stark contrast to the way, for instance, Amnesty International has historically discussed rights violations, namely, as occurring in other countries and as violated by political leaders, not everyday actors. His understanding of rights violations, by contrast, implicates his audience. Human rights violations are not just far away. In the US they are in our morning coffee and tea, in the clothes we wear, and in the land we are on – and in everything else we rely on as we go through the day. If we claim to care about human rights or humanity, Du Bois avers, then we necessarily need to be invested in restructuring ownership of land and control of labour on a global scale, and this investment needs to be our starting point and not a footnote or afterthought. To put this another way, Du Bois teaches that ethics should begin from politics.

* * *

After his speech Du Bois returned his energies to his then-stalled *Appeal*. In a 14 October letter to William Stoneman, an advisor to the UN Secretary General, he notes that '[a]lready some twelve delegations have asked to read it, and it is receiving publicity from the press'.[74] 'The case of American Negroes is not going to be kept from knowledge by denial of the right to petition', he goes on, 'no more than in the past slavery could bolster itself by silence.'[75] The petition, on his own terms, can be understood as giving the United Nations a chance to live up to its institutional potential: 'We are going to give world-wide publicity to our complaint; but first, we would like to proceed by regular process and lay this petition before the United Nations publicly and in such a manner as their Secretariat suggests.'[76]

Because it highlighted rights violations in the US, *An Appeal to the World* was understood as being on the Soviet side in the Cold War. In December 1947, the delegate from the Soviet Union brought the petition to the attention of the UN Committee on Human Rights. Despite additional support for the petition from India, Haiti and Liberia, the US delegate defeated this proposal.[77] As Levering Lewis puts it, 'Du Bois's petition was an early casualty of the new cold war civil rights politics.'[78]

By then a public champion of human rights, Eleanor Roosevelt let Walter White know that she was critical of Du Bois's ongoing public enthusiasm for *An Appeal*.[79] She also asked Du Bois to speak with her in the official US offices to the UN on Park Avenue. The meeting took place on 30 June 1948. At the meeting Du Bois suggested once again that the US put the petition on the UN agenda so as to show that it allowed true free speech – that is, to show that the US supported political rights and allowed itself to be criticised for its own rights violations. Roosevelt responded that doing so would be unwise – that no good could come from such a discussion.[80] By this point in 1948, along ideological lines, White agreed with Roosevelt that the petition would only embarrass the US in front of the Soviets.

On 1 July 1948, Du Bois sent a memo to Walter White about the petition and the meeting he had with Roosevelt, noting that the US State department did not want to put the petition on the agenda of the next General Assembly. He also described Roosevelt's personal opposition to the petition, summarising what she argued: that if 'the matter [of US-sanctioned human rights violations of Black people in the country] was discussed in the Assembly, she and her colleagues would be put in the unpleasant position of having to defend the United States'.[81] Du Bois also noted the goals of the US Department of State, which were moving along through the institutional channels in that 'the Declaration of Human Rights . . . would come up at that session and be discussed and possibly assented to'.[82] This key juxtaposition between Du Bois's vision and the UDHR implies that Du Bois's 1947 petition is part of an approach to human rights different from the one that took hold in the 1948 Universal Declaration, promoted by Eleanor Roosevelt among others and which failed to recognise the self-determination of the colonies. Therefore, in Du Bois's view, the nascent Universal Declaration insufficiently attended to the ongoing 'colonial problem'. For all of her good intentions, Roosevelt illustrated individually a broader political claim Du Bois had made in another 1947 letter, namely, that 'no people who consciously or unconsciously is oppressing another is going to agree upon a proper time when they are willing to listen to protest'.[83]

In turn Du Bois criticised White for taking a position as a consultant to the US delegation at the UN. In his memo on White's appointment, Du Bois writes:

The United States Delegation to the United Nations has expressed clearly its attitude towards matters in which the NAACP is interested; it has refused to bring the curtailment of our civil rights to the attention of the General Assembly of the United Nations; it has refused willingly to allow any other nation to bring this matter up . . . If we accept a consultantship in this delegation without a clear, open, public declaration by the Board of our position on the Truman foreign policy, our very acceptance ties us in with the reactionary, war-mongering colonial imperialism of the present administration. It is certain that no influence applied in Paris is going to have the slightest influence on our delegation . . . If, on the contrary, we are to be loaded on the Truman bandwagon, with no chance for opinion or consultation, we are headed for a tragic mistake.[84]

White responded that accepting the consultantship was not the same as supporting Truman's foreign policy. For leaking his memo to the press, which Du Bois denied doing, the NAACP board of directors said they would allow his contract to expire at the end of 1948.

The tension between Du Bois and White/Roosevelt, which I am reading as exemplifying a broader difference between decolonial and liberal approaches to human rights, was larger than just a single incident. By 1948, Du Bois was increasingly critical of the United States as an evolving power, and in that year he supported the Progressive Party candidate Henry Wallace, a position that put him against both Walter White and the NAACP board (including Roosevelt) who supported Truman and deliberately distanced themselves from communism. Du Bois thought that Truman's liberal sympathies for human rights were not radical enough given that he dropped an atomic bomb on Japan, that he provided aid to Europe but not the colonies, and that he required a loyalty oath in his administration.

At this time NAACP members were prohibited from taking partisan stances. Characteristically, Du Bois did not think this policy applied to him. He walked around NAACP offices wearing a Wallace button. Supporting Truman, the NAACP distanced itself from communism because even civil rights were associated with communism in the red-baiting US. In order to conduct its civil rights legal battles, the NAACP needed to avoid being seen as a communist organisation. Importantly, like Du Bois's position, the NAACP's position was also strategic. As Berg summarises, 'Some historians have viewed the NAACP's anticommunism as timid and opportunistic', but most concede 'that it preserved the organization and its program through the McCarthy years'.[85] The price of preservation, however, 'was the detachment of black civil rights from more radical concepts of domestic social reform and anticolonialist internationalism in favor of the narrow goals of desegregation and voting rights'.[86] Du Bois's engagement with human rights demonstrates that geopolitical priorities always inform the field of discourse. Cold

War tensions caused the US as well as prominent organisations within it to support a version of human rights that could fit within liberalism and capitalism – the minimal, narrow goals of Eleanor Roosevelt and not the maximal, expansive vision of a now-Marxist Du Bois.[87]

By and large, Du Bois did not make political claims through the language of human rights after 1948.[88] Recognising his departure from human rights claims is especially important given literature that continues to suggest, for instance, that Du Bois is 'one of the greatest sociologists of human rights and still stands as an exemplary model for human rights activists . . . worldwide'.[89] Du Bois is certainly an important sociologist and activist, but it matters that he is not an activist who should be thought of as proceeding primarily through the rhetoric of human rights.[90] He strategically used this rhetoric only briefly in his long, and always politically committed, life. In other words, I am arguing that one of Du Bois's contributions to human rights discourse is his departure from it. His reasons for that departure – that human rights claims are too conciliatory to colonialism and capitalism – merit ongoing reflection by actors invested in rights claims today.

Here it is helpful to return to Hall's definition of politics as 'the form in which the connexions are made between lived experience and the demands made upon the system'.[91] Both Roosevelt's and Du Bois's moral imaginations and practices could follow from this description, which is why Hall's next sentences are so important:

Certain kinds of politics will connect experience with demands in a meaningful relationship, will connect awareness of the nature of the system to aspiration, and aspiration for change to the agencies of change. But there are also false ways of connecting lived experience to the agency of change. And in the absence of the right kind of politics, the false connexions become the stabilizing myths of society.[92]

Roosevelt's ardent but elite liberalism promoted a vision of human rights that ultimately served as one more myth stabilising capitalist and colonial society. It remains up to activists today to shift human rights discourse and practice to a position that would be worthy of Du Bois's support.

* * *

If Du Bois's contribution to human rights discourse is his departure from it, then his example reminds those of us who still see promise in this language – and I include myself in this group – that a human rights struggle worthy of that name needs to learn from socialist and anti-colonial histories, to attend seriously to those concerns and critiques, and in turn to raise often difficult and uncomfortable questions to those around us, and to ourselves, about what it means to live a life politically committed to serving all of humanity and advancing human rights. In our present context of outrageous brutality, a brutality that falls hardest on racialised and gendered lines, a brutality that is deliberately hidden from us in the advertisements and political slogans with which we are daily bombarded, such a political commitment to humanity and human rights might look like starting from, and trusting, our feelings of immense dissatisfaction at how human life is organised around us, and working from that feeling of dissatisfaction and alienation to leverage legible demands. If pipelines violate cultural rights (going over burial grounds), political rights (free assembly), and land rights (given treaties and that much Indigenous land remains unceded), and if policing consistently violates the rights of minorities, especially racial minorities, then those interested in human rights might consider how to contribute to efforts at maintaining Indigenous sovereignty and transforming police departments into departments of public safety for all. Further, following Du Bois's connection of the personal to the structural, it is also worth considering performing alternative styles of what it means to be human in our daily lives, whether that be refusing to take certain jobs, telling someone who does not let predominant gender norms define their expression what we have learned from them, or reaching out to an Indigenous nation for permission to cross their land before we take a road trip. This is the daily work of holding open imaginaries that might otherwise remain repressed, by ourselves as much as by the state. We might also think seriously about our own positions, our positionalities, with respect to living in a settler colonial country, and how that positioning might entail contributing to struggles for land back. Finally, we might follow Du Bois to re-understand a history of human rights, starting not with the declarations of European landholders, but with the theory and practice of Africans and those descended from Africans as well as with the political rights of ancient Egyptians; and we would keep in mind that a robust contribution to human rights struggles is found in, and for Du Bois starts with, the revolts of enslaved people – 'The slave revolts were the beginnings of the revolutionary struggle for the uplift of the laboring masses in the modern world', he says in *The World and Africa*.[93] Through these relational practices, we become different kinds of humans. Part of what I am trying to suggest is that lying behind the often frustrated and deeply critical tone of Marxist analysis is an equally profound aesthetic and peaceful sensibility. In light of their continued concern for all humans, and following the recent work of the political theorist Mihaela Mihai, we might even think of Du Bois's 1940s writings, and the tradition of Black Atlantic Marxism of which he is a part, as exemplifying an 'aesthetics of care'.[94] In any case, it matters that Du Bois had the option of using human rights language when it was still largely undefined yet gaining prominence, and that he chose a different strategy. Human rights claims, after all, offer just one model of or tool for social change.

* * *

After dropping human rights language, Du Bois would return to his long-standing emphasis on pan-Africanism and continue his studies of and advocacy for communism. After he left the NAACP for the second time, he joined the Council on African Affairs. Into his eighties he was active in the international peace movement, a coalition of actors drawn from church groups to communists that was worried about nuclear weapons and critical of colonialism. He called the Soviet-sponsored 1949 World Peace Congress in Paris the greatest event he ever attended. In 1950 he would run for US Senate as part of the American Labor Party to resist conservative sentiment that was growing due to the Korean War. Suggesting that he still supported radical uses of human rights, and taking yet another stance against the NAACP official position, Du Bois endorsed Paul Robeson and William Patterson's 1951 petition to the United Nations *We Charge Genocide: The Crime of Government Against the Negro People*, which in its first few pages places the Civil Rights Congress as a 'defender of constitutional liberties, human rights, and of peace', emphasising that it is the 'implacable enemy' of any social system that 'denies democratic rights or one iota of human dignity to any human being because of color, creed, nationality, or political belief'.[95] At ninety-three – on 1 October 1961 – Du Bois applied for membership in the Communist Party USA, a protest against the Cold War, and an iconoclastic gesture given continued NAACP self-distancing from the communists. Thus, Du Bois abandoned human rights discourse when it was on the rise in the US and joined the communist party when it was on the decline[96] – he was more radical at ninety-five than twenty-five. In this series of 'treacherous choices', as Paul Gilroy describes them, Du Bois chose his bearing in a way we can learn from in choosing ours.[97]

The history of Du Bois's relationship with rights claims in the late 1940s illustrates that human rights discourse displaced, and often actively repressed, anti-colonial energy as a tradition at the UN. *Choose Your Bearing* has outlined a path for this history of displacement to include a future of convergence. But if and when that future is less and less feasible despite what we make of the present, it is Du Bois we should keep in mind. Ultimately, through his critique of human rights advocacy for its complicity with capitalism and colonialism, Du Bois asks those of us who want to maintain the use of human rights to consider the compromises of our claims, and when those compromises prevent the realisation of a beautiful life for all of humanity, to pursue not just more radical, but also more imaginative paths.

Notes

1. See Samuel Moyn, *Not Enough: Human Rights in an Unequal World*.
2. See Jeanne Morefield, *Unsettling the World: Edward Said and Political Theory* (London: Rowman & Littlefield International, 2022).
3. Perhaps Ida B. Wells offers a path here if we read the 'record' from her *The Red Record* as a verb. Such a method of recording would involve, beyond witnessing the suffering of another, challenging the official history, invoking rights, clearly making cases for the ethical validity of challenges to oppression, and calling for a new polity. This sense of 'record' resonates with how the anthropologist and dancer Deborah Thomas describes repair. 'Repair', Thomas writes, 'is practice-oriented and quotidian; it is non-eventful and deeply historical and relational. Like its nominal counterpart [reparation], repair urges us to interrogate the multiple scales of entanglement that have led us to where we are now. But where reparation seeks justice through the naming of names, the exposure of public secrets, and the articulation of chains of causality, repair looks for something else. It demands an active listening, a mutual recognizing, an acknowledging of complicity at all levels – behavioral evidence of profound interior transformations that are ongoing' (Deborah Thomas, *Political*

Life in the Wake of the Plantation: Sovereignty, Witnessing, Repair (Durham, NC: Duke University Press, 2019), p. 212). Thanks to Derefe Chevannes and AunRika Tucker-Shabazz for conversations about Wells.

4. See for example Carolyn Forché, ed., *Poetry of Witness: The Tradition in English, 1500–2001* (New York: W. W. Norton & Company, 2014). See also Steven Heighton, *Reaching Mithymna: Among the Volunteers and Refugees on Lesvos* (Windsor: Biblioasis, 2020). Is Heighton's split-second decision to travel abroad and volunteer among anarchists and fellow travellers, when he feels that his novels and poems are not making a sufficient difference in the world, problematic in light of the decolonial insights that prompted this book? Or is his impulse to work alongside other humans and attend to the suffering of those from other countries and faiths worth affirming? On a gut level, I see something beautiful in it. Cf. Paul Gilroy, '"Where every breeze speaks of courage and liberty": Offshore Humanism and Marine Xenology, or, Racism and the Problem of Critique at Sea Level', *Antipode: A Radical Journal of Geography* 50 (2018): pp. 3–22.

5. In that the human rights claims at Standing Rock were grounded in a larger context of situating ourselves in a way that centred land and ancestral knowledge, I understand Standing Rock as exemplary of a new critical theory that proceeds through a dialectic of strategy *and* receptivity, and thus as resonant with Kompridis's imaginative call for 'placing the capacity for receptivity and decentering in an unusually prominent and central normative position' (Nikolas Kompridis, *Critique and Disclosure: Critical Theory between Past and Future* (Cambridge, MA: The MIT Press, 2006), p. 187).

6. Mariátegui, *Seven Interpretive Essays on Peruvian Reality*, p. 25.

7. Ibid. p. 26.

8. Ibid. p. 31.

9. Ibid. p. 26.

10. I am thinking of 'salt' here in the sense that Aristotle uses it to talk about the need for connection over time, where salt can refer to eating together as well as to sharing tears, blood and

sweat, and so suggests intimacy, struggle, loss, achievement, effort and play. See *Nicomachean Ethics* Book VIII, Bekker 1156b.

11. Aijaz Ahmad, '*The Communist Manifesto* In Its Own Time, And In Ours' in *A World to Win: Essays on The Communist Manifesto*, ed. Prakash Karat (New Delhi: LeftWord Books, 1999), p. 17.

12. Stuart Hall, 'Political Commitment' in *Selected Political Writings*, ed. Sally Davison et al., p. 85.

13. Ibid. p. 87.

14. Ruth Marcus, 'Why Joe Biden is the antidote to this virus', *Washington Post*, 13 March 2020, <https://www.washingtonpost.com/opinions/2020/03/13/why-joe-biden-is-antidote-this-virus/>.

15. Hall, 'Political Commitment', p. 88.

16. Ibid. p. 87.

17. Stuart Hall, 'Marxist Structuralism' in Stuart Hall, *Cultural Studies 1983*, p. 115.

18. Hall, 'Political Commitment', p. 91.

19. Ibid. p. 94.

20. Ibid. p. 85.

21. Ibid. p. 103.

22. Charisse Burden-Stelly, 'Why W.E.B. Du Bois Matters', in Charisse Burden-Stelly and Gerald Horne, *W.E.B. Du Bois: A Life in American History* (Santa Barbara, CA: ABC-CLIO, 2019), p. 196.

23. The Niagara Movement was a civil rights organisation named after the Niagara Falls, Ontario meeting place to which it was forced to relocate after being denied access to hotels in Buffalo, New York.

24. Du Bois in *Horizon*, November–December 1908. Quoted in Burden-Stelly and Horne, *W.E.B. Du Bois*, p. 55.

25. Ibid.

26. Quoted in David Levering Lewis, *W.E.B. Du Bois: A Biography* (New York: Henry Holt and Company, 2009), p. 378.

27. Burden-Stelly, 'Why W.E.B. Du Bois Matters', p. 197.

28. Ibid.

29. Lewis, *W.E.B. Du Bois*, pp. 624, 549.

30. See Burden-Stelly and Horne, *W.E.B. Du Bois*, p. 144.

31. Quoted in Burden-Stelly and Horne, *W.E.B. Du Bois*, p. 70.

32. W. E. B. Du Bois, *Color and Democracy* (New York: Oxford University Press, 2007), p. 319.

33. For the argument that the traditions are separate, see Samuel Moyn, *The Last Utopia: Human Rights in History*, pp. 116, 117. For the argument that the traditions came together under the banner of self-determination, see the chapter 'From Principle to Right: The Anticolonial Reinvention of Self-Determination' in Adom Getachew, *Worldmaking after Empire: The Rise and Fall of Self-Determination* (Princeton: Princeton University Press, 2019), pp. 71–106.

34. Quoted in Gerald Horne, 'Introduction' in Du Bois, *Color and Democracy*, p. 238.

35. See Lewis, *W.E.B. Du Bois*, pp. 648–9.

36. Quoted in Lewis, *W.E.B. Du Bois*, p. 649.

37. See Lewis, *W.E.B. Du Bois*, p. 652. Showing his range across theory and practice as well as his internationalism, Du Bois had highlighted Black South Africans' lack of basic political rights in his 1943 fourth-quarter column of 'Chronicle of Race Relations' in *Phylon*. See Derek Charles Catsam, 'W.E.B. Du Bois, South Africa, and *Phylon*', in *Citizen of the World: The Late Career and Legacy of W.E.B. Du Bois*, ed. Phillip Luke Sintiere (Evanston, IL: Northwestern University Press, 2019), p. 45.

38. Bill V. Mullen, 'Russia and America' in *Citizen of the World*, p. 62.

39. Lewis, *W.E.B. Du Bois*, p. 653.

40. Ibid.

41. See Burden-Stelly and Horne, *W.E.B. Du Bois*, p. 153.

42. Du Bois, *Color and Democracy*, p. 309.

43. Ibid. p. 241.

44. Quoted in Lewis, *W.E.B. Du Bois*, p. 700.

45. Du Bois, *Color and Democracy*, p. 246.

46. Ibid. p. 248.

47. Ibid. pp. 249, 248–9. Here Du Bois echoes the language of the 1857 *Dred Scott v. Sanford* case in which Chief Justice Roger B. Taney wrote that Blacks 'had no rights which the white man was bound to respect'. Cf. Getachew, *Worldmaking after Empire*, p. 79.

48. Du Bois, *Color and Democracy*, p. 251.
49. Ibid. p. 269.
50. Ibid. p. 329.
51. Ibid. p. 251.
52. Ibid. p. 252.
53. Ibid.
54. Ibid.
55. Ibid.
56. Burden-Stelly and Horne, *W.E.B. Du Bois*, p. 158.
57. W. E. B. Du Bois, *An appeal to the world*, W.E.B. Du Bois Papers (MS 312), pp. 4, 8.
58. Ibid. p. 9.
59. Ibid. p. 12.
60. Ibid. p. 13.
61. Ibid.
62. Ibid.
63. Manfred Berg, 'Black Civil Rights and Liberal Anticommunism: The NAACP in the Early Cold War', *The Journal of American History* 94, no. 1 (2007): p. 82.
64. Burden-Stelly and Horne, *W.E.B. Du Bois*, p. 158.
65. Lewis, *W.E.B. Du Bois*, p. 672.
66. Du Bois, *Color and Democracy*, p. 327.
67. W. E. B. Du Bois, 'Human rights for all minorities, April 29, 1947', W.E.B. Du Bois Papers (MS 312), p. 1.
68. Ibid. p. 3.
69. Ibid.
70. Ibid. p. 2.
71. Ibid. p. 4.
72. Ibid. p. 6.
73. Ibid. p. 7. Cf. Glissant's line: 'When one says civilization, the immediate implication is a will to civilize. This idea is linked to the passion to impose civilization on the Other' (PR 26/PO 13).
74. W. E. B. Du Bois, *The Correspondence of W.E.B. Du Bois: Volume III: Selections, 1944–1963*, ed. Herbert Aptheker (Amherst: University of Massachusetts Press, 1978), p. 181.
75. Ibid.

76. Ibid.

77. Berg, 'Black Civil Rights and Liberal Anticommunism', p. 83.

78. Lewis, *W.E.B. Du Bois*, p. 673.

79. Ibid. p. 676.

80. Ibid.

81. Du Bois, *The Correspondence*, p. 189.

82. Ibid.

83. Ibid. p. 186. Here is the extended passage: 'No people who consciously or unconsciously is oppressing another is going to agree upon a proper time when they are willing to listen to protest. For two centuries this country declared that any protest against slavery was untimely and presumptuous; it paid for its unwillingness to listen to reason by blood and destruction. Today fourteen million Americans are deeply resentful and alarmed for themselves and their country at the continuation of color-caste, lynching, and disenfranchisement in this land. Is it not their duty to let their attitude be known, when the world asks a report on human rights and discrimination?' (ibid.).

84. Quoted in Berg, 'Black Civil Rights and Liberal Anticommunism', p. 84.

85. Berg, 'Black Civil Rights and Liberal Anticommunism', p. 76.

86. Ibid.

87. Cf. Alexandre Lefebvre, *Human Rights and the Care of the Self* (Durham, NC: Duke University Press, 2018). Lefebvre sees human rights as a touchstone for self-transformation and self-improvement. As I have argued through my treatment of participation, solidarity and feasibility, human rights need to do more than motivate self-improvement. At its best, human rights discourse allows for self-critique, connects struggles and inspires collective demands. It is not a coincidence that Lefebvre, in advancing what is ultimately an overly individualistic take on the political value of human rights, places Eleanor Roosevelt on the cover of his book, noting in the text that she is an exemplary figure of the kind of human rights practice he has in mind (see ibid. pp. 2, 189). As Du Bois's critique shows, Roosevelt's practice runs into limitations in lacking a critical

emphasis on colonial conditions and a constructive ability to make transformative demands.

88. Moyn, *Last Utopia*, p. 103.

89. Sean Elias, 'Du Bois, Race, and Human Rights', *Societies Without Borders* 4, no. 3 (2009): p. 273.

90. Du Bois's approach to capitalism through the lens of race and the perspective of the enslaved person and the sharecropper differed from Marx's starting point of the urban proletariat or Max Weber's starting point of the urban bureaucracy. In that way, Du Bois's sociology prefigured a focus on what today is called racial and colonial capitalism. For an elaboration on this point as well as a wider consideration of Du Bois as a sociologist, see José Itzigsohn and Karida L. Brown, *The Sociology of W. E. B. Du Bois: Racialized Modernity and the Global Color Line* (New York: New York University Press, 2020).

91. Hall, 'Political Commitment', p. 94.

92. Ibid.

93. For Du Bois's alternative history of rights, see *The World and Africa* (New York: Oxford University Press, 2007), p. 80. For Du Bois's alternative history of labour struggles, see ibid. p. 38.

94. Such an aesthetics, Mihai teaches, involves acknowledging a 'generalized complicity' with systemic violence while 'sabotag[ing] reductive historical scripts and prosthetically enabl[ing] spectators to see the world in its complexity, from different points of view'; ultimately, these artworks 'could open up a space for remembering and imagining differently' (Mihaela Mihai, *Political Memory and the Aesthetics of Care: The Art of Complicity and Resistance* (Stanford: Stanford University Press, 2022), pp. 4, 46). It is the argument of this chapter that Du Bois's late 1940s texts are such artworks, with *The World and Africa* remembering history differently and *Color and Democracy* imagining a different institutional order.

95. William L. Patterson, *We Charge Genocide: The Historical Petition to the United Nations for Relief from a Crime of the United States Government against the Negro People* (New York: International Publishers, 1970), p. xxvii. For discussion of Du Bois's support, see Lewis, *W.E.B. Du Bois*, p. 697.

96. See Moyn, *Last Utopia*, p. 103.

97. Paul Gilroy, *Darker than Blue: On the Moral Economies of Black Atlantic Culture* (Cambridge, MA: The Belknap Press of Harvard University Press, 2010), p. 155; see also p. 68 for a new archive of human rights.

Bibliography

Aching, Gerard. 'The "Right to Opacity" and World Literature'. *1616: Anuario de Literatura Comparada* 2 (2012): pp. 33–47.

Adonis, Mahmud Darwish and Samih al-Qasim, *Victims of a Map: A Bilingual Anthology of Arabic Poetry*. Edited by Abdullah al-Udhari. London: Saqi Books, 2005.

Adorno, Theodor. *Aspekte des neuen Rechtsradikalismus*. Berlin: Suhrkamp, 1967/2019.

Ahmad, Aijaz. *In Theory: Classes, Nations, Literatures*. New York: Verso, 1992.

——. '*The Communist Manifesto* in Its Own Time, And in Ours'. In *A World to Win: Essays on The Communist Manifesto*'. Edited by Prakash Karat. New Delhi: LeftWord Books, 1999.

Alcoff, Linda Martín. *Visible Identities: Race, Gender, and the Self*. Oxford: Oxford University Press, 2005.

Alexander, Michele. *The New Jim Crow: Mass Incarceration in the Age of Colorblindness*. New York: The New Press, 2012.

Allar, Neal. 'The Case for Incomprehension: Édouard Glissant's Poetics of Relation and the Right to Opacity'. *Journal of French and Francophone Philosophy* XXIII, no. 1 (2015): pp. 43–58.

Allard, Ladonna Bravebull. 'Why do we punish Dakota pipeline protesters but exonerate the Bundys?' *The Guardian*, 2 November 2016.

Amir, Samin. *Accumulation on a World Scale: A Critique of the Theory of Underdevelopment*. New York: Monthly Review Press, 1974.

Anzaldúa, Gloria. *Borderlands/La Frontera: The New Frontera*. San Francisco: Aunt Lute Books, 1987.

——. *The Gloria Anzaldúa Reader*. Edited by AnaLouise Keating. Durham, NC: Duke University Press, 2009.

——. *Interviews/Entrevistas*. Edited by AnaLouise Keating. New York: Routledge, 2000.

——. *Light in the Dark/Luz en lo Oscuro: Rewriting Identity, Spirituality, Reality*. Durham, NC: Duke University Press, 2015.

Archambault II, David. 'Taking a Stand at Standing Rock'. *The New York Times*, 24 August 2016.

Azoulay, Ariella Aïsha. *Potential History: Unlearning Imperialism*. New York: Verso, 2019.

Arendt, Hannah. *The Human Condition*. Chicago: University of Chicago Press, 1998.

Barreto, José-Manuel. 'Decolonial Thinking and the Quest for Decolonising Human Rights'. *Asian Journal of Social Science* 46, nos. 4–5 (2018): pp. 484–502.

Barrett, Michèle and Mary McIntosh. *The Anti-Social Family*. New York: Verso, 2015.

Bell, Derrick A. Jr. 'Brown v. Board of Education and the Interest-Convergence Dilemma'. *Harvard Law Review* 93, no. 3 (1980): pp. 518–533.

Bender, Courtney. *The New Metaphysicals: Spirituality and the American Religious Imagination*. Chicago: University of Chicago Press, 2010.

Benjamin, Ruha. 'Black AfterLives Matter: Cultivating Kinfulness as Reproductive Justice'. In *Making Kin Not Population*. Edited by Adele E. Clarke and Donna Haraway. Chicago: Prickly Paradigm Press, 2018.

Benjamin, Walter. 'Capitalism as Religion'. In *Walter Benjamin: Selected Writings 1, 1913–1926*. Edited by Marcus Bullock and Michael W. Jennings. Cambridge, MA: The Belknap Press of Harvard University Press, 2004.

Berg, Manfred. 'Black Civil Rights and Liberal Anticommunism: The NAACP in the Early Cold War', *The Journal of American History* 94, no. 1 (2007): pp. 75–96.

Berger, John. *Landscapes: John Berger on Art*. Edited by Tom Overton. New York: Verso, 2016.

Bourdieu, Pierre. *Outline of a Theory of Practice*. Cambridge: Cambridge University Press, 1977.

Brand, Dionne. *A Map to the Door of No Return: Notes to Belonging*. Toronto: Vintage Canada, 2011.

Bray, Mark. 'Beyond and Against the State: Anarchist Contributions to Human Rights History and Theory'. *Humanity: An International Journal of Human Rights, Humanitarianism, and Development* 3, no. 3 (2019): pp. 323–38.

Britton, Celia M. *Edouard Glissant and Postcolonial Theory: Strategies of Language and Resistance*. Charlottesville: University of Virginia Press, 1999.

Brown, Wendy. '"The Most We Can Hope For . . .": Human Rights and The Politics of Fatalism', *The South Atlantic Quarterly* 103, no. 2 (2004): pp. 461–2.

——. *Regulating Aversion: Tolerance in the Age of Identity and Empire*. Princeton: Princeton University Press, 2006.

——. 'Untimeliness and Punctuality: Critical Theory in Dark Times'. In Wendy Brown, *Edgework: Critical Essays on Knowledge and Politics*. Princeton: Princeton University Press, 2005.

Brown, Wendy and Janey Halley, *Left Legalism/Left Critique*. Durham, NC: Duke University Press, 2002.

Burden-Stelly, Charisse and Gerald Horne. *W.E.B. Du Bois: A Life in American History*. Santa Barbara, CA: ABC-CLIO, 2019.

Burke, Roland. *Decolonization and the Evolution of International Human Rights*. Philadelphia: University of Pennsylvania Press, 2013.

Burke, Roland, Marco Duranti and A. Dirk Moses, 'Introduction: Human Rights, Empire, and After'. In *Decolonization, Self-Determination, and the Rise of Global Human Rights Politics*. Edited by A. Dirk Moses, Marco Duranti and Roland Burke. Cambridge: Cambridge University Press, 2020.

Butler, Judith. *Frames of War: When is Life Grievable?* New York: Verso, 2009.

——. *Notes Toward a Performative Theory of Assembly*. Cambridge, MA: Harvard University Press, 2015.

Cailler, Bernadette. 'Totalité et Infini, Altérité et Relation: d'Emmanuel Levinas à Édouard Glissant'. In *Poétiques d'Edouard Glissant*. Edited by Jacques Chervrier. Paris: Presses de l'Université de Paris-Sorbonne, 1999; '*Totality and Infinity*, Alterity, and Relation'. Translated by David-Olivier Gougele. *Journal for French and Francophone Philosophy* 19, no. 1 (2011): pp. 135–51.

Campt, Tina M. 'The Opacity of Grief'. *Bomb Magazine*, 26 January 2022.

Cardenal, Ernesto. 'Las Ciudades Perdidas'. In *Nueva Antología Poética*. Mexico DF: Siglo XXI Editores, 2006.

Catsam, Derek Charles. 'W.E.B. DU Bois, South Africa, and *Phylon*'. In *Citizen of the World: The Late Career and Legacy of W.E.B. Du Bois*. Edited by Phillip Luke Sintiere. Evanston, IL: Northwestern University Press, 2019.

Césaire, Aimé. *Journal of a Homecoming/Cahier d'un retour au pays natal*. Durham, NC: Duke University Press, 2017.

Chamoiseau, Patrick and Édouard Glissant, 'When the Walls Fall: Is National Identity an Outlaw?' Translated by Jeffrey Landon Allen and Charly Verstraet. *Contemporary French and Francophone Studies* 22, no. 2 (2018): pp. 259–70.

Chi-she, Li. 'Opacity'. *Philosophy Today* 63, no. 4 (2019): pp. 859–72.

Clarke, Adele and Donna Haraway. *Making Kin Not Population*. Edited by Adele E. Clarke and Donna Haraway. Chicago: Prickly Paradigm Press, 2018.

Clifford, James. *Returns: Becoming Indigenous in the Twenty-First Century*. Cambridge, MA: Harvard University Press, 2013.

Coffineua, Lea. 'Migration as a Claim for Reparations: Connections between political agency and migration'. In *Public Seminar*, 7 December 2020.

Coulthard, Glen Sean. *Red Skin, White Masks: Rejecting the Colonial Politics of Recognition*. Minneapolis: University of Minnesota Press, 2014.

Critchley, Simon. *The Ethics of Deconstruction: Derrida and Levinas*. Edinburgh: University of Edinburgh Press, 1999.

——. *Infinitely Demanding: Ethics of Commitment, Politics of Resistance*. New York: Verso, 2007.

Çubukçu, Ayça. *For the Love of Humanity: The World Tribunal on Iraq*. Philadelphia: University of Pennsylvania Press, 2018.

——. 'Thinking against humanity'. *London Review of International Law* 5, no. 2 (2017): pp. 251–67.

Darwish, Mahmoud. *Mural*. Translated by Rema Hammami and John Berger. New York: Verso, 2017.

Davis, Benjamin P. 'Globalization/Coloniality: A Decolonial Definition and Diagnosis'. *Transmodernity: Journal of Cultural Production
of the Luso-Hispanic World* 8, no. 4 (2018): pp. 1–20.

——. 'Human Rights and Caribbean Philosophy: Implications for Teaching'. *Journal of Human Rights Practice* 12, no. 4 (2021): pp. 136–44.

——. 'The Right to Have Rights in the Americas: Arendt, Monture,
and the Problem of the State'. *Arendt Studies* 6 (2022): pp. 43–57.

——. 'What Could Human Rights Do? A Decolonial Inquiry'. *Transmodernity: Journal of Peripheral Cultural Production of the Luso-Hispanic
World* 9, no. 5 (2020): pp. 1–22.

Del Toro, Valeria M. Pelet. 'Beyond the Critique of Rights: The
Puerto Rico Legal Project and Civil Rights Litigation in America's
Colony'. *The Yale Law Journal* 128, no. 3 (2019): pp. 792–842.

Donnelly, Jack. *Universal Human Rights in Theory and Practice*. Ithaca,
NY: Cornell University Press, 2013.

Drabinski, John E. *Glissant and the Middle Passage: Philosophy, Beginning, Abyss*. Minneapolis: University of Minnesota Press, 2019.

——. *Levinas and the Postcolonial: Race, Nation, Other*. Edinburgh: Edinburgh University Press, 2011.

Drabinski, John E. and Marisa Parham, eds. *Theorizing Glissant: Sites
and Citations*. New York: Rowman & Littlefield International, 2015.

Drèze, Jean. 'Democracy and the Right to Food'. In *Human Rights
and Development*. Edited by Philip Alston and Mary Robinson.
Oxford: Oxford University Press, 2005.

Du Bois, W. E. B. *An appeal to the world*. W. E. B. Du Bois Papers
(MS 312).

——. *Color and Democracy*. New York: Oxford, 2007.

——. *The Correspondence of W.E.B. Du Bois: Volume III: Selections, 1944–1963*.
Edited by Herbert Aptheker. Amherst: University of Massachusetts
Press, 1978.

——. 'Human rights for all minorities, April 29, 1947'. W. E. B. Du
Bois Papers (MS 312).

——. *John Brown*. New York: Routledge, 2015.

——. *The World and Africa*. New York: Oxford, 2007.

Dussel, Enrique. *Ética de la Liberación en la Edad de la Globalización y de
la Exclusión*. Madrid: Editorial Trotta, 1998; *Ethics of Liberation in*

the Age of Globalization and Exclusion. Translated by Bustillo et al. Durham, NC: Duke University Press, 2013.

———. *Liberación Latinoamericana y Emmanuel Levinas*. Buenos Aires: Editorial Bonum, 1975.

Elias, Sean. 'Du Bois, Race, and Human Rights'. *Societies Without Borders* 4, no. 3 (2009): pp. 273–94.

Escobar, Arturo. *Designs for the Pluriverse: Radical Interdependence, Autonomy, and the Making of Worlds*. Durham, NC: Duke University Press, 2018.

Estes, Nick. *Our History is the Future: Standing Rock Versus the Dakota Access Pipeline, and the Long Tradition of Indigenous Resistance*. New York: Verso, 2019.

Fanon, Frantz. *Black Skin, White Masks*. Translated by Charles Lam Markmann. London: Pluto Press, 2008.

Fassin, Didier. *Humanitarian Reason: A Moral History of the Present*. Berkeley: University of California Press, 2011.

Forché, Carolyn, ed. *Poetry of Witness: The Tradition in English, 1500–2001*. New York: W. W. Norton & Company, 2014.

Friedman, Lisa. 'Standing Rock Sioux Tribe Wins a Victory in Dakota Access Pipeline Case'. *The New York Times*, 25 March 2020.

Gabel, Peter and Paul Harris. 'Building Power and Breaking Images: Critical Legal Theory and the Practice of Law'. *N.Y.U. Review of Law & Social Change* XI (1982–1983): pp. 369–411.

Gallagher, Mary. 'Ethics in the Absence of Reference: Levinas and the (Aesthetic) Value of Diversity'. *Levinas Studies* 7 (2010): pp. 95–125.

Getachew, Adom. *Worldmaking after Empire: The Rise and Fall of Self-Determination*. Princeton: Princeton University Press, 2019.

Gilroy, Paul. *Against Race: Imagining Political Culture beyond the Color Line*. Cambridge, MA: The Belknap Press of Harvard University Press, 2000.

———. *Darker than Blue: On the Moral Economies of Black Atlantic Culture*. Cambridge, MA: The Belknap Press of Harvard University Press, 2010.

———. '"Where every breeze speaks of courage and liberty": Offshore Humanism and Marine Xenology, or, Racism and the Problem of Critique at Sea Level'. *Antipode: A Radical Journal of Geography* 50 (2018): pp. 3–22.

Glissant, Édouard. *Le discours antillais*. Paris: Gallimard, 1997; *Caribbean Discourse: Selected Essays*. Translated by J. Michael Dash. Charlottesville: University of Virginia Press, 1989.

——. *Philosophie de la Relation*. Paris: Gallimard, 2009.

——. *Poétique de la Relation*. Paris: Gallimard, 1990; *Poetics of Relation*. Translated by Betsy Wing. Ann Arbor: University of Michigan Press, 1997.

——. *Traité du Tout-Monde*. Paris: Gallimard, 1997.

Gordon, Lewis. *Fear of Black Consciousness*. New York: Farrar, Straus & Giroux, 2022.

——. 'Shifting the Geography of Reason in an Age of Disciplinary Decadence'. *Transmodernity: Journal of Peripheral Cultural Production of the Luso-Hispanic World* 1, no. 2 (2011): pp. 95–104.

Graeber, David. *Toward an Anthropological Theory of Value: The False Coin of Our Own Dreams*. New York: Palgrave, 2001.

Gregg, Benjamin. *The Human Rights State: Justice within and beyond Sovereign Nations*. Philadelphia: University of Pennsylvania Press, 2016.

Griffin, James. *On Human Rights*. Oxford: Oxford University Press, 2008.

Gualdrón Ramírez, Miguel. 'Resistance and Expanse in *Nuestra América*: José Martí, with Édouard Glissant and Gloria Anzaldúa'. *Diacritics* 46, no. 2 (2018): pp. 12–29.

Guenther, Lisa. 'A Critical Phenomenology of Solidarity and Resistance in the 2013 California Prison Hunger Strikes'. In *Body/Self/Other: A Phenomenology of Social Encounters*. Edited by Luna Dolezal and Danielle Petherbridge. Albany: State University of New York Press, 2017.

Gündogdu, Ayten. 'On the ambivalent politics of human rights'. *Journal of International Political Theory* 14, no. 3 (2018): pp. 367–80.

Gutiérrez, Gustavo. *A Theology of Liberation: History, Politics, and Salvation*. Translated by Sister Caridad Inda and John Eagleson. Maryknoll, NY: Orbis, 1973.

——. *Gustavo Gutiérrez: Essential Writings*. Edited by James B. Nickoloff. Maryknoll, NY: Orbis Books, 1996.

Hall, Stuart. *Cultural Studies 1983*. Edited by Jennifer Daryl Slack and Lawrence Grossberg. Durham, NC: Duke University Press, 2016.

——. *Familiar Stranger: A Life between Two Islands*. Durham, NC: Duke University Press, 2017.

——. 'The Great Moving Right Show'. In *Selected Political Writings*. Edited by Sally Davison, David Featherstone, Michael Rustin and Bill Schwartz. Durham, NC: Duke University Press, 2017.

——. 'Political Commitment'. In *Selected Political Writings*. Edited by Sally Davison, David Featherstone, Michael Rustin and Bill Schwartz. Durham, NC: Duke University Press, 2017.

——. 'Thinking the Diaspora: Home-Thoughts from Abroad'. In *Essential Essays Vol. 2: Identity and Diaspora*. Edited by David Morley. Durham, NC: Duke University Press, 2019.

——. 'Through the Prism of an Intellectual Life'. In *Essential Essays Vol. 2: Identity and Diaspora*. Edited by David Morley. Durham, NC: Duke University Press, 2019.

Hallward, Peter. *Absolutely Postcolonial: Writing between the Singular and the Specific*. Manchester: Manchester University Press, 2002.

Haraway, Donna J. *Staying with the Trouble: Making Kin in the Chthulucene*. Durham, NC: Duke University Press, 2016.

Harcourt, Bernard. *Critique & Praxis: A Critical Philosophy of Illusions, Values, and Action*. New York: Columbia University Press, 2020.

Harris, Christopher Paul. 'For the Culture: #BlackLives Matter and the Future Yet to Come'. *The South Atlantic Quarterly* 121, no. 3 (2022): pp. 491–514.

Hartman, Saidiya. 'Wayward Lives, Beautiful Experiments, ft. Saidiya Hartman'. Rustbelt Abolition Radio, <https://rustbeltradio.org/2019/04/24/ep28/>.

Heighton, Steven. *Reaching Mithymna: Among the Volunteers and Refugees on Lesvos*. Windsor: Biblioasis, 2020.

Henry, Paget. *Caliban's Reason: Introducing Afro-Caribbean Philosophy*. New York: Routledge, 2000.

Hoff, Shannon. 'Rights and Worlds: On the Political Significance of Belonging'. *Philosophical Forum* 45, no. 4 (2014): pp. 355–73.

Hopgood, Stephen. *The Endtimes of Human Rights*. Ithaca, NY: Cornell University Press, 2013.

Howard, Emma. 'A beginner's guide to fossil fuel divestment'. *The Guardian*, 23 June 2015.

Idris, Murad, *War for Peace: Genealogies of a Violent Ideal in Western and Islamic Thought*. Oxford: Oxford University Press, 2018.

Issar, Siddhant. 'Listening to Black lives matter: racial capitalism and the critique of neoliberalism'. *Contemporary Political Theory* (2020): pp. 48–71.

Itzigsohn, José and Karida L. Brown, *The Sociology of W. E. B. Du Bois: Racialized Modernity and the Global Color Line*. New York: New York University Press, 2020.

James, Joy. '"Concerning Violence": Frantz Fanon's Rebel Intellectual in Search of a Black Cyborg'. *The South Atlantic Quarterly* 112, no. 1 (2013): pp. 57–70.

———. 'The Dead Zone: Stumbling at the Crossroads of Party Politics, Genocide, and Postracial Racism'. *South Atlantic Quarterly* 108, no. 3 (2009): pp. 459–81.

———. 'Incarceration (Un)Interrupted: Reclaiming Bodies, Lands, and Communities'. Talk given at Macalester College, 10 October 2019.

———. *Resisting State Violence: Radicalism, Gender, & Race in U.S. Culture*. Minneapolis: University of Minnesota Press, 1996.

———. 'Sorrow: The Good Soldier and the Good Woman'. In *Warfare in the American Homeland: Policing and Prison in a Penal Democracy*. Edited by Joy James. Durham, NC: Duke University Press, 2007.

Keating, AnaLouise, ed. *The Gloria Anzaldúa Reader*. Durham, NC: Duke University Press, 2009.

Keck, Margaret E. and Kathryn Sikkink. *Activists beyond Borders: Advocacy Networks in International Politics*. Ithaca, NY: Cornell University Press, 1998.

Keller, Catherine. *Cloud of the Impossible: Negative Theology and Planetary Entanglement*. New York: Columbia University Press, 2014.

———. *Political Theology of the Earth: Our Planetary Emergency and the Struggle for a New Public*. New York: Columbia University Press, 2018.

Kelly, Patrick William. *Sovereign Emergencies: Latin America and The Making of Global Human Rights Politics*. Cambridge: Cambridge University Press, 2018.

King, Tiffany Lethabo. *The Black Shoals: Offshore Formations of Black and Native Studies*. Durham, NC: Duke University Press, 2019.

Kingston, Lindsey. *Fully Human: Personhood, Citizenship, and Rights*. Oxford: Oxford University Press, 2019.

Klare, Michael. 'Low-Intensity Conflict: The War of the "Haves" against the "Have-nots'. *Christianity and Crisis* (1998).

Klose, Fabian. *Human Rights in the Shadow of Colonial Violence*. Translated by Dona Geyer. Philadelphia: University of Pennsylvania Press, 2013.

Knox, Robert. 'Marxism, International Law, and Political Strategy'. *Leiden Journal of International Law* 22, no. 3 (2009): pp. 413–36.

Kompridis, Nikolas. *Critique and Disclosure: Critical Theory between Past and Future*. Cambridge, MA: The MIT Press, 2006.

——. 'Introduction'. In *The Aesthetic Turn in Political Thought*. Edited by Nikolas Kompridis. New York: Bloomsbury, 2014.

Lebovic, Nitzan. 'Introduction: Complicity and Dissent, or Why We Need Solidarity between Struggles'. *CLCWeb: Comparative Literature and Culture* 21, no. 3 (2019): pp. 1–9.

Lefebvre, Alexandre. *Human Rights and the Care of the Self*. Durham, NC: Duke University Press, 2018.

Levering Lewis, David. *W.E.B. Du Bois: A Biography*. New York: Henry Holt, 2009.

Levinas, Emmanuel. *Ethics and Infinity: Conversations with Philippe Nemo*. Translated by Richard A. Cohen. Pittsburgh: Duquesne University Press, 1985.

——. 'Meaning and Sense'. In *Collected Philosophical Papers*. Translated by Alphonso Lingis. Dordrecht: Martinus Nijhoff, 1987.

——. *Otherwise than Being or Beyond Essence*. Translated by Alphonso Lingis. Pittsburg: Duquesne University Press, 1998.

——. *Totalité et Infini : Essai sur l'extériorité*. Leiden: Martinus Nijhoff, 1971; *Totality and Infinity: An Essay on Exteriority*. Translated by Alphonso Lingis. Pittsburgh: Duquesne University Press, 1969.

Lloyd, David and Paul Thomas. *Culture and the State*. New York: Routledge, 1998.

Loichot, Valérie. 'Between Breadfruit and Masala: Food Politics in Glissant's Martinique'. *Callaloo* 30, no. 1 (2007): pp. 124–37.

——. 'Renaming the Name: Glissant and Walcott's Reconstruction of the Caribbean Self'. *Journal of Caribbean Literature* 3, no. 2 (2002): pp. 1–12.

——. *Water Graves: The Art of the Unritual in the Greater Caribbean.* Charlottesville: University of Virginia Press, 2020.

Lorey, Isabel. *State of Insecurity: Government of the Precarious.* New York: Verso, 2015.

Lugones, María. 'Heterosexualism and the Colonial/Modern Gender System'. *Hypatia* 22, no. 1 (2007): pp. 186–209.

——. 'On Complex Communication'. *Hypatia* 21, no. 3 (2006): pp. 75–85.

Lustgarten, Abrahm. 'Oceans of Debt'. *The New York Times Magazine*, 31 July 2022.

McKittrick, Katherine. *Demonic Grounds: Black Women and the Cartographies of Struggle.* Minneapolis: University of Minnesota Press, 2006.

Mahdavi, Mojtaba. 'A Postcolonial Critique of Responsibility to Protect in the Middle East'. *Perceptions* XX, no. 1 (2015): pp. 7–36.

Maldonado-Torres, Nelson. 'Afterword: Critique and Decoloniality in the Face of Crisis, Disaster, and Catastrophe'. In *Aftershocks of the Disaster: Puerto Rico Before and After the Storm.* Edited by Yarimar Bonilla and Merison LeBrón. Haymarket Books: Chicago, 2019.

——. *Against War: Views from the Underside of Modernity.* Durham, NC: Duke University Press, 2008.

——. 'On the Coloniality of Being'. *Cultural Studies* 21, nos. 2–3 (2007): pp. 240–70.

——. 'On the Coloniality of Human Rights'. *Revista Crítica de Ciências Sociais* 114 (2017): pp. 117–36.

Mallavarapu, Siddharth. 'Colonialism and the Responsibility to Protect'. In *Theorising the Responsibility to Protect.* Edited by Ramesh Thakur and William Maley. Cambridge: Cambridge University Press, 2015.

Marcus, Ruth. 'Why Joe Biden is the antidote to this virus'. *Washington Post*, 13 March 2020.

Marion, Jean-Luc, *Being Given: Toward a Phenomenology of Givenness.* Translated by Jeffrey L. Kosky. Stanford: Stanford University Press, 2002.

Marchese, David. 'Winona LaDuke Feels That President Biden Has Betrayed Native Americans'. *New York Times*, 6 August 2021.

Mariátegui, José Carlos. *Seven Interpretive Essays on Peruvian Reality.* Translated by Marjory Urquidi. Austin: University of Texas Press, 1971.

Medina, José. *The Epistemology of Resistance: Gender and Racial Oppression, Epistemic Injustice, and Resistant Imaginations*. Oxford: Oxford University Press, 2012.

Mendieta, Eduardo. 'Editor's Introduction'. In *The Underside of Modernity: Apel, Ricoeur, Rorty, Taylor, and the Philosophy of Liberation*. Edited by Eduardo Mendieta. Atlantic Highlands, NJ: Humanity Books International, 1996.

——. *Global Fragments: Globalizations, Latinamericanisms, and Critical Theory*. Albany: State University of New York Press, 2007.

——. 'Introduction'. In *Beyond Philosophy: Ethics, History, Marxism, and Liberation Theology*. Edited by Eduardo Mendieta. Lanham, MD: Rowman & Littlefield, 2003.

——. 'The Jargon of Ontology and the Critique of Language'. In *The Aesthetic Ground of Critical Theory: New Readings of Benjamin and Adorno*. Edited by Nathan Ross. Lanham, MD: Rowman & Littlefield, 2015.

Merlo, Francesca. 'Pope: Human rights first, even if it means going against the tide'. In *Vatican News*, 10 December 2018.

Mignolo, Walter D. 'Delinking: The rhetoric of modernity, the logic of coloniality and the grammar of de-coloniality'. *Cultural Studies* 21, nos. 2–3 (2007): pp. 449–514.

——. 'The Geopolitics of Knowledge and the Colonial Difference', *The South Atlantic Quarterly* 101, no. 1 (2002): pp. 57–96.

——. 'On Decoloniality with Walter Mignolo'. Lecture given 10 February 2021.

——. 'Who Speaks for the "Human" in Human Rights?' *Hispanic Issues On Line* (2009).

Mihai, Mihaela. *Political Memory and the Aesthetics of Care: The Art of Complicity and Resistance*. Stanford: Stanford University Press, 2022.

Mills, Frederick B. *Enrique Dussel's Ethics of Liberation: An Introduction*. London: Palgrave Macmillan, 2018.

Mithlo, Nancy. *Knowing Native Arts*. Lincoln: University of Nebraska Press, 2020.

Monture-Okanee, Patricia. 'Thinking about Aboriginal Justice: Myths and Revolution'. In *Continuing Poundmaker and Riel's Quest: Presentations Made at a Conference on Aboriginal Peoples and Justice*. Edited by Richard Gosse. Saskatoon, SK: Purich, 1994.

Morefield, Jeanne, *Unsettling the World: Edward Said and Political Theory*. London: Rowman & Littlefield International, 2022.

Moses, A. Dirk. 'Empire, Resistance, and Security: International Law and the Transformative Occupation of Palestine'. *Humanity: An International Journal of Human Rights, Humanitarianism, and Development* 8, no. 2 (2017): pp. 379–409.

Mounk, Yascha. *The Age of Responsibility: Luck, Choice, and the Welfare State*. Cambridge, MA: Harvard University Press, 2017.

Moya, Paula. *Learning from Experience*. Berkeley: University of California Press, 2002.

Moyn, Samuel. *Human Rights and the Uses of History*. New York: Verso, 2017.

——. *The Last Utopia: Human Rights in History*. Cambridge, MA: The Belknap Press of Harvard University, 2010.

——. *Not Enough: Human Rights in an Unequal World*. Cambridge, MA: The Belknap Press of Harvard University Press, 2018.

Murdoch, H. Adlai. 'Édouard Glissant's Creolized World Vision: From Resistance and Relation to *Opacité*'. *Callaloo* 36, no. 4 (2013): pp. 875–90.

Murphy, Michelle. 'Against Population, Towards Afterlife'. In *Making Kin Not Population: Reconceiving Generations*. Edited by A. E. Clarke and Donna Haraway. Chicago: Prickly Paradigm Press, 2018.

Nagengast, Carole. 'Violence, Terror, and the Crisis of the State'. *Annual Review of Anthropology* 23 (1994): pp. 109–36.

Nayar, Jayan. 'The Non-Perplexity of Human Rights'. *Theory & Event* 22, no. 1 (2019): pp. 267–305.

Nemonte, Nenquimo. 'This is my message to the western world – your civilization is killing life on earth'. *The Guardian*, 12 October 2020.

Nesbitt, Nick. *Caribbean Critique: Antillean Critical Theory from Toussaint to Glissant*. Liverpool: Liverpool University Press, 2013.

Nichols, Robert. *Theft is Property!: Disposition and Critical Theory*. Durham, NC: Duke University Press, 2020.

Nkrumah, Kwame. *Neo-Colonialism: The Last Stage of Imperialism*. London: Heinemann, 1965.

Oliver, Kelly. 'Witnessing, Recognition, and Response Ethics'. *Philosophy & Rhetoric* 48, no. 4 (2015): pp. 473–93.

Ortega, Mariana. 'Decolonial Woes and Practices of Un-knowing'. *Journal of Speculative Philosophy* 31, no. 3 (2017): pp. 504–16.

——. *In-Between: Latina Feminist Phenomenology, Multiplicity, and the Self*. Albany: State University of New York Press, 2016.

Paccacerqua, Cynthia M. 'Gloria Anzaldúa's Affective Logic of *Volverse Una*'. In *Hypatia: A Journal of Feminist Philosophy* 31, no. 2 (2016): pp. 334–51.

Parris, LaRose T. *Being Apart: Theoretical and Existential Resistance in Africana Literature*. Charlottesville: University of Virginia Press, 2015.

Patterson, William L. *We Charge Genocide: The Historical Petition to the United Nations for Relief from a Crime of the United States Government against the Negro People*. New York: International Publishers, 1970.

Pérez, Emma. *The Decolonial Imaginary: Writing Chicanas into History*. Bloomington: Indiana University Press, 1999.

Perugini, Nicola and Neve Gordon. *The Human Right to Dominate*. Oxford: Oxford University Press, 2015.

Price, Richard. '*Créolisation*, Creolization, and *Créolité*'. *Small Axe* 21 no. 1 (2017): pp. 211–19.

Puar, Jasbir. *The Right to Maim: Debility, Capacity, Disability*. Durham, NC: Duke University Press, 2017.

Puchner, Martin. *Poetry of the Revolution: Marx, Manifestos, and the Avant-Gardes*. Princeton: Princeton University Press, 2006.

Quijano, Aníbal. 'Coloniality and Modernity/Rationality', *Cultural Studies* 21, no. 2 (2007): pp. 168–78.

——. 'Coloniality of Power, Eurocentrism and Latin America'. *Nepantla: Views from the South* 1, no. 3 (2000): pp. 533–80.

Raffoul, François. *The Origins of Responsibility*. Bloomington: Indiana University Press, 2010.

Ratner, Steven. 'International law and political philosophy: Uncovering new linkages'. *Philosophy Compass* (2018): p. 4.

Rivera, Mayra. *Poetics of the Flesh*. Durham, NC: Duke University Press, 2015.

Rodney, Walter. *How Europe Underdeveloped Africa*. New York: Verso, 2018.

Roelofs, Monique. *The Cultural Promise of the Aesthetic*. New York: Bloomsbury, 2014.

Rothberg, Michael. *The Implicated Subject: Beyond Victims and Perpetrators*. Stanford: Stanford University Press, 2019.

Said, Edward W. *Reflections on Exile and Other Essays*. Cambridge, MA: Harvard University Press, 2002.

——. *Reflections on Exile and Other Essays*. London: Granta Books, 2000.

——. *Representations of the Intellectual*. New York: Vintage, 1994.

Sandoval, Chela. *Methodologies of the Oppressed*. Minneapolis: University of Minnesota Press, 2000.

Scheper-Hughes, Nancy. *Death Without Weeping: The Violence of Everyday Life in Brazil*. Berkeley: University of California Press, 1992.

——. 'The Primacy of the Ethical: Propositions for a Militant Anthropology'. *Current Anthropology* 36, no. 3 (1995): pp. 409–40.

Schlesinger, Stephen. 'Ghosts of Guatemala's Past'. *New York Times*, 3 June 2011, <https://www.nytimes.com/2011/06/04/opinion/04 schlesinger.html>.

Schlesinger, Stephen and Stephen Kinzer. *Bitter Fruit: The Story of the American Coup in Guatemala*. Cambridge, MA: Harvard University Press, 2005.

Schram, Sanford F. *The Return of Ordinary Capitalism: Neoliberalism, Precarity, Occupy*. Oxford: Oxford University Press, 2015.

Sealey, Kris F. *Creolizing the Nation*. Evanston, IL: Northwestern University Press, 2020.

Sharpe, Christina. *In the Wake: On Blackness and Being*. Durham, NC: Duke University Press, 2016.

Sheth, Falguni. *Toward a Political Philosophy of Race*. Albany: State University of New York Press, 2009.

Sikka, Sonia. 'The Delightful Other: Portraits of the Feminine in Kierkegaard, Nietzsche, and Levinas'. In *Feminist Interpretations of Emmanuel Levinas*. Edited by Tina Chanter. University Park: The Pennsylvania State University Press, 2001.

Sikkink, Kathryn. *Evidence for Hope: Making Human Rights work in the 21st Century*. Princeton: Princeton University Press, 2017.

——. *The Hidden Face of Rights: Toward a Politics of Responsibilities*. New Haven, CT: Yale University Press, 2020.

Simpson, Audra. *Mohawk Interruptus: Political Life across the Borders of Settler States*. Durham, NC: Duke University Press, 2014.

Slaughter, Joseph R. *Human Rights Inc.: The World Novel, Narrative Form, and International Law*. New York: Fordham University Press, 2007.

Solnit, Rebecca. 'Big oil coined "carbon footprints" to blame us for their greed. Keep them on the hook'. *The Guardian*, 23 August 2021.

——. 'The light from Standing Rock: beautiful struggle shows the power of protest'. *The Guardian*, 6 December 2016.

——. 'Standing Rock protests: this is only the beginning'. *The Guardian*, 12 September 2016.

Spivak, Gayatri Chakravorty. *An Aesthetic Education in the Era of Globalization*. Cambridge, MA: Harvard University Press, 2013.

——. 'Responsibility'. *boundary 2* 21, no. 3 (1994): pp. 19–64.

——. 'supplementing marxism'. In *Whither Marxism? Global Crises in International Perspective*. Edited by Bernd Magnus and Stephen Cullenberg. New York: Routledge, 1994.

Stoler, Ann Laura. *Haunted by Empire: Geographies of Intimacy in North American History*. Durham, NC: Duke University Press, 2006.

Stonebridge, Lyndsey. *Placeless People: Writing, Rights, and Refugees*. Oxford: Oxford University Press, 2018.

Suárez-Krabbe, Julia. *Race, Rights and Rebels: Alternatives to Human Rights and Development from the Global South*. London: Rowman & Littlefield International, 2016.

TallBear, Kim. 'Making Love and Relations Beyond Settler Sex and Family'. In *Making Kin Not Population*. Edited by Adele E. Clarke and Donna Haraway. Chicago: Prickly Paradigm Press, 2018.

Tarrow, Sidney. *Power in Movement: Social Movement and Contentious Politics*. Cambridge: University of Cambridge Press, 2011.

Thomas, Deborah. *Political Life in the Wake of the Plantation: Sovereignty, Witnessing, Repair*. Durham, NC: Duke University Press, 2019.

Towell, Larry. 'The End of the Beginning: Closing Standing Rock'. *Magnum Photos*.

Trouillot, Michel-Rolph. 'Anthropology and the Savage Slot: The Poetics and Politics of Otherness'. In *Recapturing Anthropology: Working in the Present*. Edited by Richard Fox. Santa Fe, NM: School of American Research Press, 1991.

Tuck, Eve and K. Wayne Yang. 'Decolonization is not a metaphor'. *Decolonization: Indigeneity, Education & Society* 1, no. 1 (2012): pp. 1–40.

Vázquez-Arroyo, Antonio. *Political Responsibility: Responding to Predicaments of Power*. New York: Columbia University Press, 2016.

Walcott, Derek. *The Poetry of Derek Walcott 1948–2013*. New York: Farrar, Straus & Giroux, 2014.

Walcott, Ronaldo. *The Long Emancipation: Moving toward Black Freedom*. Durham, NC: Duke University Press, 2021.

Wampole, Christy. *Rootedness: The Ramifications of a Metaphor*. Chicago: The University of Chicago Press, 2016.

Watson, Mike. 'An Interview with François Maspero: "A Few Misunderstandings"'. Translated by David Broder. Verso Blog.

Weil, Simone. 'Cold War Policy in 1939'. In *Selected Essays*. Translated by Richard Rees. Eugene, OR: Wipf & Stock, 1962.

——. 'Human Personality'. In *Simone Weil: An Anthology*. Edited by Siân Miles. New York: Penguin, 2005.

——. *The Need for Roots: Prelude to a Declaration of Duties Toward Mankind*. Translated by Arthur Wills. London: Routledge, 2010; *L'enracinement: Prélude à une déclaration des devoirs envers l'être humain*. Paris: Gallimard, 1949.

——. 'New Facts about the Colonial Problem in the French Empire'. In *Simone Weil on Colonialism: An Ethic of the Other*. Edited and Translated by J. P. Little. Lanham: Rowman & Littlefield, 2003.

——. *On the Abolition of all Political Parties*. Translated by Simon Leys. New York: New York Review of Books, 2013.

——. 'Reflections concerning the Causes of Liberty and Social Oppression'. In *Oppression and Liberty*. Translated by Arthur Wills and John Petrie. New York: Routledge, 2001.

——. *Waiting for God*. Translated by Emma Craufurd. New York: HarperCollins, 2009.

Weir, Allison. 'Collective Love as Public Freedom: Dancing Resistance. Ehrenreich, Arendt, Kristeva, and Idle No More'. *Hypatia* 32, no. 1 (2017): pp. 19–34.

——. *Identities and Freedom: Feminist Theory between Power and Connection*. Oxford: Oxford University Press, 2013.

Weitz, Eric. *A World Divided: The Global Struggle for Human Rights in the Age of Nation-States*. Princeton: Princeton University Press, 2019.

Weizman, Eyal. *The Least of All Possible Evils: Humanitarian Violence from Arendt to Gaza*. New York: Verso, 2011.

Whyte, Jessica. 'Human Rights and the Collateral Damage of Neoliberalism'. *Theory & Event* 20, no. 1 (2017): pp. 137–51.

——. *The Morals of the Market: Human Rights and the Rise of Neoliberalism*. London: Verso, 2019.

Wilder, Gary. *Freedom Time: Negritude, Decolonization, and the Future of the World*. Durham, NC: Duke University Press, 2015.

Willet, Cynthia. *Maternal Ethics and Other Slave Moralities*. New York: Routledge, 1995.

Williams, Randall. *The Divided World: Human Rights and Its Violence*. Minneapolis: University of Minnesota Press, 2010.

Young, Iris Marion. *Responsibility for Justice*. Oxford: Oxford University Press, 2011.

Young, Robert J. C. *Postcolonialism: An Historical Introduction*. Oxford: Wiley, 2016.

Yountae, An. *The Decolonial Abyss: Mysticism and Cosmopolitics from the Ruins*. New York: Fordham University Press, 2016.

Index

Note: End-of-chapter notes are indicated by the page number followed by the letter n and the note number, e.g. 31n74 relates to note 74 on page 31.